心理学专业英语

English in Psychology

主 编　田新华　任铭静
副主编　马玉红　王　朓

哈尔滨工业大学出版社

内容简介

为了提高我国高校双语教学水平,拓展学生的专业领域知识,组织心理学专业教师和英语专业教师共同编写了本书。

本书包括三部分内容。第一部分为专业阅读,共 10 章,前 9 章各章包括 3 篇文章。第 1 篇选自经典教材,主要阐述基本原理;第 2 篇选自经典专著,拓展专业知识;第 3 篇选自学术期刊或专业网站,把握最新最前沿的学术动态。第 10 章包括 8 篇文章,专题介绍应用心理学研究新进展。每篇文章后列出本篇文章关键词的英汉对照、难句翻译、学术论文撰写常用句型、思考题等。第二部分为附属篇,主要包括心理学专业的国内外相关学术信息,如国内外专业学术期刊、心理学研究所及协会等。第三部分列出了专业词汇和参考文献,供读者参考。

本书可作为各类大专院校学生双语教学或专业英语教学的教材,也可供自学者使用。

图书在版编目(CIP)数据

心理学专业英语/田新华,任铭静主编. —哈尔滨:哈尔滨工业大学出版社,2017.2(2021.7 重印)
ISBN 978-7-5603-6463-6

Ⅰ.①心… Ⅱ.①田… ②任… Ⅲ.①心理学-英语-高等学校-教材 Ⅳ.①B84

中国版本图书馆 CIP 数据核字(2017)第 025017 号

策划编辑	田新华
责任编辑	丁桂焱
封面设计	卞秉利
出版发行	哈尔滨工业大学出版社
社　　址	哈尔滨市南岗区复华四道街 10 号　邮编 150006
传　　真	0451-86414749
网　　址	http://hitpress.hit.edu.cn
印　　刷	哈尔滨市工大节能印刷厂
开　　本	880mm×1230mm　1/32　印张 11.25　字数 380 千字
版　　次	2017 年 2 月第 1 版　2021 年 7 月第 4 次印刷
书　　号	ISBN 978-7-5603-6463-6
定　　价	38.00 元

(如因印装质量问题影响阅读,我社负责调换)

21世纪专业英语系列丛书
编委会

主　任　赵毓琴
副主任　闫纪红
编　委　于云玲　马玉红　王　旸　王　星
　　　　　王　洋　王　朓　王艳薇　王倩玉
　　　　　任　丽　任　莉　任铭静　刘秀杰
　　　　　李　莉　李慧杰　杨　皓　吴　迪
　　　　　张凌岩　陈　楠　岳文赫　项　睿
　　　　　栾　岩　葛乃晟
总策划　田新华

前　言

随着经济社会的发展,人们的生活水平得到了提高,当物质需求得到满足后,人们对精神的需求就会随之提高。为适应经济全球化的发展趋势,满足国内广大学生和读者了解、学习和借鉴国外先进的心理学专业理论,了解心理学前沿动态的需求,使学生通过阅读大量英语文章来扩充词汇量,提高熟练获取信息和独立阅读原著的能力,我们编写了本书。

本书主要内容由专业阅读、专业学术信息和专业词汇三部分组成。

第一部分为主干内容,共 10 章。主要包括心理学主要学派及其理论、行为的生物学基础、感觉与知觉、认知与语言、动机与情感、人格、心理混乱症、社会心理学以及专题:应用心理学研究新进展等。

第二部分的主要内容为心理学专业的国内外相关专业学术信息,如国外著名期刊、国内心理学研究所及协会等,可供读者了解最新心理学专业学术动态。

第三部分基本涵盖了心理学领域的专业术语和常用词汇。

本书具有以下特点:

第一,内容全面,时代感强。涵盖了心理学的多方面内容,文章选自近年英美国家原版教材和期刊。

第二,内容实用,针对性强。专业学术信息部分提供了详尽的了解专业学术信息的渠道,能够有效促进学生的专业发展。

第三,注释合理,可读性强。选文中的难点和重点词汇、句子都配有相应的中文解释和实用例句,能够激发学生进一步学习的积极性。

本书适用范围较广，可作为高等院校心理学等专业英语教学教材，也可供心理咨询人士和自学者参考使用。

本书由哈尔滨工业大学田新华、任铭静任主编，由主讲本科生、研究生心理学课的第一主编拟定编写提纲和编写模块、提出文献遴选路径、撰写每章及专题导读等，由主讲英语的第二主编负责组织副主编马玉红、王胧等共同翻译和编写，最后由主编统稿、定稿。

在编写过程中，我们参考了部分著作和文献，在此一并向相关作者等表示感谢。由于编写时间仓促，且编者水平及经验有限，书中不妥和疏漏之处在所难免，恳请广大读者批评指正。

编　者

2016 年 12 月

CONTENTS

PART ONE ACADEMIC READING
第一部分 专业阅读

1 An Introduction to Psychology ·· 3
  心理学简介
  ❖ 本章导读 ··· 3
  1.1 What Is Psychology ··· 4
      什么是心理学
  1.2 Approaches to Psychology ····································· 12
      心理学入门
  1.3 Intuition ·· 22
      直觉
2 Main Schools in Psychology and Their Theories ············· 33
  心理学主要学派及其理论
  ❖ 本章导读 ··· 33
  2.1 The Interpretation of Dreams ································· 33
      梦的解析
  2.2 Unlearned Behavior: Emotion ································ 44
      非习得的行为:情绪
  2.3 The Postulates of a Structural Psychology ··············· 52
      构造心理学公设
3 The Biology Underlying Behavior ··································· 64
  行为的生物学基础
  ❖ 本章导读 ··· 64
  3.1 The Nervous System: An Overview ························ 64
      神经系统:概述
  3.2 A Tour Through the Brain ···································· 71
      大脑结构一览

3.3 Behavior and the Nervous System: Input/Output Boxes within Input/Output Boxes ……… 80
行为与神经系统:输入/输出装置内部的输入/输出装置

4 Sensation and Perception ……… 88
感觉与知觉
❖ 本章导读 ……… 88
4.1 Sensation: Receiving Messages about the World ……… 88
感觉:接收关于世界的讯息
4.2 Perception: Interpreting Sensory Messages ……… 97
知觉:解释感官讯息
4.3 Pain and Why It Hurts ……… 107
疼痛与为什么感到疼痛

5 Cognition and Language ……… 116
认知与语言
❖ 本章导读 ……… 116
5.1 How Do We Think? ……… 116
我们如何思考?
5.2 Language: Symbolic Communication ……… 126
语言:符号的交际
5.3 Concept Formation and Problem Solving: Understanding and Managing Two Key Components of Higher Order Cognition ……… 136
概念形成与问题解决:理解和使用两个关键的高级认知组成部分

6 Motivation and Emotion ……… 145
动机与情感
❖ 本章导读 ……… 145
6.1 An Overview of Emotion and Motivational Concept ……… 145
情感与动机综述
6.2 Arousal Theory ……… 154
激励理论
6.3 Employee Motivation: Theory and Practice ……… 162
员工动机的理论与实践

7 Personality 169
人格
❖ 本章导读 169
7.1 Major Perspectives on Personality 169
关于人格的主要观点
7.2 Is Behavior Really Consistent 177
行为真的是前后一致的吗
7.3 Contextualized Personality: Traditional and New Assessment Procedures 186
背景人格:传统的和新的评估程序

8 Psychological Disorders 195
心理混乱症
❖ 本章导读 195
8.1 Understanding Abnormality 195
解读心理反常行为
8.2 Anxiety States 202
焦虑状态
8.3 Social Phobia 210
社会恐惧症

9 Social Psychology 220
社会心理学
❖ 本章导读 220
9.1 The Nature of Social Psychology 220
社会心理学的本质
9.2 Schemas and Stereotypes 229
图式与定型
9.3 Objects, Decision Considerations and Self-Image in Men's and Women's Impulse Purchases 237
男人和女人冲动购买的对象、决定和自我形象

10 Feature: New Development of Applied Psychology 248
专题:应用心理学研究新进展
❖ 本章导读 248

10.1	Health and Stress ·················· 249
	健康与压力
10.2	Stress and Personality ·················· 258
	压力与人格
10.3	Initiation and Maintenance of Health Behaviors ········ 269
	启动及维持健康行为
10.4	Changing Behavior Can Improve Your Health ······ 281
	改变行为能改善健康
10.5	Psychology: Is It Applied Enough ·················· 283
	心理学:它的应用是否足够
10.6	Theory-Based Health Behavior Change: Developing, Testing, and Applying Theories for Evidence-Based Interventions ·················· 284
	基于理论的健康行为的改变:开发、测试和以证据为基础的干预应用理论
10.7	Positive Health ·················· 286
	积极健康
10.8	Positive Psychology and the Illness Ideology: Toward a Positive Clinical Psychology ·················· 288
	积极心理学和疾病意识:对于积极临床心理学

PART TWO　ACADEMIC INFORMATION
第二部分　专业学术信息

国外著名期刊 ·················· 293
国外心理学协会 ·················· 294
国内心理学研究所及协会 ·················· 297
国内期刊 ·················· 300

PART THREE GLOSSARY
第三部分　专业词汇

词汇表 ·················· 305
REFERENCES ·················· 344

PART ONE
ACADEMIC READING

第一部分 专业阅读

An Introduction to Psychology
心理学简介

【本章导读】 本章是全书的引言部分,阐述心理学的基本概念和研究内容。第 1 篇文章介绍心理学的概念、目的及其与相关社会学学科的差异。心理学用科学的手段研究行为和心理活动,同时研究一个个体的生理、心理及其所处的外在环境对行为及心理活动产生的影响。心理学研究的主要目的是描述、理解、预测并控制或改变行为及心理活动。心理学属于社会学的一种,与其他社会学学科有一定的相关性,同时又有很大的区别。与其他学科相比,心理学更依赖实验及观察,更重视个体研究,更充分利用生物学知识。第 2 篇文章介绍了几个重要的心理学研究方法,包括心理分析的研究方法、行为主义研究方法、人本主义研究方法、认知研究方法和生物学研究方法。第 3 篇文章首先阐述心理学的两个研究方法即直觉和推理之间的区别,指出直觉可能产生的错误。其次,指出思想产生的难易度具有连续性,对技术的精心掌握会使研究者更容易得出有价值的答案和有效的组织信息的方法。

1.1 What Is Psychology
什么是心理学

In 1945, a 15-year-old Jewish girl named Anne Frank died of typhus at Bergen-Belsen, a notorious Nazi death camp. She had spent the previous two years with her parents, her sister, and four others in a cramped apartment in Amsterdam, hiding from German troops occupying Holland. Unable to go outside, the group depended entirely on Christian friends for food and other necessities. Anne, who was a gifted writer and astute observer, recorded in her diary the fears, frustrations, and inevitable clashes of people forced to live 24 hours a day in close proximity①. Yet she never despaired or lost her sense of wonder at life's joys. With humor and grace, she described the pleasure of family celebrations, the thrill of first love, the excitement of growing up. Shortly before the Gestapo discovered the hideout, Anne wrote, "It's really a wonder that I haven't dropped all my ideals, because they seem so absurd and impossible to carry out. Yet I keep them, because in spite of everything I still believe that people are really good at heart. I simply can't build up my hopes on a foundation consisting of confusion, misery, and death."

Many years later, and thousands of miles away, Charles "Tex" Watson grew up, apparently uneventfully, in a small American town. A handsome boy, Charles attended church, earned high grades, and competed successfully in football, basketball, and track. During his junior year in high school his fellow students named him the outstanding member of his class. Then, a few years after leaving home for college, Watson fell in with the Charles Manson cult. Manson was a charismatic figure who convinced his followers that he was divinely chosen to lead them and demanded their blind obedience. In 1969, on Manson's orders, the cult savagely slaughtered seven innocent people in Los Angeles. Tex Watson, the young man who had earlier seemed so full of promise, cold-bloodedly carved his initials on the chest of one of the victims.

Why did Anne Frank, living in the constant shadow of death, retain her love of humanity? Why did Tex Watson, who apparently had everything to live for, turn to brutal acts of violence? How can we explain why some people are overwhelmed by petty problems, while others, faced with real difficulties, remain mentally healthy? What principles can help us understand why some human beings are confident players in the game of life, while others angrily reject its basic rules?

If you have ever asked yourself such questions, welcome to the world of psychology. You <u>are about to explore</u> a discipline that studies the many complexities and contradictions of human behavior. Psychologists <u>take as their subject</u> the entire spectrum of brave and cowardly, wise and silly, intelligent and foolish, beautiful and brutish things that human beings do[②]. Their aim: to examine and explain how human beings—and animals, too—learn, remember, solve problems, perceive, feel, and get along with others.

Many people, when they hear the word psychology, think immediately of mental disorders and abnormal behavior. But psychologists do not <u>confine their attention to</u> extremes of behavior. They are just as likely to focus on common place experiences—experiences as universal and ordinary as rearing children, remembering a shopping list, daydreaming, and even gossiping. Most of us, after all, are neither saints nor sinners but a curious combination of both positive and negative qualities. Psychology, <u>in short, is not only about</u> martyrs and murderers; <u>it is also about</u> you.

Definition

Psychology has always had a way of outgrowing its definitions. At the start of this century, most psychologists considered psychology to be the study of mental life, the mind, or consciousness. Within a few years, however, such definitions came under attack as vague and unscientific. As we shall see, between the 1920s and the 1950s many psychologists preferred to define their discipline as the study of behavior, because what people do—unlike what they think or feel—can be directly observed and measured. But this definition also came under attack. To those who still wanted to study thinking, dreaming, and all the other fascinating things that go on between people's ears, confining psychology to behavior made <u>no more</u> sense <u>than</u> confining literature to short stories or history to descriptions of military battles[③]. Today, most psychologists are willing to make room for both behavior and mind in their work. We define psychology as the scientific study of behavior and mental processes and how they are affected by an organism's physical state, mental state, and external environment.

Main Goals

Psychology's main goals are straightforward: to (a) describe, (b) understand, (c) predict, and (d) control or modify behavior and mental processes. In a sense, every human being is an amateur psychologist, because everyone wants to describe, understand, predict, and control behavior and mental processes, both their own and those of other people. Suppose your best friend has just nagged you for the three hundredth time about your tendency to subsist solely on pizza, potato chips, and soda pop[④]. You might describe the behavior ("Frieda is always badgering me about the way I eat"); attempt to understand its cause ("She's a health nut"); make a prediction about the future ("If I don't do something, I'm going to be nagged for the rest of my life"); and try to bring about a change ("I'll eat wheat germ and drink carrot juice once a week, and then maybe she'll leave me alone").

But if psychologists' goals are the same as everyone else's, what makes psychology a special discipline? The answer is that most people form opinions about human behavior and experience in a casual way. Most psychologists, in contrast, follow rigorous and systematic procedures. They resist reaching for conclusions until they have evidence that can be checked and verified by other⑤. They test their ideas.

Psychology's Relatives

Psychology belongs to a family of disciplines known as the social sciences. All of these sciences encourage us to analyze human problems objectively and to search for reliable patterns in behavior. But there are some important differences in emphasis. Sociology is the study of groups and institutions within society. In general, sociologists pay less attention than psychologists do to personality traits and individual differences. However, one specialty, social psychology, falls on the border between psychology and sociology; it focuses on how social groups and situations affect an individual's behavior, and vice versa. Anthropology <u>is concerned with</u> the physical and cultural origins and development of the human species. Anthropologists typically focus on a large social unit—a tribe, a community or even an entire society. In contrast, most psychologists study behavior only in their own society, and they take specific behaviors or mental processes as the topic for analysis, rather than the society itself. Economics is the study of how people produce, distribute, and consume goods and services. Political science is the study of political behavior and the establishment and conduct of government. Each of these two sciences bites off a piece of the behavioral pie; in contrast, psychology searches for general principles of human nature.

Of all the social sciences, psychology relies most heavily on laboratory experiments and observations. At the same time it is the most personal of the social sciences, focusing more than the others on the individual and his or her well-being. Psychology also makes more use of biological information than the other disciplines do.

from: Psychology, Carole Wade & Carol Tavris, Harper Collins College Publishers, 1993

Words and Expressions

typhus	n.	['taifəs]	斑疹伤寒
notorious	adj.	[nəu'tɔːriəs]	恶名昭彰的;声名狼藉的
cramped	adj.	[kræmpt]	狭窄的
astute	adj.	[ə'stjuːt]	敏锐的;精明的
proximity	n.	[prɔk'simiti]	接近;邻近
hideout	n.	['haidaut]	躲藏处
uneventfully	adv.	[ˌʌni'ventfuli]	太平无事地
cult	n.	[kʌlt]	异教
charismatic	adj.	[ˌkæriz'mætik]	有吸引力的
divinely	adv.	[di'vainli]	凭借上帝的力量
slaughter	v.	['slɔːtə]	屠杀
carve	v.	[kɑːv]	刻;雕刻
initial	n.	[i'niʃəl]	(名字的)首字母
humanity	n.	[hjuː'mæniti]	人性
brutal	adj.	['bruːtl]	残忍的;冷酷的
petty	adj.	['peti]	小的;琐碎的
spectrum	n.	['spektrəm]	范围
cowardly	adj.	['kauədli]	胆小的;怯懦的
brutish	adj.	['bruːtiʃ]	残酷的
perceive	v.	[pə'siːv]	察觉
disorder	n.	[dis'ɔːdə]	紊乱;疾病
abnormal	adj.	[æb'nɔːməl]	反常的
commonplace	adj.	['kɔmənpleis]	平凡的;普通的
rear	v.	[riə]	养育

saint	n.	[seint]	道德崇高的人
sinner	n.	['sinə]	罪人
martyr	n.	['mɑːtə]	烈士
outgrow	v.	[aut'grəu]	变大了便不再适用
vague	adj.	[veig]	不明确的;含糊的
organism	n.	['ɔːgənizəm]	生物;有机体
amateur	adj.	['æmətə(r)]	业余的
nag	v.	[næg]	困扰;使烦恼
subsist	v.	[səb'sist]	维持生活
solely	adv.	['səu(l)li]	仅仅
badger	v.	['bædʒə]	困扰
nut	n.	[nʌt]	狂热者
germ	n.	[dʒəːm]	芽
rigorous	adj.	['rigərəs]	严密的
procedure	n.	[prə'siːdʒə]	步骤
verify	v.	['verifai]	证明;证实
institution	n.	[ˌinsti'tjuːʃən]	制度
specialty	n.	['speʃəlti]	专业
distribute	v.	[dis'tribju(ː)t]	分配
establishment	n.	[is'tæbliʃmənt]	体制
conduct	n.	['kɔndʌkt]	行为;管理

Difficult Sentences

① Anne, who was a gifted writer and astute observer, recorded in her diary the fears, frustrations, and inevitable clashes of people forced to live 24 hours a day in close proximity.
安妮是一个很有天分的作家,具有敏锐的观察力。她在日记中记载了人们被迫一天24小时挤在一起时感受到的恐惧、失望和难免产生的冲突。

② Psychologists take as their subject the entire spectrum of brave and cowardly, wise and silly, intelligent and foolish, beautiful and brutish things that human beings do.

被心理学家纳入其研究范围的所有人类行为包括:勇敢和怯懦的,明智和愚蠢的,聪明和笨拙的,美好的及残酷的行为。

③ To those who still wanted to study thinking, dreaming, and all the other fascinating things that go on between people's ears, confining psychology to behavior made no more sense than confining literature to short stories or history to descriptions of military battles.

对那些仍想要研究思维、做梦和其他大脑中令人感兴趣的活动的人来说,仅把心理学作为行为的研究就如同仅把文学作为短篇小说的研究或者仅把历史作为对军事战争的描述一样,是没有道理的。

④ Suppose your best friend has just nagged you for the three hundredth time about your tendency to subsist solely on pizza, potato chips, and soda pop.

假设你最好的朋友已经跟你唠叨第三百遍了,劝你不要只吃比萨、薯条,只喝汽水。

⑤ They resist reaching for conclusions until they have evidence that can be checked and verified by others.

除非他们得到的证据能被他人检验和证实,否则他们不会得出结论。

Phrases and Patterns

1. be about to explore... 将要探究……
   You are about to explore a discipline that studies the many complexities and contradictions of human behavior.
   你将要探究一门研究人类行为的复杂特征及矛盾特征的学科。
   We are about to explore several solutions to the problem.
   我们将要探讨几种解决该问题的方法。

2. take as their subject... 将……纳入其研究范围

The research group takes the behaviors of young people as their subject.

这个研究小组把年轻人的行为作为他们的研究对象。

3. confine one's attention to... 仅仅关注……

   But psychologists do not confine their attention to extremes of behavior.

   但心理学家们并不是仅仅关注极端的行为。

   Let's confine our attention to the most urgent matter at present.

   让我们主要关注目前最紧急的事。

4. ..., in short, is not only about...; it is also about... 简而言之,不仅是关于……同时也关于……

   Psychology, in short, is not only about martyrs and murderers; it is also about you.

   简而言之,心理学不仅仅是关于烈士和凶手,它还与你自己有关。

   This, in short, is not about your own interest; it is also about the public interest.

   简而言之,这不仅与你个人的利益相关,还与公共利益相关。

5. no more...than... 和……一样;都不……

   He is no more diligent than you.

   和你一样,他也不勤奋。(他和你一样不勤奋)

6. be concerned with... 与……相关

   Anthropology is concerned with the physical and cultural origins and development of the human species.

   人类学与人类的物质文化渊源及发展有关。

   In contrast, the clinical psychological literature has been concerned with the excessive buying of compulsive shoppers.

   相反,临床心理学的著作与购物成瘾者的过度购买行为相关。

1.2 Approaches to Psychology
心理学入门

The Psychoanalytic Approach to Psychology

The psychoanalytic approach was started and developed mainly by Sigmund, a Viennese doctor who specialised in neurology. Freud became interested in hysteria—the manifestation of physical symptoms without physical causes—and became convinced that unconscious mental causes were responsible not just for this disorder but for all disorders and even "normal" personality[①]. Freud developed techniques for treating the unconscious causes of mental disorders and built up an underlying explanatory theory of how human personality and abnormality develop from childhood.

Freud's theory and approach were influenced by the technology of the time (such as the steam engine), and his early work with Charcot, the Parisian hypnotist, and Breuer, the pioneer of the cathartic method. Freud's psychoanalytic approach had a great impact on psychology and psychiatry, and was developed in different ways by other psychoanalysts such as Jung, Adler, Klein, Anna Freud (his daughter), and Erickson.

Psychoanalysis Proposes:

Unconscious Processes—the major causes of behaviour come from that part of the mind which we have no direct awareness of.

Psychic Determinism—all we say and do has a cause (usually unconscious), even slips of the tongue of "Freudian slip".

Hydraulic Drives—behaviour is motivated by the two basic instinctual drives, the sex drive from Eros and life instinct, and the aggression drive from Thanatos the death instinct. The drives create psychic energy which will build up (like steam in a steam engine) and create tension and anxiety if it cannot be released in some form.

Psychodynamic Conflict—different parts of the unconscious mind are in constant struggle as the rational ego and moralistic superego seek to control the id expressing its sexual and aggressive urges.

Stages of Development—personality is shaped as the drives are modified by different conflicts at different times in childhood.

Freud used the case study method when treating his clients (seeing them individually several times a week for many months), and deeply analysed and interpreted all they said and did. Two techniques Freud used for investigating the unconscious were:

Free Association—involving the uninhibited expression of thought associations, no matter how bizarre or embarrassing, from the client to the analyst.

Dream Analysis—the "royal road to the unconscious". The analyst attempts to decode the symbols and unravel the hidden meaning (the latent content) of a dream from the dreamer's report (the manifest content).

The Behaviorist Approach to Psychology

The behaviorist approach was influenced by the philosophy of empiricism (which argues that knowledge comes from the environment via the senses, since humans are like a "tabula rasa", or blank slate, at birth) and the physical sciences (which emphasize scientific and objective methods of investigation)[2].

Watson started the behaviorist movement in 1913 when he wrote an article entitled "Psychology as the behaviorist views it", which set out its main principles and assumptions. Drawing on earlier work by Pavlov, behaviorists such as Watson, Thorndike and Skinner proceeded to develop theories of learning (such as classical and operant conditioning) that they attempted to use to explain virtually all behaviour.

The behaviorist approach dominated experimental psychology until the late 1950s, when its assumptions and methods became increasingly criticized by ethologists and cognitive psychologists. The behaviourist theories have been modified to provide more realistic explanations of how learning can occur, for example by psychologists such as Bandura with his social learning theory.

The Behaviorists Believed:

1. the majority of all behavior is learned from the environment after birth (behaviorism takes the nurture side of the nature-nurture debate), and so psychology should investigate the laws and products of learning and behaviour is determined by the environment, since we are merely the total of all our past learning experiences, free will is an illusion.

2. only observable behaviour not minds should be studied if psychology is to be an objective science, since we cannot see into other people's minds, and if we ask them about their thoughts they may lie, not know, or just be mistaken.

The behaviorists adopted a very nomothetic approach, using strict laboratory experimentation, usually conducted on animals such as rates or pigeons. Animals were tested because the behaviorists believed: the laws of learning were universal; there was only a quantitative difference between animals and humans; animals are practically and ethically more convenient to test.

The Humanistic Approach to Psychology

The humanistic movement developed in America in the early 1960s, and was termed the third force in psychology since it aimed to replace the two main approaches in the subject at that time, behaviourism and psychoanalysis. Influenced by gestalt psychology's idea of studying whole unites, and existential philosophy with its belief in conscious free will, humanists argued that behaviourism's artificial and dehumanizing approach and psychoanalysis's gloomy determinism were insufficient to provide a complete psychology[3].

The humanistic approach armed to investigate all the uniquely human aspects of experience such as love, hope, creativity, etc. and emphasized the importance of the individual's interaction with the environment. Humanists, such as Maslow, believed that every individual has the need to self-actualise or reach their potential, and Rogers developed client-centred therapy to help individuals in this process of self-actualization.

Bugental, the first president of the American Association for Humanistic Psychology, described some of its fundamental assumptions:

A proper understanding of human nature can only be gained from studying humans, not other animals.

Psychology should research areas that are meaningful and important to human existence, not neglect them because they are too difficult. Psychology should be applied to enrich human life.

Psychology should study internal experience as well as external behaviour and consider that individuals can show some degree of free will.

Psychology should study the individual case (an idiographic method) rather than the average performance of groups (a nomothetic approach).

In general, humanistic psychologists assume that the whole person should be studied in their environmental context.

Humanists take a phenomenological approach, investigation the individual's conscious experience of the world. For this reason they employ the idiographic case study method, and use a variety of individualistic techniques such as flexible open ended interviews and the

Q-sort technique, where the participant is given one hundred different statements on cards, such as "I don't trust my emotions" or " I have an attractive personality" which they have to sort into piles for personal relevance.

The Cognitive Approach to Psychology

The cognitive approach began to revolutionize psychology in the late 1950s and early 1960s, to become the dominant paradigm in the subject by the 1970s. Interest in mental processes had been gradually resurrected through the work of people like Tolman and Piaget, but it was the arrival of the computer that gave cognitive psychology the terminology and metaphor it needed to investigate human minds.

Cognitive psychology compares the human mind to a computer, suggesting that we too are information processors and that it is possible and desirable to study the internal mental processes that lie between the stimuli we receive and the responses we make[④]. Cognition means "knowing" and cognitive processes refer to the ways in which knowledge is gained, used and retained. Therefore, cognitive psychologists have studied perception, attention, memory, thinking, language, and problem solving.

Cognitive psychology has influenced and integrated with many other approaches and areas of study to produce, for example, social learning theory, cognitive neuropsychology, and artificial intelligence.

Cognitive Psychologists Assume That:

1. mental processes can and should be investigated scientifically.
2. models of psychological functions can be proposed.
3. research on these models can be carried out to confirm, refute or modify them by testing observable behaviour and conscious report.
4. cognitive processes actively organize and manipulate information

that we receive—humans are not merely passive responders to their environment.

Cognitive psychologists mostly employ a nomothetic approach to discover human cognitive processes, but have also adopted idiographic techniques at times:

Laboratory experimentation—for example, many subjects have been exposed to memory tests under strictly controlled conditions.

Case study—Piaget studied the cognitive development of his children using the clinical interview methods.

The Biological Approach to Psychology

Sometimes known as the physiological, biopsychological, neurophysiological, nativist (considering nature rather than nurture) or innate approach. The biological approach to psychological matters has integrated with and run parallel to the rest of psychological thought since early Greek times—the Greek physician Galen suggested that personality and temperament may be linked to the levels of body fluids such as blood and bile in the body[5].

As knowledge of human anatomy, physiology, biochemistry, and medicine developed, important insights for human behaviour and experience were gained. Penfield for example mapped the role of various areas of the cerebral cortex through microelectrode simulation with conscious patients. Sperry investigated the effects of splitting the cerebral hemispheres on consciousness and psychological function. The field will progress still further as the technology to isolate the effects of genes and scan the living brain develops.

Biologically Orientated Psychologists Assume That:

1. all that is psychological is first physiological—that is since the mind appears to reside in the brain, all thoughts, feelings and behaviours

ultimately have a physical/ biological cause.

2. human genes have evolved over millions of years to adapt behaviour to the environment. Therefore, much behaviour will have a genetic basis.

3. psychology should, therefore, investigate the brain, nervous system, endocrine system, neurochemistry, and genes.

4. it is also useful to study why human behaviour has evolved in the way it has, the subject of evolutionary/ sociobiological theory.

The biological approach mainly adopts a nomothetic approach to generalize biological influences on behaviour to all humans with similar physiology, but finds the use of particular "special case studies" very useful.

Most common techniques include laboratory experimentation—stimulating, giving drugs to, or removing parts of the body to see what effect it has on behaviour; and laboratory observations—controlled observations of physical processes, e.g. sleep.

from: *Advanced Psychology Through Diagram*, *Grhame Hill*, *Oxford University Press*, 1998

Words and Expressions

neurology	n.	[njuə'rɔlədʒi]	神经学;神经病学
hysteria	n.	[his'tiəriə]	歇斯底里;癔症
abnormality	n.	[ˌæbnɔː'mæliti]	变态
psychiatry	n.	[sai'kaiətri]	精神病学;精神病治疗法
Eros	n.	['irɔs, 'erɔs]	爱神;愿望;性爱
Thanatos	n.	['θænətɔs]	死的愿望
ego	n.	['iːgəu]	自我
superego	n.	[ˌsuːpər'egəu]	超我
id	n.	[id]	本我
empiricism	n.	[em'pirisizəm]	经验主义
ethologist	n.	[iː'θɔlədʒist]	生态学研究者;习性学者

nomothetic	adj.	[ˌnɔməˈθetik]	基于普遍性科学规律的
dehumanizing	adj.	[diːˈhjuːmənaiziŋ]	失去人性的
self-actualise	v.	[ˌselfˈæktjuəlaiz]	自我实现
phenomenological	adj.	[fiˌnɔminəˈlɔdʒikəl]	现象的
neuropsychology	n.	[ˌnjuərəusaiˈkɔlədʒi]	神经心理学
physiological	adj.	[ˌfiziəˈlɔdʒikəl]	生理学的
biopsychological	adj.	[ˈbaiəusaikɔˈlɔdʒikəl]	生物心理学的；精神生物学的
nativist	n.	[ˈneitivist]	先天论者；本土主义者
anatomy	n.	[əˈnætəmi]	解剖学
biochemistry	n.	[ˈbaiəuˈkemistri]	生物化学
microelectrode	n.	[ˌmaikrəuiˈlektrəud]	微电极
endocrine	n.	[ˈendəukrain]	内分泌
sociobiological	adj.	[ˌsəuʃiəuˌbaiəˈlɔdʒikəl]	社会生物学的

psychoanalytic approach	心理分析的研究方法
unconscious mental causes	无意识心理原因
unconscious process	无意识过程
psychic determinism	精神决定论
hydraulic drive	液压传动
psychodynamic conflict	心理动力冲突
behaviorist approach	行为主义研究方法
stages of development	发展阶段
free association	自由联想
case study	个案研究
dream analysis	梦的分析
theories of learning	学习理论
humanistic approach	人本主义研究方法
whole unit	单位整体
conscious free will	有意识的自由意志

client-centred therapy	以求诊者为中心的治疗法
internal experience	内在经验
individual case	个案
idiographic case study method	特殊规律个案研究法
Q-sort technique	Q 分类技术
cognitive approach	认知研究方法
artificial intelligence	人工智能
information processor	信息处理器
internal mental process	内在心理加工
biological approach	生物学研究方法
cerebral cortex	大脑皮质
psychological function	心理机能

Difficult Sentences

① Freud became interested in hysteria—the manifestation of physical symptoms without physical causes—and became convinced that unconscious mental causes were responsible not just for this disorder but for all disorders and even "normal" personality.

弗洛伊德对癔病很感兴趣。癔症是没有身体原因的身体症状的表现。他还确信无意识的精神原因不仅仅是这种疾病而且是所有疾病甚至"正常的"人格的起因。

② The behaviourist approach was influenced by the philosophy of empiricism (which argues that knowledge comes from the environment via the senses, since humans are like a "tabula rasa", or blank slate, at birth) and the physical sciences (which emphasize scientific and objective methods of investigation).

行为主义研究方法受经验主义和自然科学的影响。前者认为知识通过感官来自于外部环境,因为人类在出生时就像是一张"白板"。后者强调科学和客观的研究方法。

③ Influenced by gestalt psychology's idea of studying whole unites, and existential philosophy with its belief in conscious free will, humanists argued that behaviourism's artificial and dehumanizing approach and psychoanalysis's gloomy determinism were insufficient to provide a complete psychology.

在格式塔心理学研究单位整体的思想和相信有意识的自由意志的存在哲学的影响下,人本主义者认为行为主义的人为的和不人道的方法以及心理分析那令人沮丧的决定论不能充分地提供一个完整的心理学。

④ Cognitive psychology compares the human mind to a computer, suggesting that we too are information processors and that it is possible and desirable to study the internal mental processes that lie between the stimuli we receive and the responses we make.

认知心理学把人的大脑比作计算机,并认为我们都是信息处理器,界于我们接收到的刺激和做出的反应之间的内部心理活动也可能很值得去研究。

⑤ The biological approach to psychological matters has integrated with and run parallel to the rest of psychological thought since early Greek times—the Greek physician Galen suggested that personality and temperament may be linked to the levels of body fluids such as blood and bile in the body.

自早期的希腊时期,对心理学问题的生物学研究方法已结合了其他的心理学思想并与它们平行发展。当时希腊哲学家盖伦认为个性和气质与诸如血液和胆汁这样的体液的水平有关。

Phrases and Patterns

1. specialise in 专门研究;专门从事
    The psychoanalytic approach was started and developed mainly by Sigmund, a Viennese doctor who specialised in neurology.
    心理分析的研究方法主要是由弗洛伊德提出并发展的,他是维也纳一位专门研究神经病学的医生。
2. a variety of 多种的
For this reason they employ the idiographic case study method, and use a variety of individualistic techniques such as flexible open ended interviews and the Q-sort technique...
因此,他们使用了特殊规律个案研究法并且还使用了多种个体技术,如灵活的、开放式的访问和Q分类技术……
These opportunities were also presented in a variety of contexts.
这些机会在多种情况下呈现。
3. run parallel to... 与……平行
This design incorporates several grids into the plan at different angles that run parallel to the surrounding roads, the railway lines, and the train station plaza.
此设计安排了各式的单元网格,从不同角度与周围道路、铁道及火车站广场相平行。

1.3 Intuition
直觉

From its earliest days, the research that Tversky and I conducted was guided by the idea that intuitive judgments occupy a position—perhaps corresponding to evolutionary history—between the automatic operations of perception and the deliberate operations of reasoning[①]. Our first joint article examined systematic errors in the casual statistical judgments of statistically sophisticated researchers. Remarkably, the intuitive judgments of these experts did not conform to statistical principles with which they were thoroughly familiar. In particular, their intuitive statistical inferences and their estimates of statistical power showed a striking lack of sensitivity to the effects of sample size. We were impressed by the persistence of discrepancies between statistical intuition and statistical knowledge, which we observed both in ourselves and in our colleagues. We were also impressed by the fact that significant research decisions, such as the choice of sample size for an experiment, are routinely guided by the flawed intuitions of people who know better②. In the terminology that became accepted much later, we held a two-system view, which distinguished intuition from reasoning. Our research focused on errors of intuition, which we studied both for their intrinsic interest and for their value as diagnostic indicators of cognitive mechanisms.

The Two-System View

The distinction between intuition and reasoning has been a topic of considerable interest in the intervening decades. In particular, the differences between the two modes of thought have been invoked <u>in attempts to</u> organize seemingly contradictory results in studies of judgment under uncertainty. There is considerable agreement on the characteristics that distinguish the two types of cognitive processes, which Stanovich and West labeled System 1 and System 2. The operations of System 1 are fast, automatic, effortless, associative, and difficult to control or modify. The operations of System 2 are slower, serial, effortful, and deliberately controlled; they are also relatively flexible and potentially rule-governed. The operating characteristics of System 1 are similar to the features of perceptual processes. On the other hand, the operations of System 1, like those of System 2, are not restricted to the processing of current stimulation. Intuitive judgments deal with concepts as well as with percepts, and can be evoked by language.

The perceptual system and the intuitive operations of System 1 generate impressions of the attributes of objects of perception and thought. These impressions are not voluntary and need not be verbally explicit. In contrast, judgments are always explicit and intentional, whether or not they are overtly expressed. Thus, System 2 is involved in all judgments, whether they originate in impressions or in deliberate reasoning. The label "intuitive" is applied to judgments that directly reflect impressions. One of the functions of System 2 is to monitor the quality of both mental operations and overt behavior. The explicit judgments that people make (whether overt or not) are endorsed, at least passively, by System 2. Kahneman and Frederick suggested that the monitoring is normally quite lax, and allows many intuitive judgments to be expressed, including some that are erroneous.

Shane Frederick has used simple puzzles to study cognitive self-monitoring, as in the following example: "A bat and a ball cost USD 1.10 in total. The bat costs USD 1 more than the ball. How much does the ball cost?" Almost everyone reports an initial tendency to answer "10 cents" because the sum USD 1.10 separates naturally into USD 1 and 10 cents, and 10 cents is about the right magnitude. Frederick found that many intelligent people yield to this immediate impulse: 50% (47/93) of Princeton students, and 56% (164/293) of students at the University of Michigan gave the wrong answer. Clearly, these respondents offered a response without checking it. The surprisingly high rate of errors in this easy problem illustrates how lightly the output of System 1 is monitored by System 2: people are not accustomed to thinking hard, and are often content to trust a plausible judgment that quickly comes to mind[3]. Remarkably, errors in this puzzle and in others of the same type were significant predictors of relative indifference to delayed rewards (high discount rates), and of cheating.

The Accessibility Dimension

The core concept of the present analysis of intuitive judgments and preferences is accessibility—the ease with which particular mental contents come to mind. A defining property of intuitive thoughts is that they come to mind spontaneously, like percepts. To understand intuition, then, we must understand why some thoughts are accessible and others are not. The concept of accessibility is applied more broadly in this treatment than in common usage. Category labels, descriptive dimensions (attributes, traits), values of dimensions, all can <u>be described as</u> more or less accessible, for a given individual exposed to a given situation at a particular moment.

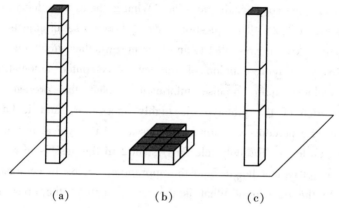

Figure 1.1 **Figure of blocks**

For an illustration of differential accessibility, consider Figure 1.1 (a) and (b). As we look at the object in Figure 1.1 (a), we have immediate impressions of the height of the tower, the area of the top block, and perhaps the volume of the tower. Translating these impressions into units of height or volume requires a deliberate operation, but the impressions themselves are highly accessible. For other attributes, no perceptual impression exists. For example, the total area that the blocks would cover if the tower were dismantled is not perceptually accessible, though it can be estimated by a deliberate procedure, such as multiplying the area of a block by the number of blocks[④]. Of course, the situation is reversed with Figure 1.1(b). Now the blocks are <u>laid out</u> and an impression of total area is immediately accessible, but the height of the tower that could be constructed with these blocks is not.

Some relational properties are accessible. Thus, it is obvious at a glance that Figure 1.1(a) and (c) are different, but also that they are more similar to each other than either is to Figure 1.1(b). And some statistical properties of ensembles are accessible, while others are not. For an example, consider the question "What is the average length of the lines in Figure 1.2?" This question is easy. When a set of objects of the same general kind is presented to an observer—whether simultaneously or successively—a representation of the set is computed automatically, which includes quite precise information about the average. The representation of the prototype is highly accessible, and it has the character of a percept: we form an impression of the typical line without choosing to do so. The only role for System 2 in this task is to map this impression of typical length onto the appropriate scale. In contrast, the answer to the question "What is the total length of the lines in the display?" does not come to mind without considerable effort.

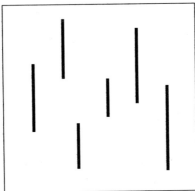

Figure 1.2 Figure of lines

These perceptual examples serve to establish a dimension of accessibility. At one end of this dimension we find operations that have the characteristics of perception and of the intuitive System 1: they are rapid, automatic, and effortless. At the other end are slow, serial and effortful operations that people need a special reason to undertake. Accessibility is a continuum, not a dichotomy, and some effortful operations demand more effort than others. The acquisition of skill selectively increases the accessibility of useful responses and of productive ways to organize information. The master chess player does not see the same board as the novice, and the skill of visualizing the tower that could be built from an array of blocks could surely be improved by prolonged practice[⑤].

from: *Maps of Bounded Rationality: A Perspective on Intuitive Judgment and Choice*, *Prize Lecture, December 8, 2002, by Daniel Kahneman, Princeton University, Department of Psychology, Princeton, NJ08544, USA*

Words and Expressions

intuitive	*adj.*	[inˈtju(ː)itiv]	直觉的
correspond	*v.*	[ˌkɔrisˈpɔnd]	符合;相当;相应
automatic	*adj.*	[ˌɔːtəˈmætik]	自动的;无意识的;机械的
perception	*n.*	[pəˈsepʃən]	感知;感觉
deliberate	*adj.*	[diˈlibəreit]	深思熟虑的;审慎的
conform	*v.*	[kənˈfɔːm]	符合
inference	*n.*	[ˈinfərəns]	推论
estimate	*n.*	[ˈestimeit]	估计;评估
sensitivity	*n.*	[ˌsensiˈtiviti]	敏感
persistence	*n.*	[ˈpəsistəns]	坚持;持续
discrepancy	*n.*	[disˈkrepənsi]	相差;差异;矛盾
terminology	*n.*	[ˌtəːmiˈnɔlədʒi]	术语学

英文	词性	音标	中文
intrinsic	adj.	[in'trinsik]	固有的;内在的;本质的
diagnostic	adj.	[ˌdaiəg'nɔstik]	特征的
indicator	n.	['indikeitə]	指示物
intervene	v.	[ˌintə'vi:n]	(指时间)介于其间
invoke	v.	[in'vəuk]	求助于;使用或应用
contradictory	adj.	[ˌkɔntrə'diktəri]	反驳的;反对的;矛盾的
cognitive	adj.	['kɔgnitiv]	认知的;认识的
associative	adj.	[ə'səuʃjətiv]	联想的
serial	adj.	['siəriəl]	连续的
deliberately	adv.	[di'libərətli]	故意地;审慎地
flexible	adj.	['fleksəbl]	灵活的
potentially	adv.	[pə'tenʃ(ə)li]	潜在地
perceptual	adj.	[pə'septjuəl]	知觉的
percept	n.	['pə:sept]	知觉的对象
evoke	v.	[i'vəuk]	唤起;引起
attribute	n.	[ə'tribju(:)t]	属性;品质;特征
voluntary	adj.	['vɔləntəri]	故意的
verbally	adv.	['və:bəli]	用言辞地
explicit	adj.	[iks'plisit]	清楚的
originate	v.	[ə'ridʒineit]	起源;发生
endorse	v.	[in'dɔ:s]	核准;批准或给予支持
lax	adj.	[læks]	松的;松懈的;不严格的
erroneous	adj.	[i'rəunjəs]	错误的;不正确的
initial	adj.	[i'niʃəl]	最初的
magnitude	n.	['mægnitju:d]	大小;数量
respondent	n.	[ris'pɔndənt]	回答者
lightly	adv.	['laitli]	轻松地;容易地
plausible	adj.	['plɔ:zəbl]	似是而非的
indifference	n.	[in'difrəns]	不关心
accessibility	n.	[ˌæksesi'biliti]	易接近;可到达

dimension	n.	[di'menʃən]	因素
spontaneously	adv.	[spɔn'teinjəsli]	自然地;本能地
differential	adj.	[ˌdifə'renʃəl]	差别的;关于或显出差别的
dismantle	v.	[dis'mæntl]	拆开;分解
procedure	n.	[prə'siːdʒə]	方式;完成某事的途径
reverse	v.	[ri'vəːs]	交换……的位置;使变位
construct	v.	[kən'strʌkt]	建造;构造
ensemble	n.	[əːn'sɑːmbl]	整体;全体
simultaneously	adv.	[siməl'teiniəsli]	同时地
successively	adv.	[sək'sesivli]	接连着;继续地
compute	v.	[kəm'pjuːt]	计算;估计
prototype	n.	['prəutətaip]	原型
undertake	v.	[ˌʌndə'teik]	着手做;从事
continuum	n.	[kən'tinjuəm]	统一体
dichotomy	n.	[dai'kɔtəmi]	二分法
novice	n.	['nɔvis]	新手;初学者
prolonged	adj.	[prə'lɔŋd]	延长的

| sample size | | | 试样量;样本大小 |
| cognitive mechanism | | | 认知机构 |

Difficult Sentences

① From its earliest days, the research that Tversky and I conducted was guided by the idea that intuitive judgments occupy a position—perhaps corresponding to evolutionary history—between the automatic operations of perception and the deliberate operations of reasoning.

从最早开始,Tversky 和我做的研究的指导思想就是:直觉判断介于无意识的感觉活动和深思熟虑的推理活动之间——这或许与进化的历史相符。

② We were also impressed by the fact that significant research decisions, such as the choice of sample size for an experiment, are routinely guided by the flawed intuitions of people who know better.

同时,我们还发现,重要的研究决策,如做实验用的样本量的选择,往往被有头脑的人的错误直觉所引导。

③ The surprisingly high rate of errors in this easy problem illustrates how lightly the output of System 1 is monitored by System 2: people are not accustomed to thinking hard, and are often content to trust a plausible judgment that quickly comes to mind.

人们在这个简单问题上的犯错率如此之高说明了系统 1 的输出很容易受到系统 2 的监控:人们不习惯冥思苦想,往往满足于相信迅速想到的似是而非的判断。

④ For example, the total area that the blocks would cover if the tower were dismantled is not perceptually accessible, though it can be estimated by a deliberate procedure, such as multiplying the area of a block by the number of blocks.

例如,如果塔被拆除,这些木块所占的总面积靠感觉无法知道,尽管可以用一种审慎的方法,如用每一块的面积乘以块数来估算出面积。

⑤ The master chess player does not see the same board as the novice, and the skill of visualizing the tower that could be built from an array of blocks could surely be improved by prolonged practice.

杰出的棋手与新手看棋盘的方式不一样。当然,我们完全可以通过长时间的练习提高从一堆木块设想出能盖出的塔的模样的能力。

Phrases and Patterns

1. in attempts to 企图;用以

   In particular, the differences between the two modes of thought have been invoked in attempts to organize seemingly contradictory results in studies of judgment under uncertainty.

尤其是当人们在需要做出不确定判断的研究中想要理清似乎矛盾的结果时,往往会用到这两种思维模式的差异。

Purchasing consumer goods is thus a significant element in the construction and maintenance of consumers' self-identities, in the attainment of social status, and in attempts to make oneself "feel better".

消费商品的购买是消费者构建和维持自我身份、取得社会地位和企图使自己感觉更好的一个重要因素。

2. yield to 屈服;让步

Frederick found that many intelligent people yield to this immediate impulse.

弗雷德里克发现很多聪明的人往往会有这种直接的冲动。

3. be described as 被描述成;可以说

Category labels, descriptive dimensions (attributes, traits), values of dimensions, all can be described as more or less accessible, for a given individual exposed to a given situation at a particular moment.

对于一个在特定时间、特定环境下的特定的人来说,可以说或多或少都可以了解范畴标志、描述的因素(属性、特征)和属性的价值。

He could be described as radical, more than idealist.

可以说他是激进的,比说他理想主义更确切。

4. lay out 放下;摊开

Now the blocks are laid out and an impression of total area is immediately accessible, but the height of the tower that could be constructed with these blocks is not.

现在,这些木块被放下摊平,你立刻就可以感知它们占据的总面积,但是却无法知道可以用这些木块搭建的塔的高度。

Questions

1. What is psychology and what are its main goals?
2. What are the assumptions of each approach to psychology?
3. What methods of investigation does each approach employ?

2

Main Schools in Psychology and Their Theories
心理学主要学派及其理论

【本章导读】 本章的3篇文章选自于心理学主要学派的代表人物的经典著作。第1篇文章《梦的解析》节选自精神分析学派创始人弗洛伊德的同名原著第6章,介绍了梦的内容和梦的思想的相关关系。第2篇文章《非习得的行为:情绪》节选自行为主义心理学创建人 Watson 的《从行为主义者的眼光来看心理学》的第6章,介绍了什么是情绪,同时宣传了他的心理学主张即以客观观察法来观察行为。第3篇文章《构造心理学公设》节选自构造心理学派代表人物 Titchener 的《心理学评论》第7卷,他试图从经验的构造方面去说明人的整个心理。

2.1 The Interpretation of Dreams
梦的解析

The Dream Work

Every attempt that has hitherto been made to solve the problem of dreams has dealt directly with their manifest content as it is presented in our memory. All such attempts have endeavored to arrive at an interpretation of dreams from their manifest content or (if no interpretation was attempted) to form a judgement as to their nature on the basis of that same manifest content. We are alone in taking something else into account. We have introduced a new class of psychical material between the manifest content of dreams and the conclusions of our enquiry: namely, their latent content, or (as we say) the "dream-thoughts", arrived at by means of our procedure. It is from these dream-thoughts and not from a dream's manifest content that we disentangle its meaning. We are thus presented with a new task which had no previous existence: the task, that is, of investigating the relations between the manifest content of dreams and the latent dream-thoughts, and of tracing out the processes by which the latter have been changed into the former.

The dream-thoughts and the dream-content are presented to us like two versions of the same subject-matter in two different languages. Or, more properly, the dream-content seems like a transcript of the dream-thoughts into another mode of expression, whose characters and syntactic laws it is our business to discover by comparing the original and the translation. The dream-thoughts are immediately comprehensible, as soon as we have learnt them. The dream-contents, on the other hand, is expressed as it were in a pictographic script, the characters of which have to be transposed individually into the language of the dream – thoughts. If we attempted to read these characters according to their pictorial value instead of according to their symbolic relation, we should clearly be led into error. Suppose I have a picture-puzzle, a rebus, in front of me. It depicts a house with a boat on its roof, a single letter of the alphabet, the figure of a running man whose head has been conjured away, and so on. Now I might be misled into raising objections and declaring that the picture as a whole and its component parts are nonsensical. A boat has no business to be on the roof of a house, and a headless man cannot run.

Moreover, the man is bigger than the house; and if the whole picture is intended to represent a landscape, letters of the alphabet are out of place in it since such objects do not occur in nature. But obviously we can only form a proper judgement of the rebus if we put aside criticisms such as these of the whole composition and its parts and if, instead, we try to replace each separate element by a syllable or word that can be represented by that element in some way or other①. The words which are put together in this way are no longer nonsensical but many form a poetical phrase of the greatest beauty and significance. A dream is a picture—puzzle of this sort and our predecessors in the field of dream—interpretation have made the mistake of treating the rebus as a pictorial composition; and as such it has seemed to them nonsensical and worthless.

The Work of Displacement

In making our collection of instances of condensation in dreams, the existence of another relation, probably of no less importance, had already become evident②. It could be seen that the elements which stand out as the principal components of the manifest content of the dream are far from playing the same part in the dream-thoughts. And, as a corollary, the converse of this assertion can be affirmed: What is clearly the essence of the dream-thoughts need not be represented in the dream at all. The dream is, as it were, differently centred from the dream-thoughts—its content has different elements as its central point. Thus in the dream of the botanical monograph, for instance, the central point of the dream-content was obviously the element "botanical"; whereas the dream-thoughts were concerned with the complications and conflicts arising between colleagues from their professional obligations, and further with the charge that I was in the habit of sacrificing too much for the sake of my hobbies. The element "botanical" has no place whatever in this core of the dream-thoughts, unless it was loosely connected with it by an antithesis—the fact that botany never had a place among my favourite studies. In my patient's Sappho dream the central position was occupied by climbing up and down and being up above and down below; the dream-thoughts, however, dealt with the dangers of sexual relations with people of an inferior social class. So that only a single element of the dream-content, though that element was expanded to a disproportionate extent. Similarly, in the dream of the may-beetles, the topic of which was the relations of sexuality to cruelty, it is true that the factor of cruelty emerged in the dream-content; but it did so in another connection and without any mention of sexuality, that is to say, divorced from its context and consequently transformed into something extraneous. Once again, in my dream about my uncle, the fair beard which formed its centre-point seems to have had no connection in its meaning with my ambitious wishes which, as we saw, were the core of the dream thoughts. Dreams such as these give a justifiable impression of "displacement". In complete contrast to these examples, we can see that in the dream of Irma's injection the different elements were able to retain, during the process of construction the dream, the approximate place which they occupied in the dream-thoughts. This further relation between the dream-thoughts and the dream-content, wholly variable as it is in its sense or direction, is calculated at first to create astonishment. If we are considering a psychical process in normal life and find that one out of its several component ideas has been picked out and has acquired a special degree of vividness in consciousness, we usually regard this effect as evidence that a specially high amount of psychical value—some particular degree of interest—attaches to this predominant idea. But we now discover that, in the case of the different elements of the dream-thoughts, a value of this kind does not persist or is disregarded in the process of dream-formation. There is never any doubt as to which of the elements of the dream-thoughts have the highest psychical value; we learn that by direct judgement. In the course of the formation of a dream these essential elements, charged, as they are, with intense interest, may be treated as though they were of small value, and their place may be taken in the dream-thoughts there can be no question[3]. At first sight it looks as though no attention whatever is paid to the psychical intensity of the various ideas in making the choice among them for the dream, and as though the only thing considered is the greater or less degree of multiplicity of their determination. What appears in dreams, we might suppose, is not what is important in the dream-thoughts but what occurs in them several times over. But this hypothesis does not greatly assist our understanding of dream-formation, since from the nature of things it seems clear that the two factors of multiple determination and inherent psychical value must necessarily operate in the same sense. The ideas which are most important among the dream-thoughts will almost certainly be those which occur most often in them, since the different dream-thoughts will, as it were, radiate out from them. Nevertheless a dream can reject elements which are thus both highly stressed in themselves and reinforced from many directions, and can select for its content other elements which possess only the second of these attributes.

In order to solve this difficulty we shall make use of another impression derived from our enquiry into the overdetermination of the dream-content. Perhaps some of those who have read that enquiry may already have formed an independent conclusion that the overdetermination of the elements of dreams is no very important discovery, since it is a self-evident one. For in analysis we start out from the dream elements and note down all the associations which lead off from them; so that there is nothing surprising in the fact that in the thought-material arrived at in this way we come across these same elements with peculiar frequency. I cannot accept this objection; but I will myself put into words something that sounds not unlike it. Among the thoughts that analysis brings to light are many which are relatively remote from the kernel of the dream and which look like artificial interpolations made for some particular purpose[④]. That purpose is easy to divine. It is precisely that they constitute a connection, often a forced and far-fetched one, between the dream-content and the dream-thoughts; and if these elements were weeded out of the analysis the result would often be that the component parts of the dream-content would be left not only without overdetermination but without any satisfactory determination at all[⑤]. We shall be led to conclude that the multiple determination which decides what shall be included in a dream is not always a primary factor in dream-construction but is often the secondary product of a psychical force which is still unknown to us. Nevertheless multiple determination must be of importance in choosing what particular elements shall enter a dream, since we can see that a considerable expenditure of effort is used to bring it about in cases where it does not arise from the dream-material unassisted.

It thus seems plausible to suppose that in the dream-work a psychical force is operating which on the one hand strips the elements which have a high psychical value of their intensity, and on the other hand, by means of overdetermination, creates from elements of low psychical value new values, which afterwards find their way into the dream-content. If that is so, a transference and displacement of psychical intensities occurs in the process of dream-formation, and it is as a result of these that the difference between the text of the dream-content and that of the dream-thoughts comes about. The process which we are here presuming is nothing less than the essential portion of the dream-work; and it deserves to be described as "dream-displacement". Dream-displacement and dream-condensation are the two governing factors to whose activity we may in essence ascribe the form assumed by dreams.

Nor do I think we shall have any difficulty in recognizing the psychical force which manifests itself in the facts of dream-displacement. The consequence of the displacement is that the dream-content no longer resembles the core of the dream-thoughts and that the dream gives no more than a distortion of the dream-wish which exists in the unconscious. But we are already familiar with dream distortion. We traced it back to the censorship which is exercised by one psychical agency in the mind over another. Dream-displacement is one of the chief methods by which that distortion is achieved. *Is fecit cui profuit*. (Latin, means it is the way that can form dreams.) We may assume, then, that dream-displacement comes about through the influence of the same censorship—that is, the censorship of endopsychic defence.

The question of the interplay of these factors—of displacement, condensation and overdetermination—in the construction of dreams, and the question which is a dominant factor and which a subordinate one—all of this we shall leave aside for later investigation. But we can state provisionally a second condition which must be satisfied by those elements of the dream-thoughts which make their way into the dream: they must escape the censorship imposed by resistance. And henceforward in interpreting dreams we shall take dream-displacement into account as an undeniable fact.

from: *The Interpretation of Dreams*, Sigmund Freud, Wordsworth, 1997

Words and Expressions

hitherto	adv.	[ˌhiðə'tu:]	迄今;至今
psychical	adj.	['saikikəl]	灵魂的;精神的
latent	adj.	['leitənt]	潜在的;潜伏的;隐藏的

disentangle	v.	['disin'tæŋgl]	解脱;解开纠结;松开;解决(纠纷)
syntactic	adj.	[sin'tæktik]	依据造句法的
pictographic	adj.	[,piktə'græfik]	象形文字的
pictorial	adj.	[pik'tɔːriəl]	图示的
rebus	n.	['riːbəs]	(猜字的)画谜
nonsensical	adj.	[nɔn'sensikəl]	无意义的;荒谬的
displacement	n.	[dis'pleismənt]	移置;转移;取代;置换;位移;排水量
condensation	n.	[kɔnden'seiʃən]	浓缩
corollary	n.	[kə'rɔləri]	必然的结果;系;推论
botanical	adj.	[bə'tænik(ə)l]	植物学的
monograph	n.	['mɔnəugrɑːf]	专论
antithesis	n.	[æn'tiθisis]	对立面
extraneous	adj.	[eks'treinjəs]	无关系的;外来的;[化]外部裂化;[化]新异反射
justifiable	adj.	['dʒʌstifaiəbl]	有理由的
multiplicity	n.	[,mʌlti'plisiti]	多样性
radiate	v.	['reidieit]	放射;辐射;传播;广播
attribute	n.	[ə'tribju(ː)t]	属性;品质;特征;加于;归结于
interpolation	n.	[in,təːpəu'leiʃən]	篡改;插补
expenditure	n.	[iks'penditʃə]	支出;花费
plausible	adj.	['plɔːzəbl]	似是而非的
transference	n.	['trænsfərəns]	移动;转送;转让
manifest	v.	['mænifest]	表明;证明
distortion	n.	[dis'tɔːʃən]	扭曲;变形;曲解;失真
censorship	n.	['sensəʃip]	审查机构;审查制度
endopsychic	adj.	[,endəu'saikik]	灵魂中的

dream-work	梦的运作
manifest-content	梦的显意
dream-thoughts	梦的思想
pictographic script	象形文字的原稿
work of displacement	梦的转移作用
botanical monograph	植物学专论
psychical process	心理过程
dream-content	梦的内容
dream-displacement	梦的转移
dream-condensation	梦的凝缩

Difficult Sentences

① But obviously we can only form a proper judgement of the rebus if we put aside criticisms such as these of the whole composition and its parts and if, instead, we try to replace each separate element by a syllable or word that can be represented by that element in some way or other.

想对这幅画谜做出正确解释,只有抛弃这些对其整体和各部分的反对意见,并用每一个成分所代表的音节或词来代替该成分。

② In making our collection of instances of condensation in dreams, the existence of another relation, probably of no less importance, had already become evident.

当我们收集"梦凝缩"的例子时,我们就已注意到了另外一种重要性不亚于凝缩作用的因素。

③ In the course of the formation of a dream these essential elements, charged, as they are, with intense interest, may be treated as though they were of small value, and their place may be taken in the dream-thoughts there can be no question.

在梦形成时,那些富有强烈兴趣的重要部分往往成了次要部分,反而被某些"梦思"中次要的部分所代替。

④ Among the thoughts that analysis brings to light are many which are relatively remote from the kernel of the dream and which look like artificial interpolations made for some particular purpose.

通过梦的分析所找出的意念中,有些已与梦的核心相去甚远而变成了似乎是为了某种特定目的而设的人为添加物。

⑤ It is precisely that they constitute a connection, often a forced and far-fetched one, between the dream-content and the dream-thoughts; and if these elements were weeded out of the analysis the result would often be that the component parts of the dream-content would be left not only without overdetermination but without any satisfactory determination at all.

正是它们构成了"梦的内容"与"梦思"之间的联系,通常是一种牵强的联系。如果在分析中剔除这些元素,那么,结果通常是梦的内容中的构成部分不只是没有过度判断,连差强人意的判断都做不到。

Phrases and Patterns

1. take ... into account 重视;考虑

   We are alone in taking something else into account.

   在这方面我们有不同的考虑。

   Moreover, they further point to the need to supplement traditional global assessments of personality with more contextual ones that take into account situational influences.

   此外,他们进一步指出,有必要更多地考虑到情境影响的情景评估来补充传统的综合人格评估。

2. have no business to do 无权利做某事;不可能做某事

   A boat has no business to be on the roof of a house, and a headless man cannot run.

   一只小船不可能摆放在屋顶上,一个无头的人不可能跑动。

3. in the habit of 有……的习惯;常常

...whereas the dream-thoughts were concerned with the complications and conflicts arising between colleagues from their professional obligations, and further with the charge that I was in the habit of sacrificing too much for the sake of my hobbies.

同时,梦的思想与同事之间从工作义务中引起的复杂和冲突有关系,甚至跟我常常为了我的个人爱好而牺牲很多的个人习惯有关系。

He's not in the habit of drinking a lot.
他不习惯多喝酒。

4. on the one hand... on the other hand... 一方面……另一方面……
It thus seems plausible to suppose that in the dream-work a psychical force is operating which on the one hand strips the elements which have a high psychical value of their intensity, and on the other hand, by means of overdetermination, creates from elements of low psychical value new values, which afterwards find their way into the dream-content.

大概可以这样假设:在梦的运作下,一种精神力量一方面将其本身精神价值较高的单元所含的精神强度予以降低,而另一方面,利用过度判断的方法,可以从精神价值较低的单元中塑造出新的价值,此后这些新价值在梦的内容中得以表现。

We may regard mind, on the one hand, as a complex of processes, shaped and moulded under the conditions of the physical organism. We may regard it, on the other hand, as the collective name for a system of functions of the psychophysical organism.

一方面,我们可以把意识当作一种复杂的过程,在身体机能状况下形成。另一方面,我们还可以把它当成心理物理机体功能系统的集合名词。

5. in essence 本质上;大体上;其实
Dream-displacement and dream-condensation are the two governing factors to whose activity we may in essence ascribe the form assumed

by dreams.

其实,"梦的转移"与"梦的凝缩"有可能是我们剖析梦的结构的两大决定性因素。

The two arguments are in essence the same.

这两个论点大致相同。

2.2 Unlearned Behavior: Emotion
非习得的行为:情绪

Introduction

In the last three chapters we have been concerned with the details of sensory-motor adjustment. We turn next to man as a reacting organism, and specifically to some of the reactions which belong to his hereditary equipment. Human action as a whole can be divided into hereditary modes of response (emotional and instinctive), and acquired modes of response (habit). Each of these two broad divisions is capable of subdivisions. It is obvious both from the standpoint of common-sense and of laboratory experimentation that the hereditary and acquired forms of activity begin to overlap early in life. Emotional reactions become wholly separated from the stimuli that originally called them out, and the instinctive positive reaction tendencies displayed by the child soon become overlaid with the organized habits of the adult[①]. This process of masking or dovetailing of activities is a part of the general process of organization. The separation between hereditary reaction modes and acquired reaction modes can thus never be made absolute. Fortunately in most connections psychology is not called upon to draw a sharp distinction between hereditary and acquired reactions. In making laboratory studies, however, it is sometimes necessary for us to study the details of hereditary response. We find it simpler in such cases to overemphasize for the time the definiteness of the separation. This is unquestionably a legitimate mode of procedure in science. Few biological problems permit of any other treatment. In order to accomplish this at all we have to adopt a genetic method. We have to start with the baby's advent (we would start before if it were not for possible injure to mother and child) and follow his development step by step, noting the first appearance of the hereditary forms of reaction, their course and effect upon the moulding of the child's whole personality; and the early beginnings of acquired modes of response. Undoubtedly learning begins in utero (there is no reason to suppose that conditioned reflexes do not begin there), and probably several hereditary modes of action (particular types of reflexes) run their entire course in utero. But we are entering here upon a field which just at present is purely speculative.

What Is an Emotion?

Hard and fast definitions are not possible in the psychology of emotion, but formulations are possible and sometimes help us to group our facts. A formulation which will fit a part of the emotional group of reactions may be stated as follows: An emotion is a hereditary "pattern-reaction" involving profound changes of the bodily mechanism as a whole, but particularly of the visceral and glandular systems[2]. By pattern-reaction we mean that the separate details of response appear with some constancy, with some regularity and in approximately the same sequential order each time the exciting stimulus is presented. It is obvious that if this formulation is to fit the facts, the general condition of the organism must be such that the stimulus can produce its effect. A child alone in a house on a stormy night with only a dim candle burning may display the reaction of fear at the mournful hoot of an owl. If the parents are at hand and the room is well lighted, the stimulus may pass unreacted to.

Stimulus then in this sense is used in a broad way to refer not only to the exciting object but also to the general setting. There is implied also the fact that the general state of the organism must be sensitive (capable of being stimulated) to this form of stimulus at the moment. This condition is very important. A young man may be extremely sensitive to the blandishments of every female he meets while in the unmarried state and may show considerable excitement and over-reaction on such occasions. In most cases, he becomes considerably less sensitive after being happily married. This formulation may seem somewhat roundabout—somewhat like saying that a stimulus is an emotional stimulus only when you get the pattern-reaction, but this is very nearly the case. Possibly we can illustrate most easily what we mean by choosing an example from animal life. When the naturalist comes suddenly upon a young sooty tern under four days of age, it lies stock still (it is capable of very rapid locomotion): It can be pushed about or rolled over without explicit forms of response appearing. The moment the intruder moves away, the fledgling may hop to its feet and dash away or give one of its instinctive cries. The pattern-reaction, that is, the explicit observable pattern, is very simple indeed—a death feint or posture. Such a type of response which is quite common is the animal world. In order to bring about such a tremendous variation in behavior in an animal usually so active there must be a profound modification of the organic processes. We shall see later that the locus of the effect is principally in the visceral system. Often, however, the skeletal musculature is involved in the pattern. A serviceable way to mark off an emotional reaction from an instinctive reaction is to include in the formulation of emotion a factor which may be stated as follows: The shock of an emotional stimulus throws the organism for the moment at least into a chaotic state[3]. When in the first shock of an emotional state, the subject makes few adjustments to objects in his environment. In contrast to this stand the instincts as we shall see farther on. The subject in an instinctive act usually does something: he throws his hand up for defense, blinks his eyes or ducks his head; runs away; he bites, scratches, kicks and grasps whatever his hand touches. We may express our formulation in convenient terms somewhat as follows: when the adjustments called out by the stimulus are internal and confined to the subject's body, we have emotion, for example, blushing; when the stimulus leads to adjustment of the organism as a whole to objects, we have instinct, for example, defense responses, grasping, etc. Emotions seldom appear alone. The stimulus usually calls out emotional instinctive and habit factors simultaneously[4].

Additional Formulation

The above formulation fits only the more stereotyped forms of emotional response as seen, for example, in the states popularly called blushing, anger, fear and shame. When we take into account the whole group of phenomena in which we see emotional manifestations in adults, a pronounced modification is necessary. Apparently the hereditary pattern as a whole gets broken up. At any rate it largely disappears (the parts never wholly disappear) except under unusual conditions, and there can be noted only a reinforcement or inhibition of the habit and instinctive (exaggerated and depressed reflexes, for example) activities taking place at the moment. We mean to imply here only the generally observed facts typified by such popular expressions as "He is working at a low ebb today" "His tone is low" "He's a gloom"; in psychopathology when this phase is more marked, depression are spoken of. The opposite picture is popularly portrayed by such expressions as "Jones is full of pep today" "he is excited" "happy" "he is working with a punch"; in psychopathology, the exaggerated type of this behavior is termed manic. It will be noted that these expressions refer to the activity level at which all of an individual's acts are accomplished, that is, they do not refer to the pattern type of emotion. Only in pathological cases, or in the case of normals in periods of a cataclysmic nature, such as war, earthquake, and the sudden death of loved ones, do we get a complete return to the original and more infantile type of emotional response.

Observation would seem to suggest the following formulation: Organized activity (hereditary and acquired) may go on and usually does go on at a given level. We may call the most usual the normal level or level of equilibrium. It varies with different individuals and one can determine it even with respect to a single individual only after observing him for a considerable time. We may note further that an individual at one time may exhibit more energy, push or pep than normal, for example, during and immediately, after a cold shower; we may call this the excited level. Again at times he works at a level lower than normal, for example, when in trouble, after money losses or illness; we may call this the depressed level.

Without neurologizing too much, we may venture the assumption that in adults environmental factors have brought about the partial inhibition of the more external features of the primitive pattern types of emotion. The implicit, mainly glandular and smooth muscular side of the pattern, remains. The emotionally exciting object releases important internal secretions which, without initiation new (part) reactions, reinforce or inhibit those actually in progress. This hypothesis would account for changes in level. Only in rare cases do we see mere changes in level. Usually when such changes occur, certain auxiliary or additional part reactions appear, such as we see in whistling while at work, keeping time with the feet, drumming on the table, biting the finger nails. These types of reaction are singled out and spoken of in some detail under the head Emotional Outlets.

The Genetic Study of Emotion in the Child

Unfortunately for the subject of psychology, few experiments have been made upon the emotional life of the child under anything like as favorable conditions as obtain in the study of animals[5]. Our observations upon the child are similar to those which were made upon animals before Thorndike and Lloyd Morgan introduced the experimental method. Until very recently, in spite of volumes written upon it, discussion has been of the armchair variety. The superstition that the human infant is too fragile for study is giving way to a more sensible viewpoint. It has proven practicable in some laboratories to take infants from birth and to study them from the same point of view that animals are studied, giving due consideration to those factors in behavior which do not appear in animal response. But unfortunately this work is handicapped because there are no facilities in maternity wards for keeping the mother and child under close observation for years, a condition which is indispensable for real systematic work.

from: *Psychology from the Standpoint of a Behaviorist*, Waston J. B., 1919

Words and Expressions

hereditary	adj.	[hi'reditəri]	遗传的
dovetailing	adj.	[dʌv'teiliŋ]	燕尾连接楔形接合
legitimate	adj.	[li'dʒitimit]	合法的;合理的
moulding	n.	['məuldiŋ]	塑造
personality	n.	[ˌpə:sə'næliti]	个性;人格
inutero	n.	[in'ju:tərəu]	在子宫内;未出生
formulation	n.	[ˌfɔ:mju'leiʃən]	明确地表达;简洁陈述
instinct	n.	['instiŋkt]	本能
visceral	adj.	['visərəl]	内脏的

glandular	adj.	['glændjulə]	腺(状)的
locomotion	n.	[ˌləukə'məuʃ(ə)n]	运动
modification	n.	[ˌmɔdifi'keiʃən]	修改；修正
skeletal	adj.	['skelitl]	骨骼的
musculature	n.	['mʌskjulətʃə]	肌肉组织
chaotic	adj.	[kei'ɔtik]	混乱的；无秩序的
manifestation	n.	[ˌmænifes'teiʃən]	显示；表现
reinforcement	n.	[ˌriːin'fɔːsmənt]	加强
psychopathology	n.	[ˌsaikəupə'θɔlədʒi]	精神病理学
manic	adj.	['meinik]	狂躁的
pathological	adj.	[ˌpæθə'lɔdʒikəl]	病理的；病态的
infantile	adj.	['infəntail]	婴儿的
equilibrium	n.	[ˌiːkwi'libriəm]	平衡
secretion	n.	[si'kriːʃən]	分泌
auxiliary	adj.	[ɔːg'zilijəri]	辅助的
facility	n.	[fə'siliti]	设备

common-sense	常识(尤指判断力)
hereditary modes of response	遗传的反应模式
acquired modes of response	习得的反应模式
genetic method	遗传研究法
stereotyped form	刻板形式
activity level	活动水平
normal level	正常水平
level of equilibrium	平衡水平
excited level	兴奋水平
depressed level	抑郁水平
internal secretion	内分泌物
conditioned reflex	条件反射

Difficult Sentences

① Emotional reactions become wholly separated from the stimuli that originally called them out, and the instinctive positive reaction tendencies displayed by the child soon become overlaid with the organized habits of the adult.
情绪的反应与原来引起它们的刺激可以完全分离,孩童所表现出来的本能的积极反应趋向很快被成年人的有条理的习惯所覆盖。

② An emotion is a hereditary "pattern-reaction" involving profound changes of the bodily mechanism as a whole, but particularly of the visceral and glandular systems.
情绪是一种遗传的"反应模式",包括整个身体构造的完全变化,最显著的是内脏和腺体的变化。

③ The shock of an emotional stimulus throws the organism for the moment at least into a chaotic state.
情绪刺激的震动至少在那个时候把机体置于混乱状态中。

④ The stimulus usually calls out emotional instinctive and habit factors simultaneously.
刺激通常把情绪性的本能因素及习惯因素同时激发起来。

⑤ Unfortunately for the subject of psychology, few experiments have been made upon the emotional life of the child under anything like as favorable conditions as obtain in the study of animals.
对心理学学科而言不幸的是,对孩子情感生活所做的实验,所依赖的条件很少像研究动物时的实验条件那么有利。

Phrases and Patterns

1. draw a sharp distinction between ... and ... 对……与……加以区别
   Fortunately in most connections psychology is not called upon to draw a sharp distinction between hereditary and acquired reactions.

幸而心理学通常用不着在遗传的反应模式和习得的反应模式二者之间作严格的区别。

You can draw a distinction between deductive and inductive reasoning in this way: In deductive reasoning, the conclusion is derived through the use of general rules, whereas in inductive reasoning, a conclusion is inferred from specific examples.

你可以用这种方法来对演绎推理和归纳推理加以区别:在演绎推理中,结论是通过使用普遍规则得出的;而在归纳推理中,结论是从特定的例子中推断出来的。

2. enter upon(on) 着手开始

But we are entering here upon a field which just at present is purely speculative.

不过我们着手开始研究的领域现在还纯粹是推想而已。

3. as we shall see farther on 后面我们会了解到

In contrast to this stand the instincts as we shall see farther on.

本能与此相反,讲到以后章节我们便知道。

4. account for 说明

This hypothesis would account for changes in level.

这个假设会说明水平的变化。

The suspect couldn't account for his time that night.

嫌疑犯解释不清楚那天晚上他的时间安排。

2.3 The Postulates of a Structural Psychology
构造心理学公设

Biology, defined in its widest sense as the science of life and of living things, falls into three parts, or may be approached from any one of three points of view. We may enquire into the structure of an organism, without regard to function—by analysis determining its component parts, and by synthesis exhibiting the mode of its formation from the parts①. Or we may enquire into the function of the various structures which our analysis has revealed, and into the manner of their interrelation as functional organs. Or, again, we may enquire into the changes of form and function that accompany the persistence of the organism in time, the phenomena of growth and of decay. Biology, the science of living things, comprises the three mutually interdependent sciences of morphology, physiology, and ontogeny②.

This account is, however, incomplete. The life which forms the subject matter of science is not merely the life of an individual; it is species life, collective life, as well. Corresponding to morphology, we have taxonomy or systematic zoology, the science of classification. The whole world of living things is here the organism, and species and sub-species and races are its parts. Corresponding to physiology, we have that department of biology—it has been termed "oecology"—which deals with questions of geographical distribution, of the function of species in the general economy of nature. Corresponding to ontogeny we have the science of phylogeny (in Cope's sense): the biology of evolution, with its problems of descent and of transmission.

We may accept this scheme as a "working" classification of the biological sciences. It is indifferent, for may present purpose, whether or not the classification is exhaustive, as it is indifferent whether the reader regards psychology as a subdivision of biology or as a separate province of knowledge. The point which I wish now to make is this: that, employing the same principle of division, we can represent modern psychology as the exact counterpart of modern biology. There are three ways of approaching the one, as there are the three ways of approaching the other; and the subject matter in every case may be individual or general. A little consideration will make this clear.

1. We find a parallel to morphology in a very large portion of

"experimental" psychology. The primary aim of the experimental psychologist has been to analyze the structure of mind; to ravel out the elemental processes from the tangle of consciousness, or (if we may change the metaphor) to isolate the constituents in the given conscious formation. His task is a vivisection, but a vivisection which shall yield structural, not functional results. He tries to discover, first of all, what is there and in what quantity, not what it is there for. Indeed, this work of analysis bulks so largely in the literature of experimental psychology that a recent writer has questioned the right of the science to its adjective, declaring that an experiment is something more than a measurement made by the help of delicate instruments. And there can be no doubt that much of the criticism passed upon the new psychology depends on the critic's failure to recognize its morphological character. We are often told that our treatment of feeling and emotion, of reasoning, of the self is inadequate; that the experimental method is valuable for the investigation of sensation and idea, but can carry us no farther. The answer is that the results gained by dissection of the "higher" processes will always be disappointing to those who have not themselves adopted the dissector's standpoint. Protoplasm consists, we are told, of carbon, oxygen, nitrogen, and hydrogen; but this statement would prove exceedingly disappointing to one who had thought to be informed of the phenomena of contractility and metabolism, respiration and reproduction[③]. Taken in its appropriate context, the jejuneness of certain chapters in mental anatomy, implying, as it does, the fewness of the mental elements, is a fact of extreme importance.

2. There is, however, a functional psychology, over and above this psychology of structure. We may regard mind, on the one hand, as a complex of processes, shaped and moulded under the conditions of the physical organism. We may regard it, on the other hand, as the collective name for a system of functions of the psychophysical organism.

The two points of view are not seldom confused. The phrase "association of ideas", e.g., may denote either the structural complex, the associated sensation group, or the functional process of recognition and recall, the associating of formation to formation. <u>In the former</u> sense it is morphological material, <u>in the latter</u> it belongs to what I must name (the phrase will not be misunderstood) a physiological psychology.

Just as experimental psychology is to a large extent concerned with problems of structure, so is "descriptive" psychology, ancient and modern, chiefly occupied with problems of function. Memory, recognition, imagination, conception, judgment, attention, apperception, volition, and a host of verbal nouns, wider or narrower in denotation, connote, in the discussions of descriptive psychology, functions of the total organism. That their underlying processes are psychical in character is, so to speak, an accident; for all practical purposes they stand upon the same level as digestion and locomotion, secretion and excretion. The organism remembers, wills, judges, recognizes, etc., and is assisted in its life-struggle by remembering and willing. Such functions are, however, rightly included in mental science, in as much as they constitute, in sum, the actual, working mind of the individual man. They are not functions of the body, but functions of the organism, and they may—nay, they must—be examined by the methods and under the regulative principles of a mental "physiology". The adoption of these methods does not at all prejudice the ultimate and extra-psychological problem of the function of mentality <u>at large</u> in the universe of things[4]. Whether consciousness really has a survival-value, as James supposes, or whether it is a mere epiphenomenon, as Ribot teaches, is here an entirely irrelevant question.

It cannot be said that this functional psychology, despite what we may call its greater obviousness to investigation, has been worked out either with as much patient enthusiasm or with as much scientific accuracy as has the psychology of mind structure. It is true, and it is a truth which the experimentalist should be quick to recognize and emphasize, that there is very much of value in "descriptive" psychology. But it is also true that the methods of descriptive psychology cannot, in the nature of the case, lead to results of scientific finality. The same criticism holds, as things stand, of individual psychology, which is doing excellent pioneer work in the sphere of function. Experimental psychology has added much to our knowledge, functional as well as structural, of memory, attention, imagination, etc., and will, in the future, absorb and quantify the results of these other, new coordinate branches. Still, I do not think that anyone who has followed the course of the experimental method, in its application to the higher processes and states of mind, can doubt that the main interest throughout has lain in morphological analysis, rather than in ascertainment of function. Nor are the reasons far to seek. We must remember that experimental psychology arose by way of reaction against the faculty psychology of the last century. This was a metaphysical, not a scientific, psychology. There is, in reality, a great difference between, say, memory regarded as a function of the psychophysical organism, and memory regarded as a faculty of the substantial mind. At the same time, these two memories are nearer together than are the faculty memory and the memories or memory complexes of psychological anatomy. There is, further, the danger that, if function is studied before structure has been fully elucidated, the student may <u>fall into</u> that acceptance of teleological explanation which is fatal to scientific advance: witness, if witness be necessary, the recrudescence of vitalism in physiology. Psychology might thus put herself for the second time, and no less surely though by different means, under the dominion of philosophy. In a word, the historical conditions of psychology rendered it inevitable that, when the time came for the transformation from philosophy to science, problems should be formulated, explicitly or implicitly, as static rather than dynamic, structural rather than functional. We may notice also the fact that elementary morphology is intrinsically an easier study than elementary physiology, and that scientific men are so far subject to the law of inertia, whose effects we see in the conservatism of mankind at large, that prefer the continued application of a fruitful method to the adoption of a new standpoint for the standpoint's sake.

I may, perhaps, digress here for a moment, to raise and attempt to answer two questions which naturally suggest themselves: the questions whether this conservatism is wise, and whether it is likely to persist. I believe that both should be answered in the affirmative. As has been indicated above, the morphological study of mind serves, as no other method of study can, to enforce and sustain the thesis that psychology is a science, and not a province of metaphysics; and recent writing shows clearly enough that this truth has need of constant reiteration. Moreover, there is still so much to be done in the field of analysis (not simply analysis of the higher processes, though these will of course benefit in the long run, but also analysis of perception and feeling and idea) that a general swing of the laboratories towards functional work would be most regrettable. It seems probable, if one may presume to read the signs of the times, that experimental psychology has before it a long period of analytical research, whose results, direct and indirect, shall ultimately serve as basis for the psychology of function; unless, indeed—and this is beyond predicting—the demands laid upon psychology by the educationalist become so insistent as partially to divert the natural channels of investigation.

The remaining four psychologies may be dismissed with a briefer mention.

3. Ontogenetic psychology, the psychology of individual childhood and adolescence, is now a subject of wide interest, and has a large

literature of its own.

4. Taxonomic psychology is not yet, and in all likelihood will not be, for some time to come, anything more than an ingredient in "descriptive", and a portion of individual, psychology. It deals with such topics as the classification of emotions, instincts and impulses, temperaments, etc., the hierarchy of psychological "selves", the typical mind of social classes (artists, soldiers, literary men), and so forth.

5. The functional psychology of the collective mind is, as might be expected, in a very rudimentary condition. We can delimit its sphere and indicate its problems; minor contributions to it may be found here and there in the pages of works upon psychology, logic, ethics, aesthetics, sociology, and anthropology; and a few salient points—the question, e. g. of the part played by the aesthetic sentiment in the make-up of a national mind—have been touched upon in essays. But we must have an experimental physiology of individual mind, before there can be any great progress.

6. Lastly, the labors of the evolutionary school have set phylogenetic psychology upon a fairly secure foundation, and the number of workers is a guarantee of rapid advance in our understanding of mental development[⑤].

from: *Psychological Review*, 1898, *Vol.* 7, 449 ~ 465

Words and Expressions

postulate	n.	[ˈpɔstjuleit]	假定;基本条件;基本原理
synthesis	n.	[ˈsinθisis]	综合;合成
accompany	v.	[əˈkʌmpəni]	陪伴;伴奏
decay	n.	[diˈkei]	腐朽;腐烂;衰减;衰退
comprise	v.	[kəmˈpraiz]	包含;由……组成
morphology	n.	[mɔːˈfɔlədʒi]	[生物]形态学;形态论 [语法]词法;词态学

physiology	n.	[ˌfizi'ɔlədʒi]	生理学
ontogeny	n.	[ɔn'tɔdʒini]	[生]个体发生;个体发生学
taxonomy	n.	[tæk'sɔnəmi]	分类法;分类学
zoology	n.	[zəu'ɔlədʒi]	动物学
oecology	n.	[iː'kɔlədʒi]	生态学;社会生态学
phylogeny	n.	[fai'lɔdʒini]	语系发生;发展史
constituent	n.	[kən'stitjuənt]	委托人;要素
bulk	v.	[bʌlk]	显得大;显得重要
metaphysical	adj.	[ˌmetə'fizikəl]	形而上学的;纯粹哲学的;超自然的
elucidate	v.	[i'ljuːsideit]	阐明;说明
recrudescence	n.	[ˌriːkruː'desns]	复发;再发作
dominion	n.	[də'minjən]	主权;领土;统治权;支配;控制
metabolism	n.	[mə'tæbəlizəm]	新陈代谢
apperception	n.	[ˌæpə'sepʃən]	领悟;知觉
volition	n.	[vəu'liʃən]	意志
secretion	n.	[si'kriːʃən]	分泌;分泌物(液)
excretion	n.	[eks'kriːʃən]	(动植物的)排泄;排泄物
epiphenomenon	n.	[ˌepifi'nɔminən]	附带现象;偶发症状
rudimentary	adj.	[ruːdi'mentəri]	根本的;未发展的
aesthetics	n.	[iːs'θetiks]	美学;美术理论;审美学;美的哲学
salient	adj.	['seiljənt]	易见的;显著的;突出的;跳跃的

species life	物种的生命
systematic zoology	系统动物学
general economy of nature	普通自然经济
experimental psychology	实验心理学

functional psychology	机能主义心理学
psychology of structure	构造心理学
physiological psychology	生理心理学
faculty psychology	官能心理学
psychological anatomy	心理解剖学
taxonomic psychology	分类心理学
phylogenetic psychology	进化心理学

Difficult Sentences

① We may enquire into the structure of an organism, without regard to function—by analysis determining its component parts, and by synthesis exhibiting the mode of its formation from the parts.

我们可以不考虑功能,只分析判断有机体的组成部分,揭示其各部分的形成方式,从而探讨有机体的结构。

② Biology, the science of living things, comprises the three mutually interdependent sciences of morphology, physiology, and ontogeny.

生物学作为研究生物的科学,包括形态学、生理学和发育学三个相互依赖的科学。

③ Protoplasm consists, we are told, of carbon, oxygen, nitrogen, and hydrogen; but this statement would prove exceedingly disappointing to one who had thought to be informed of the phenomena of contractility and metabolism, respiration and reproduction.

据我们所知,原形质包括碳、氧、氮和氢,但是这种说法使了解收缩、新陈代谢、呼吸和生殖现象的人倍感失望。

④ The adoption of these methods does not at all prejudice the ultimate and extra-psychological problem of the function of mentality at large in the universe of things.

采用这种方法,完全不排斥世界万物中心理机能最终极的和超出心理学外的问题。

⑤ Lastly, the labors of the evolutionary school have set phylogenetic psychology upon a fairly secure foundation, and the number of workers is a guarantee of rapid advance in our understanding of mental development.

最后,进化派把进化心理学建立在一个稳固的基础上,研究人员的数量保证了我们可以快速深入地理解心理发展。

Phrases and Patterns

1. without regard to 不考虑;不遵守

   We can not come to the conclusion without regard to other's advice.
   我们不能不考虑他人的建议就得出结论。
   Anyone who behaves without regard to the rules will not be welcome.
   不遵守规则的人不会受欢迎。

2. correspond to 相应;符合

   Corresponding to physiology, we have that department of biology—it has been termed "oecology"—which deals with questions of geographical distribution, of the function of species in the general economy of nature.
   我们有与生理学相对应的、被叫作社会生态学的生物系,它处理地理分布的问题和普通自然经济中的物种功能的问题。
   Corresponding to ontogeny we have the science of phylogeny (in Cope's sense): the biology of evolution, with its problems of descent and of transmission.
   与个体发展学相对应,我们有科普派的语系发展史学,即研究世系和传播的进化生物学。

3. in the former ... in the latter ... 前者……后者……

   In the former sense it is morphological material, in the latter it belongs to what I must name (the phrase will not be misunderstood) a physiological psychology.

根据前者,功能心理学是形而上的物质;根据后者,它属于我命名的生理心理学(这个名词不会导致误解)。

4. at large 详尽;普遍

We may notice also the fact that scientific men are so far subject to the law of inertia, whose effects we see in the conservatism of mankind at large.

我们也许会注意到科学研究人员受到惯性规律的影响,我们详尽地看到它在人类的保守性上的作用。

5. fall into 落入;陷于(混乱,错误等);注入;开始;分成;属于

There is, further, the danger that, if function is studied before structure has been fully elucidated, the student may fall into that acceptance of teleological explanation which is fatal to scientific advance: witness, if witness be necessary, the recrudescence of vitalism in physiology.

于是,这就存在一个危险,如果在完全阐明结构之前研究功能,这个学生可能陷入对科学发展具有毁灭性的目的论解释:必要的话,可以证明生理学中的生机说会重新复苏。

The specimens fall into three categories.

这些标本被分作三类。

Questions

1. In the case of different elements of the dream-thoughts, does a value persist in the process of dream-formation?
2. Are dream-displacement and dream-condensation the two governing factors? And briefly explain it.
3. What are the two parts, according to Watson, of human actions as a whole divided into?
4. According to the Watson, in the psychology of emotion, what are possible and sometimes can help us to group our facts?

5. Please give the definitions of biology, morphology, physiology, and ontogeny. And explain their relations.
6. Does anyone who has followed the course of the experimental method doubt that the main interest has lain in morphological analysis, rather than in ascertainment of sensations?

3

The Biology Underlying Behavior
行为的生物学基础

【本章导读】 本章阐述心理学的生物学基础。第1篇文章是对神经系统的概述。由大脑和脊椎神经构成的中枢神经系统是身体中处理信息、做出决策的主要器官。由传送信息的神经网络构成的外围神经系统是身体中的通信系统。第2篇文章是对大脑结构及主要功能的简介。后脑主要控制睡眠、做梦、呼吸、心率、信息筛选、警觉、平衡感、肌肉协调等。前脑控制情感、记忆、思想等。大脑皮层控制视觉、知觉、听觉、记忆、情感、语言理解、自发动作、决策、创造性思维、主动行动等。第3篇文章描述神经系统在结构及功能上的一些基本构成特征。

3.1 The Nervous System: An Overview
神经系统:概述

Of all the structures we inherit, the one that is most closely associated with our human identity is the nervous system because it regulates the estimated 50 trillion cells of the human body. As members of the species homo sapiens, we all receive a human nervous system, although each one has its own set of idiosyncracies. The nervous system plays the dominant role in coordinating and conducting. A number of the divisions of the nervous system will concern us.

Central Nervous System

Instead of the robot's computer, people have a central nervous system (CNS), composed of the brain and spinal cord. In handling the tasks it was designed for, the CNS is vastly more powerful than any computer that has been built. Some computer scientists estimate that the brain's overall data-processing capability is 10 trillion bits of information per second. The current generation of computers is estimated to be about a tenth as efficient[①].

The brain is the master information-processing, decision-making organ of the body. Receiving messages from the receptors, it integrates the information with past experiences, evaluates the data, and makes the plans that guide our actions. Besides governing what we choose to do, the brain manages many actions over which we have little awareness of control. It integrates vital functions, such as circulation and respiration. It supervises the fulfilling of bodily needs, including those for food and sleep. It manages the fuel supply as well.

Despite gross similarities, brains and computers are strikingly different. Computers process information serially at a rapid rate. The brain works more slowly but deals with information coming in over thousands of parallel channels. In the brain we find intricate cross-links between the parallel channels. The computer—by comparison—is backward. The brain is active as long as we are alive. It is working as people use language, think, solve problems, or recollect—pursuits that are not necessarily initiated by sensory stimulation[②]. It is diligent in monitoring the internal environment, even while we sleep. Signals from the senses blend into, modify, and are modified by the brain's ongoing activity. The brain, in turn, has a hand in controlling what the senses bring in. It can allow access to certain sensory messages and block others[3].

The spinal cord is often thought of as an extension of the brain. But the reverse can be argued. Since spinal cords existed before brains in evolutionary history, the brain can be considered an extension of the spinal cord. In any case, the spinal cord and the brain are quite similar. The spinal cord is the simpler of the two in organization and function.

The cord performs a number of roles. Acting as a go-between, it sends information to the brain; and it receives messages from the brain, which it routes to other parts of the body[4]. In addition, the cord integrates and coordinates sensory data—about pressure, touch, temperature, and pain—that are headed for the brain. The cord helps protect the body from damage, too, by serving as an intermediary for many reflexes. A reflex (such as withdrawing one's hand from a hot stove) is a very rapid, involuntary response to a stimulus, often a potentially dangerous one. The spinal cord is also involved in voluntary movements.

Peripheral Nervous System

Human beings have a communications system, the peripheral nervous system. It includes a network of information-carrying cables, or nerves, which connect the various components. The peripheral system contains all the nervous system structures bordering or lying outside the brain and spinal cord. ("Peripheral" means "on the border") The peripheral system is divided into two major parts: somatic and autonomic nervous systems.

The somatic nervous system enables us to make voluntary actions, to move about and to behave as we choose to.

The autonomic nervous system (ANS) contains nerves which relay messages between the CNS and the so-called involuntary muscles. The involuntary muscles include those that control glands and internal organs. The autonomic nervous system functions autonomously, or on its own, to maintain our bodies in proper working order and to regulate the fuel supply so that we can act as we need to[⑤]. If you have to run across a busy intersection, for instance, the ANS speeds the heart and routes blood to the muscles to supply more oxygen and, consequently, more energy. It takes no conscious effort on your part. Though we think of the ANS as autonomous, it is influenced by the CNS, the endocrine system, and environmental events. While some people are not aware of being able to directly modify the action of the autonomic system, it can be done. Eastern mystics who have learned to slow their hearts or stick pins in their skin without pain or bleeding demonstrate this clearly.

from: *Introduction to Psychology*, Linda L. Davidoff, McGraw-Hill Education, 1987

Words and Expressions

inherit	v.	[in'herit]	经遗传而获得
regulate	v.	['regjuleit]	管理；控制
idiosyncrasy	n.	[ˌidiə'siŋkrəsi]	（个人的）气质；习性
coordinate	v.	[kəu'ɔːdineit]	协调；调节
conduct	v.	['kɔndʌkt]	管理
capability	n.	[ˌkeipə'biliti]	能力
receptor	n.	[ri'septə]	感觉器官；感受体
integrate	v.	['intigreit]	使成一体；使结合；使合并
circulation	n.	[ˌsəːkju'leiʃən]	循环
respiration	n.	[ˌrespi'reiʃən]	呼吸
gross	adj.	[grəus]	显著的
serially	adv.	['siəriəli]	连续地
intricate	adj.	['intrikit]	错综复杂的

英文	词性	音标	中文
cross-link	n.	[ˈkrɔsliŋk]	交叉结合
recollect	v.	[ˌrekəˈlekt]	回忆；记忆
pursuit	n.	[pəˈsjuːt]	事务
initiate	v.	[iˈniʃieit]	开始；创始
sensory	adj.	[ˈsensəri]	知觉的；感觉的；感觉中枢的
diligent	adj.	[ˈdilidʒənt]	勤勉的；勤奋的
monitor	v.	[ˈmɔnitə]	监控
reverse	n.	[riˈvəːs]	相反
route	v.	[ruːt]	按规定路线发送
intermediary	n.	[ˌintəˈmiːdiəri]	中间物；媒介物
reflex	n.	[ˈriːfieks]	反射（作用）；本能的反应
involuntary	adj.	[inˈvɔləntəri]	不受意志控制的；不由自主的
peripheral	adj.	[pəˈrifərəl]	周围的；外面的
component	n.	[kəmˈpəunənt]	构成要素
somatic	adj.	[səuˈmætik]	细胞体的
autonomic	adj.	[ˌɔːtəuˈnɔmik]	自主的
relay	v.	[ˈriːlei]	转达；转播
gland	n.	[glænd]	腺
intersection	n.	[ˌintə(ː)ˈsekʃən]	交叉
endocrine	adj.	[ˈendəukrain]	内分泌（腺）的
mystic	n.	[ˈmistik]	神秘主义者
pin	n.	[pin]	大头针；别针

homo sapiens	人类；现代人
central nervous system	中枢神经系统
spinal cord	脊椎神经
peripheral nervous system	外围神经系统
somatic nervous system	细胞体神经系统
autonomic nervous system	自主神经系统

Difficult Sentences

① The current generation of computers is estimated to be about a tenth as efficient.
据估计,现今计算机的处理信息的能力只能达到人脑的大约十分之一。

② It is working as people use language, think, solve problems, or recollect—pursuits that are not necessarily initiated by sensory stimulation.
当人们使用语言、思考、解决问题或回忆时,大脑就在工作——这些活动不一定由感觉刺激引起。

③ It can allow access to certain sensory messages and block others.
它可以使我们接收到某些感官信息,也可以阻止我们收到某些信息。

④ Acting as a go-between, it sends information to the brain; and it receives messages from the brain, which it routes to other parts of the body.
作为中介,它把信息传给大脑,从大脑那里接受信息,再把信息按一定路线发送到身体的各个部分。

⑤ The autonomic nervous system functions autonomously, or on its own, to maintain our bodies in proper working order and to regulate the fuel supply so that we can act as we need to.
自主神经系统自主或独立地工作,维护身体的正常运转,调节能量供应,使我们能够完成需要完成的活动。

Phrases and Patterns

1. play ... role in 在……中发挥作用
   The nervous system plays the dominant role in coordinating and conducting.
   神经系统在协调和控制上发挥主要作用。

This change indicates that feedback from various systems of the body can directly influence the arousal system and suggests that bodily systems may also play a role in the length of arousal episodes.

这个变化说明身体各系统的反应能直接影响激励系统,身体各系统在激励长度上也可能起到了重要作用。

2. integrate ... with ... 将……和……结合

    Receiving messages from the receptors, it integrates the information with past experiences, evaluates the data, and makes the plans that guide our actions.

    大脑从感觉器官那里收到信息,将信息与以往的经历结合在一起,评价信息,然后制订计划指导我们的行为。

    The biological approach to psychological matters has integrated with and run parallel to the rest of psychological thought since early Greek times—the Greek physician Galen suggested that personality and temperament may be linked to the levels of body fluids such as blood and bile in the body.

    自早期的希腊时期,对心理学问题的生物学研究方法已结合了其他的心理学思想并与它们平行发展。当时希腊哲学家盖伦认为个性和气质与体液的水平如血液和胆汁有关。

3. have little awareness of 几乎没意识到

    Besides governing what we choose to do, the brain manages many actions over which we have little awareness of control.

    除了管理我们想做的事情,大脑还控制很多我们几乎没意识到要去控制的活动。

    I have little awareness of the changes around me.

    我几乎没意识到周围的变化。

4. be diligent in 认真地做

    It is diligent in monitoring the internal environment, even while we sleep.

    即使是在我们睡觉时,大脑也在认真地监控内部环境。

They are very diligent in keeping records.
他们十分认真地做记录。

5. have a hand in 参与或介入某事物

He had a hand in the research.
他参与了此项研究。

6. while... 尽管……但是……

While some people are not aware of being able to directly modify the action of the autonomous system, it can be done.
尽管一些人没有意识到能够直接改变自主系统的行为,但事实是它们能做到这一点。

While many similarities existed in the aims that students had (making new friends, getting good grades, and so forth), the students anticipated using quite different strategies to accomplish their ends.
尽管学生的目标有许多相似之处(交新朋友、获得好成绩等),但是他们期望使用不同的策略来达到目的。

3.2 A Tour Through the Brain
大脑结构一览

Neurosurgeon Joseph Bogen once suggested that a 30-story replica of the brain be built so that people could learn about brain anatomy the way they learn about a neighborhood—by strolling through it[①]. No one has followed up on that suggestion, so we must do with an imaginary tour. Pretend, then, that you have shrunk to microscopic size and that you are wending your way through the "soul's frail dwelling house".

The Hindbrain: Vital Functions

Our guided tour begins at the base of the skull, with the brain stem, which began to evolve some 500 million years ago in segmented worms.

The brain system looks like a stalk rising out of the spinal cord. Pathways to and from upper areas of the brain pass through its two main structures, the medulla and the pons②.

The pons is involved in sleeping, waking, and dreaming. The medulla is responsible for functions that do not have to be consciously willed, such as breathing and heart rate.

Another important structure, is the reticular activating system (RAS). This dense network of neurons, which has connections with many higher areas of the brain, screens incoming information. Irrelevant information is filtered out. Important information is passed on to higher centers. The RAS also arouses the higher centers when something happens that demands their attention. Without the RAS, we could not be alert, nor perhaps even conscious.

Standing on the brain stem and looking toward the back part of the brain, we see a structure about the size of a small fist, bulging out from the pons. It is the cerebellum, or "lesser brain", which contributes to a sense of balance and coordinates the muscles so that movement is smooth and precise. If your cerebellum were damaged, you would probably become clumsy and uncoordinated. You might have trouble using a pencil, threading a needle, or riding a bicycle.

The Forebrain: Emotions, Memory, and Thought

The largest part of the brain is the forebrain. The complexity of the human brain's circuitry far exceeds that of any computer in existence, and much of its most complicated wiring is packed into the uppermost part of the brain, the cerebrum, where the higher forms of thinking take place③. Compared to many other creatures we may be ungainly, feeble, and thin-skinned, but our well-developed cerebrum enables us to overcome these limitations and creatively control our environment, for better or for worse.

The cauliflower-like cerebrum is divided into two separate halves or cerebral hemispheres, connected by a large band of fibers called the corpus callosum. In general, the right hemisphere is in charge of the left side of the body, and vice versa. The two sides also have somewhat different talents.

One of the structures in the forebrain is the thalamus, the busy traffic officer of the brain. As sensory messages come into the brain, the thalamus directs them to various higher centers.

Beneath the thalamus sits a tiny, bean-shaped structure called the hypothalamus. The small size of the hypothalamus is no indicator—of its importance. It is involved in powerful drives associated with the survival of both the individual and the species—hunger, thirst, emotion, sex, and reproduction. It regulates body temperature by triggering sweating or shivering. It controls the complex operations of the autonomic nervous system.

Hanging down from the hypothalamus, connected to it by a short stalk, is a cherry-sized structure that is not made up of neurons[4]. It is the pituitary gland, an endocrine gland. The pituitary is often called the body's "master gland" because it controls many other endocrine glands. The master, however, is really only a supervisor. The true boss is the hypothalamus. The hypothalamus sends chemicals to the pituitary that tell it when to "talk" to the various endocrine glands. The pituitary, in turn, sends hormonal orders to the glands.

The hypothalamus has many connections to a set of loosely interconnected structures that form a sort of border on the underside of the brain's "Cauliflower". Together these structures make up the limbic system of the brain. The limbic system is heavily involved in emotions, such as rage and fear, that we share with other animals.

An important part of the limbic system is the hippocampus, which has a shape that must have reminded someone of a sea horse, for that is what its name means. This structure is larger in human beings than in any other species. One of its duties seems to be to compare sensory messages with what the brain has learned to expect about the world. When expectations are met, the hippocampus tells the reticular activating system, the brain's arousal center, to "cool it".

The Cerebral Cortex: The Brain's Thinking Cap

Working our way right up through the top of the brain, we find that the forebrain is covered by several thin layers of densely packed cells known collectively as the cerebral cortex⑤. Cell bodies in the cortex are crowded together and produce a grayish tissue; hence the term gray matter. In other parts of the brain and nervous system, long, myelin-covered axons prevail, producing white matter. The cortex contains almost three-fourths of all the cells in the human brain. In only 1 square inch of the cortex there are around 10 000 miles of synaptically connected nerve cells. In the entire cortex there are enough connections to stretch from the earth to the moon and back again, and then back to the moon.

Standing atop the cortex, we note that it has many deep crevasses and wrinkles. The folds and fissures in the brain's surface enable it to contain its billions of neurons without requiring us to have the heads of giants—heads that would be too big to permit birth.

The cerebral cortex can be divided into four distinct regions, or lobes:

1. The occipital lobes are at the lower back part of the brain. <u>Among other things</u>, they contain the visual cortex, where visual signals are processed. Damage to the visual cortex can cause impaired visual recognition or blindness.

2. The parietal lobes are at the top of the brain. They contain the somatosensory cortex, which receives information about pressure, pain, touch, and temperature from all over the body. The sensory information

tells you what the movable parts of your body are doing at every moment. Different parts of the somatosensory cortex are associated with different body parts. The areas associated with the hands and the face are disproportionately large because these parts are particularly sensitive.

3. The temporal lobes are at the sides of the brain, just above the ears, behind the temples. They are involved in memory, perception, emotion, and language comprehension, and they contain the auditory cortex, which processes sounds.

4. The frontal lobes, as their name indicates, are located toward the front of the brain, just under the skull in the area of the forehead. They contain the motor cortex, which issues orders to the 600 muscles of the body that produce voluntary movement. They also seem to be responsible for the ability to make plans, think creatively, and take initiative.

Scientists have long known that the frontal lobes must have something to do with personality. Various sorts of damage to the frontal lobes, including tumors and war injuries, suggest that they are involved in planning, goal setting, and intention, or what is commonly called "will". They govern the ability to do a series of tasks in the proper order and to stop doing them at proper time.

from: *Psychology*, *Carole Wade & Carol Tavris*, *Harper Collins College Publishers*, 1993

Words and Expressions

neurosurgeon	n.	[ˌnjuərəu'sə:dʒən]	神经外科医生
replica	n.	['replikə]	复制品;复写;酷似
anatomy	n.	[ə'nætəmi]	解剖结构
microscopic	adj.	[maikrə'skɔpik]	微小的
wend	v.	[wend]	走;离开
hindbrain	n.	['haindbrein]	后脑
skull	n.	[skʌl]	头盖骨;头骨

segmented	adj.	['segməntid]	分割的;分段的
stalk	n.	[stɔːk]	柄;柄状物
medulla	n.	[me'dʌlə]	延髓;骨髓
pons	n.	[pɔnz]	脑桥
will	v.	[wil]	用意志力使;主观促成
reticular	adj.	[ri'tikjulə]	网状的
bulge	v.	[bʌldʒ]	凸起
screen	v.	[skriːn]	审查
filter	v.	['filtə]	过滤
cerebellum	n.	[ˌseri'beləm]	小脑
clumsy	adj.	['klʌmzi]	笨拙的;手脚不灵活的
forebrain	n.	['fɔːˌbrein]	前脑
circuitry	n.	['səːkitri]	电路系统;电路图
wiring	n.	['waiəriŋ]	线路
pack	v.	[pæk]	挤(塞,装)满
cerebrum	n.	['seribrəm]	大脑
ungainly	adj.	[ʌn'geinli]	笨拙的
feeble	adj.	['fiːbl]	弱的;软弱的
cauliflower	adj.	['kɔːliflauə]	花椰菜
cerebral	adj.	['seribrəl]	大脑的
hemisphere	n.	['hemisfiə]	大脑半球
fiber	n.	['faibə]	纤维物质
thalamus	n.	['θæləməs]	视神经床;丘脑
hypothalamus	n.	[ˌhaipəu'θæləməs]	丘脑下部
drive	n.	[draiv]	(人的)本能需要;欲望
trigger	v.	['trigə]	触发;引起
neuron	n.	['njuərɔn]	神经元
pituitary	adj.	[pi'tju(ː)itəri]	脑垂体的
gland	n.	[glænd]	腺
endocrine	adj.	['endəukrain]	内分泌的

hormonal	adj.	[hɔːˈməunəl]	荷尔蒙的
limbic	adj.	[ˈlimbik]	边的
hippocampus	n.	[ˌhipəˈkæmpəs]	海马
cap	n.	[kæp]	盖
tissue	n.	[ˈtisjuː]	组织
myelin	n.	[ˈmaiəli(ː)n]	髓磷脂;髓鞘
axon	n.	[ˈæksɔn]	(神经细胞的)轴突
prevail	v.	[priˈveil]	普遍
synaptically	adv.	[siˈnæptikəli]	突触地
crevasse	n.	[kriˈvæs]	裂缝;裂隙
fissure	n.	[ˈfiʃə]	裂缝;裂隙
lobe	n.	[ləub]	(脑、肺等的)叶
temple	n.	[ˈtempl]	太阳穴
issue	v.	[ˈiʃuː]	发布
tumor	n.	[ˈtjuːmə]	肿瘤

dwelling house	住宅
brain stem	脑干
reticular activating system	网状激活系统
cerebral cortex	大脑皮层
gray matter	灰白质
white matter	白质
occipital lobe	枕叶
visual cortex	视觉皮层
parietal lobe	顶叶
somatosensory cortex	身体感觉皮层
temporal lobe	颞叶
auditory cortex	听觉皮层
frontal lobe	前叶
motor cortex	运动皮层

Difficult Sentences

① Neurosurgeon Joseph Bogen once suggested that a 30-story replica of the brain be built so that people could learn about brain anatomy the way they learn about a neighborhood—by strolling through it.

神经外科医生 Joseph Bogen 曾经建议做一个模拟的有三十层楼高的大脑,这样一来人们就能像了解整个街坊那样去了解大脑的结构——在其中闲逛。

② Pathways to and from upper areas of the brain pass through its two main structures, the medulla and the pons.

来自或通向大脑上部的各条路径都穿过两个重要的结构:骨髓和脑桥。

③ The complexity of the human brain's circuitry far exceeds that of any computer in existence, and much of its most complicated wiring is packed into the uppermost part of the brain, the cerebrum, where the higher forms of thinking take place.

人脑线路图的复杂性大大超过现存的计算机的复杂性。它的很多最复杂的线路都密布在脑的最上方即大脑,也就是进行高级思维活动的区域。

④ Hanging down from the hypothalamus, connected to it by a short stalk, is a cherry-sized structure that is not made up of neurons.

在丘脑下部悬挂的是一个只有樱桃大小的结构,这个结构通过一个很短的柄状物与丘脑下部相连,它是由神经元构成的。

⑤ Working our way right up through the top of the brain, we find that the forebrain is covered by several thin layers of densely packed cells known collectively as the cerebral cortex.

当我们继续往上走,走到脑的顶部,我们会发现前脑覆盖着几个细胞薄层。这些细胞层是由密布在一起的细胞构成的,它们合起来被叫作大脑皮层。

Phrases and Patterns

1. follow up on... 对……进一步采取措施
   No one has followed up on that suggestion, so we must do with an imaginary tour.
   没有人真的照着这一建议去做,所以我们只能做这样一个虚拟观光。

2. be responsible for 决定;是……的原因
   The medulla is responsible for functions that do not have to be consciously willed, such as breathing and heart rate.
   骨髓决定不必用意识和意志控制的功能,如呼吸和心率。

3. compare to... 与……相比
   Compared to many other creatures we may be ungainly, feeble, and thin-skinned, but our well-developed cerebrum enables us to overcome these limitations and creatively control our environment, for better or for worse.
   与许多其他的生物相比,我们可能更笨拙、软弱和敏感。但是我们发育良好的大脑可以使我们克服障碍,创造性地控制环境——或是改善环境或是破坏环境。

4. among other things 除了别的以外;其中
   Among other things, they contain the visual cortex, where visual signals are processed.
   其中,它们包含处理视觉信号的视觉皮层。

5. as its name indicates 正如其名暗示地那样
   The frontal lobes, as their name indicates, are located toward the front of the brain, just under the skull in the area of the forehead.
   前叶,正如其名暗示地那样,朝向脑的前部,就在前脑的颅骨下面。

3.3 Behavior and the Nervous System: Input/Output Boxes within Input/Output Boxes
行为与神经系统:输入/输出装置内部的输入/输出装置

Two general presumptions accepted to one degree or another by most neurobiologists underlie this discussion. The first is that behavior and the nervous system are in some sense the same thing: all aspects of behavior correspond in one way or another to phenomena of nervous system structure and function. The second general presumption is that an understanding of nervous system structure and function provides special advantages for better understanding behavior. An implication of the first general principle is that the Harvard Law ought to be understandable in terms of properties of the nervous system, and of the second is that knowing something of how the nervous system works should help to make sense of the Law[①]. The following is a description of some basic organizational features of nervous system structure and function relevant to these considerations.

To a good first approximation, the nervous system can be regarded as an input/output device for information which is made up of interconnected input/output information devices which are in turn themselves made up of input/output information devices[②]. A convenient stopping point for what might, perhaps correctly, be regarded as an infinite regress is at the level of neurons, the cells which represent similar building blocks for all parts of the nervous system[③]. Each neuron is itself an input/output device, receiving information (typically from other neurons) on receptor surfaces and transmitting information (typically to other neurons) from specialized effector regions. Two aspects of this picture are particularly important to appreciate, both at the level of the neuron and at the levels of each of the successive larger boxes of which they are a part. The first is that one can, with a fairly high degree of rigor, identify and independently monitor inputs and outputs. The second is that the input/output relationship of neurons is in general neither obvious nor stereotyped. It depends on intrinsic properties of the neuron itself, properties which can and do vary from neuron to neuron. That one can identify and independently monitor inputs and outputs, and in many cases control the former, provides the experimental ability to show the dependence of input/output relationships on intrinsic properties and, if one chooses, to characterize aspects of those properties, a point of substantial importance to what follows[④].

The same two principles hold for the nervous system as a whole, the highest level input/output box under consideration here (there is every reason to believe that a similar analysis could be usefully extended to still higher levels of organization, one in which individual organisms represent interconnected input/output boxes from which emerge, for example, properties of social organization). Like neurons, the nervous system has reasonably well-defined inputs (sensory neurons, the generally quite small percentage of the total neuronal population which consists of neurons whose receptor surfaces are outside the nervous system, rather than in contact with other neurons) and outputs (a second distinct set of neurons, including motoneurons, again generally a quite small percentage, whose effector regions are outside the nervous system, rather than in contact with other neurons). Here too, the input/output relations are neither obvious nor stereotyped (individual organisms behave differently from one another). They depend on intrinsic properties of the nervous system as a whole, a reality which can (as with neurons) be both verified and explored because of the ability to control inputs and monitor outputs.

Between the level of the nervous system as a whole, and that of neurons, there are a variety of levels of organization at which the description of interconnected input/output boxes each with significant intrinsic properties continues to hold[⑤]. The neocortex, for example, has well defined input and output connections (restricted to other areas of the nervous system), and an internal organization which influences its input/output characteristics. So too does the spinal cord, which is interconnected by input and output pathways to other parts of the nervous system, and has, as well, associated sensory and motor neurons. These in turn are made up of smaller interconnected input/output boxes, each with characterizable and distinct intrinsic properties, such as different cortical regions and spinal cord segments associated respectively with forelimbs and hindlimbs. There is no unique way to describe the interconnected boxes within boxes which represent levels of organization between neurons and the nervous system as a whole, and <u>it remains to be seen</u> whether there is some best way. Regardless, the more general point holds. One can identify (perhaps inevitably with some degree of arbitrariness) at several levels of organization systems of related neurons with well-defined inputs and outputs, each having intrinsic organizations which are significant for determining their input/output characteristics[⑥].

from: *Variability in Brain Function and Behavior*, *Paul Grobstein*, *Department of Biology*, *Bryn Mawr College*, *Bryn Mawr*, *Pennsylvania* 19010, *published in The Encyclopedia of Human Behavior*, *Volume* 4, (*V. S. Ramachandran*, *editor*), *Academic Press*, 1994 (*pp* 447~458), *copyright by Academic Press*, *Inc.*

Words and Expressions

presumption   *n.*   [priˈzʌmpʃən]   推测;假定
neurobiologist   *n.*   [ˌnjuərəubaiˈɔlədʒist] 神经生物学家

underlie	v.	[ˌʌndə'lai]	成为……根据；作为……的基础
approximation	n.	[əˌprɔksi'meiʃən]	接近；过程或结果
device	n.	[di'vais]	装置；设计
interconnected	adj.	[ˌintə(ː)kə'nektid]	互相连接的
infinite	adj.	['infinit]	无穷大的；无限的
regress	n.	['riːgres]	退路
neuron	n.	['njuərɔn]	神经细胞；神经元
effector	n.	[i'fektə]	神经效应器
successive	adj.	[sək'sesiv]	连续的
rigor	n.	['rigə]	精确
stereotyped	adj.	['steriəutaipt]	套用陈规的
intrinsic	adj.	[in'trinsik]	固有的；内在的；本质的
substantial	adj.	[səb'stænʃəl]	重要的；有价值的；坚固的
distinct	adj.	[dis'tiŋkt]	截然不同的；独特的
motoneuron	n.	[ˌməutə'njuərɔn]	运动神经元
verify	v.	['verifai]	证实
neocortex	n.	[ˌniəu'kɔːteks]	新（大脑）皮层
characterizable	adj.	['kæriktəraizəbl]	可描述的
cortical	adj.	['kɔːtikəl]	皮质的；有关脑皮层的
forelimb	n.	['fɔːlim]	前肢
hindlimb	n.	['haindlim]	（动物或昆虫的）后肢；下肢
arbitrariness	n.	['ɑːbitrərinis]	任意

nervous system	神经系统
building block	积木
spinal cord	脊髓
sensory neurons	感觉神经元
motor neurons	运动神经元

Difficult Sentences

① An implication of the first general principle is that the Harvard Law ought to be understandable in terms of properties of the nervous system, and of the second is that knowing something of how the nervous system works should help to make sense of the Law.

第一个一般原则的意义在于,关于神经系统的特性方面哈佛定律应该可以理解;第二个原则的意义在于,一旦我们对神经系统的作用规律有一些了解的话,我们就能理解哈佛定律。

② To a good first approximation, the nervous system can be regarded as an input/output device for information which is made up of interconnected input/output information devices which are in turn themselves made up of input/output information devices.

第一种恰当的近似性描述是:神经系统可以被看作一个信息输入/输出装置。这个装置同时又是由其他若干相互连接的信息输入/输出装置构成的,而这些相互连接的装置各自本身仍然是由信息输入/输出装置构成的。

③ A convenient stopping point for what might, perhaps correctly, be regarded as an infinite regress is at the level of neurons, the cells which represent similar building blocks for all parts of the nervous system.

神经元层是由一些细胞构成的。这些细胞代表神经系统各个部分的类似的基本构成元件。它们是一个回归点的方便的起点。这个回归点,确切地讲,或许可以被描述成无穷大。

④ That one can identify and independently monitor inputs and outputs, and in many cases control the former, provides the experimental ability to show the dependence of input/output relationships on intrinsic properties and, if one chooses, to characterize aspects of those properties, a point of substantial importance to what follows.

人们可以识别并独立地监控输入和输出,而且往往可以控制输入。这一点使人们可以在实验室里显示输入/输出关系对神经元固有特性的依赖。同时,如果人们愿意的话,还能够描述那些特性的特征,而做到这一点将对后续的工作至关重要。

⑤ Between the level of the nervous system as a whole, and that of neurons, there are a variety of levels of organization at which the description of interconnected input/output boxes each with significant intrinsic properties continues to hold.

在整个神经系统层与神经元层之间,有很多层次的结构。在这些层次中,彼此相连的输入/输出装置各自都具有显著的内在特性。上面提到的原则同样适用于对这些装置的描述。

⑥ One can identify (perhaps inevitably with some degree of arbitrariness) at several levels of organization systems of related neurons with well-defined inputs and outputs, each having intrinsic organizations which are significant for determining their input/output characteristics.

人们可以(或许不可避免地带有某种程度的任意性)在各个结构层发现具有明确的输入和输出的相互关联的神经元系统。每个神经元系统都有内在的结构,这些结构对于断定它们的输入/输出特征至关重要。

Phrases and Patterns

1. correspond to... 与……相当/相符

   The first is that behavior and the nervous system are in some sense the same thing: all aspects of behavior correspond in one way or another to phenomena of nervous system structure and function.

   第一个假定是行为和神经系统在某种程度上是一回事:行为的各个方面都在某种程度上与神经系统的结构和功能的现象相符。

   The process of perceptual constancy means that we automatically adjust our perceptions to correspond to what we have learned about the physical world, rather than relying solely on changing stimulus input.

知觉常性的过程意味着我们自动地调整知觉来符合我们已经认识到的物质世界,而非完全依赖于变化的刺激输入。

2. in general 一般而言

The second is that the input/output relationship of neurons is in general neither obvious nor stereotyped.

第二,神经元的输入/输出关系一般而言不明显,同时也没有固定的模式。

But in general, people's central traits, according to trait theorists, incline them to behave similarly in many different contexts.

但是一般而言,据特性理论家所说,人们的主要特性使他们在很多不同的环境下做出相似的行为。

3. vary from ... to 根据……不同

It depends on intrinsic properties of the neuron itself, properties which can and do vary from neuron to neuron.

它取决于神经元固有的内在特性。这些特性有可能而且事实上也的确根据不同的神经元发生变化。

These are the basic strategies, though the mix in the final "recipe" will vary from workplace situation to situation.

以上这些就是基本策略,尽管最后一条的混合会根据工作环境的不同而变化。

4. hold for 适用于

The same two principles hold for the nervous system as a whole, the highest level input/output box under consideration here.

这两个原则适用于整个神经系统,即这里讨论的最高层次的输入/输出装置。

The theory holds for all of the three situations.

这个理论适用于所有这三种情况。

5. It remains to be seen 尚待分晓

There is no unique way to describe the interconnected boxes within boxes which represent levels of organization between neurons and the nervous system as a whole, and it remains to be seen whether there is some best way.

在这些装置内是相互连接的装置,它们体现神经元与整个神经系统之间的各个层次的结构。描述这些装置没有唯一的方式。是否能发现某个最好的方法还尚待分晓。

It remains to be seen whether his theory is right.

他的理论是否正确,还尚得分晓。

Questions

1. What are the major functions of the central nervous system and the peripheral nervous system?
2. Can you give a brief description of the vital functions of the brain?

4

Sensation and Perception
感觉与知觉

【本章导读】 本章主要介绍了人的感觉与知觉系统。第1篇文章介绍感觉,即人从外部世界接受的讯息是如何被转化并被传送到大脑的,同时介绍了主要研究感官限制、感官适应性及相关论题的精神物理学。第2篇文章介绍知觉,集中讨论了视觉、知觉常性、深度知觉的十条线索以及个体和文化对知觉的影响。第3篇文章用闸门控制理论说明疼痛是如何产生的,还列出了一些控制疼痛的方法。

4.1 Sensation: Receiving Messages about the World
感觉:接收关于世界的讯息

We are aware of an outside world and the internal world of our own bodies only because we have a number of sense organs able to receive messages. These organs enable us to see, hear, taste, smell, touch, balance, and experience such feelings as body stiffness, soreness, fullness, warmth, pleasure, pain, and movement. Sense organs operate through sensory receptor cells, which receive outside forms of energy (light, vibrations, heat) and translate them into neural impulses that can be transmitted to the brain for interpretation①. Sense organs do the job of the basketball announcer who translates what he or she sees into words that can be transmitted on the radio. The process of receiving information from the outside world, translating it, and transmitting it to the brain is called sensation②. The process of interpreting that information and forming images of the world is called perception.

Stimuli: What Messages Can Be Received?

A key concept you will run into frequently throughout this text is stimulus, which <u>refers to</u> any aspect of the outside world that directly influences our behavior or conscious experience. The term stimulus comes from the action of stimulating sensory receptor cells.

Virtually anything that can excite receptor cells can be a stimulus. When you take a seat at a dinner party, the chair is a stimulus through your senses of sight and touch. When you begin to eat, the food becomes a stimulus through your senses of taste, smell, and sight. If the room is too hot, the temperature acts as a stimulus through the sensory receptors in your skin. The compliments you lavish on your hosts are also stimuli, which increase your chances of being invited for dinner again. Whenever a person is aware of, or in some other way responds to, a part of the outside world, she or he receives a stimulus.

When I say that any part of the outside world can be a stimulus, I am using the term outside broadly. Even parts of the internal world of the body can be stimuli. If you eat too much at the dinner party, the bloated stretching of your stomach is a very noticeable stimulus.

Transduction: Translating Messages for the Brain

Energy from stimuli cannot go directly to the brain. Light, sound, and other kinds of energy from the outside world are not able to travel through the nerves, and the brain cannot "understand" what they mean.

To be useful to the brain, sensory messages must be translated into neural impulses that the neurons carry and the brain understands. The translation of one form of energy into another is called transduction.

Sense organs transduce sensory energy into neural energy. This is accomplished in the sense organ by the sensory receptor cells, which are specialized neurons that are excited by specific kinds of sensory energy and give off neural impulses from their axons[3]. Some sensory receptor cells are sensitive to sound, some to light, some to chemicals, and so on. But, in every case, the receptor cells give off coded neural impulses that carry the transduced sensory message to one of the sensory areas of the brain. The sense organs themselves (such as the ear, eye, and nose) are constructed in special ways that expose the receptor cells to sensory energy and help them transduce it into neural impulses. At the center of every sense organ are receptor cells that do the transducing.

Note that we can be aware of a stimulus only if we have receptor cells that can transduce it. For example, we cannot see radio waves or hear some high-frequency tones, and we find some chemicals to be "tasteless" and "odorless" because we do not have receptors that can transduce these kinds of stimuli. Although a radio wave is just as real as the light reflected to our eyes from an apple, we cannot transduce the radio wave. We know that radio waves exist only because radios physically transduce them into sound waves, which are in turn transduced by our ears into neural messages to the brain. There are many forms of energy in the world that we are not aware of because we do not have receptor cells that can transduce them (see Figure 4.1). If our planet were visited by aliens with sensory receptors sensitive only to forms of energy different from our own sensory receptors, they would experience a world entirely different from the one we experience[4].

The visual receptor cells of bees allow them to transduce ultraviolet light better than we can with our normal visual receptor cells. Therefore, bees "see" more of this form of energy. The flower on the left is as the human sees it; the bee, however, is able to see an ultraviolet "landing strip" on the flower that we do not see.

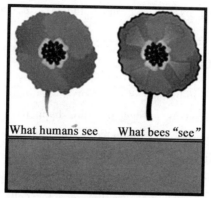

Figure 4.1 What humans see and what bees "see"

Sensory Limits: How Strong Must Messages Be?

Even when we have receptor cells that can transduce a kind of sensory message, not every message will be strong enough to be detected. The term threshold refers to the lower limits of sensory experience. The two primary kinds of thresholds are (a) the smallest magnitude of a stimulus that can be detected and (b) the smallest difference between two stimuli that can be detected.

The absolute threshold is the smallest magnitude of a stimulus that can be detected. Measuring such thresholds is no simple matter. People differ considerably in their sensitivity to weak stimuli, and the sensitivity of each of us differs from time to time. For this reason, absolute thresholds <u>are defined as</u> the magnitude of a stimulus that subjects can detect half the time. The smallest difference between two stimuli that can be detected half the time is called the difference threshold. For example, the smallest change in intensity of your stereo that you can distinguish as "louder" 50 percent of the time is your difference threshold for that stimulus. Detailed knowledge of absolute and difference thresholds has, in fact, been used by the electronics industry to design better stereo systems.

Sensory Adaptation

Recall that an individual's sensitivity to a stimulus differs from time to time. There are many reasons why this happens, such as fatigue or inattention, but sensory adaptation is one of the major causes. When a stimulus is continuously present or repeated at short intervals, the sensation that the same amount of sensory energy causes becomes gradually weaker, largely because the receptor cells become fatigued. When I was a teenager, I frequently went skin diving in an extremely cold spring in central Florida. At first the water was almost unbearably cold; when I jumped in from the dock, the intensity of the cold grabbed my attention so totally that for a moment I felt like only the cold skin of a person rather than a whole person. But after a few minutes the water felt comfortably cool. The water did not change in temperature, of course, but the sensation changed considerably because the temperature receptors in the skin adapted to the temperature of the water. This is sensory adaptation. It happens to some extent in all the senses; loud sounds and offensive odors, fortunately, also seem less intense as time goes by.

Psychophysics

The specialty area within the field of psychology that studies sensory limits, sensory adaptation, and related topics is called psychophysics. The subject matter of this field is the relationship between the physical properties of stimuli and the psychological sensations they produce[5]. Psychophysics is an important field because frequently there is not a direct or simple relationship between stimuli and sensations. Because our knowledge of the outside world is limited to what our sensations tell us, we need to understand under what conditions our sensations do not directly reflect the physical nature of the stimulus. Sensory adaptation is a process that alters the relationship between stimuli and sensations, but numerous other circumstances provide examples of this lack of a one-to-one relationship. The concept of the difference threshold provides another good example.

A fact about difference thresholds that has captured the attention of psychophysicists since the nineteenth century is that the size of the difference threshold increases as the strength of the stimulus increases. When a stimulus is strong, changes in it must be bigger to be noticed than when the stimulus is weak. You can see this for yourself the next time you turn on a three-way light in a dark room. Most three-way bulbs provide light energy in three approximately equal steps (such as a 50-, 100-, and 150-watt bulb), but the greatest difference in brightness in the room is noticeable after the first click of the switch—the sofa that you just tripped over in the darkness is now plainly visible. Turning up the light to the next level adds a less noticeable increase in perceived brightness, and the third level adds even less in apparent brightness. At each level of increasing illumination, the difference threshold is greater, so the perceived increase in brightness is less. If you were to turn on another 50-watt bulb at this point—with the three-way bulb at its highest illumination—you might not see any increase in apparent brightness because your difference threshold is so high.

The ability to detect small changes in the intensity of weak stimuli, but only large changes in the intensity of strong stimuli, was first formally noted by German psychophysicist Ernst Weber. Today this phenomenon is known as Weber's Law. Interestingly, the amount of the change needed to be detected half the time (the different threshold) is almost always in direct proportion to the intensity of the original stimulus. Thus, if a waiter holding a tray on which four glasses had been placed is just able to detect the added weight of one glass, he would just be able to feel the added weight from two more glasses if the tray were already holding eight glasses. The amount of detectable added weight would always be in the same proportion, in this case 1/4.

What is the relevance of this bit of information? Weber's law tells us that what we sense is not always the same as the energy that enters the sense organ. The same magnitude of physical change in intensity can be obvious one time, yet would go undetected under different circumstances. This fact has important practical implications. Suppose, for example, that you are chosen to help design the instruments for a new airplane. The pilot wants an easier way to monitor the plane's altitude, so you put in a light that increases in intensity as the plane nears the earth—the lower the altitude, the more intense the light. That way, you assume, the pilot can easily monitor changes in altitude by seeing changes in brightness. Right? According to Weber's Law, this would be a dangerous way to monitor altitude. At high altitudes, the intensity of the light would be low, so small changes could be detected easily; at low altitudes, however, the intensity would be so great that large changes in altitude—even fatal ones—might not be noticed. That is why the people who design instruments for airplanes, cars, and the like need to know about psychophysics.

from: *An Introduction to Psychology*, Benjamin B. Lahey, *McGraw-Hill Education*, 2001

Words and Expressions

neural	*adj.*	['njuərəl]	神经系统的;神经中枢的
impulse	*n.*	['impʌls]	神经脉冲
sensation	*n.*	[sen'seiʃən]	感觉

perception	n.	[pə'sepʃən]	知觉
stimulus	n.	['stimjuləs]	刺激物
bloated	adj.	['bləutid]	发胀的
transduction	n.	[træns'dʌkʃən]	换能;转换
transduce	v.	[trænz'dju:s]	转换
axon	n.	['æksɔn]	(神经的)轴突
threshold	n.	['θreʃhəuld]	阈
magnitude	n.	['mægnitju:d]	量;大小
sensitivity	n.	['sensi'tiviti]	敏感;灵敏(度)
subject	n.	['sʌbdʒikt]	受实验者
psychophysics	n.	['saikəu'fiziks]	精神物理学

sense organs	感觉器官
sensory receptor cells	感觉接收细胞
neural impulse	神经脉冲
absolute threshold	绝对阈值
difference threshold	差别阈限
sensory adaptation	感觉适应
skin diving	轻装潜水

Difficult Sentences

① Sense organs operate through sensory receptor cells, which receive outside forms of energy (light, vibrations, heat) and translate them into neural impulses that can be transmitted to the brain for interpretation.

感觉器官是通过感官接收细胞进行工作的。感官接收细胞接收外部能量(光、振动、热)并把它们转化为能够被传送到大脑进行解释的神经脉冲。

② The process of receiving information from the outside world, translating it, and transmitting it to the brain is called sensation.

从外部世界接收信息，进行解释并把它传送到大脑的过程被称为感觉。

③ This is accomplished in the sense organ by the sensory receptor cells, which are specialized neurons that are excited by specific kinds of sensory energy and give off neural impulses from their axons.

在感觉器官中这是通过感官接收细胞实现的。感官接收细胞是被特定的感官能量激活并从神经轴突释放神经脉冲的专门神经细胞。

④ If our planet were visited by aliens with sensory receptors sensitive only to forms of energy different from our own sensory receptors, they would experience a world entirely different from the one we experience.

假如外星人拜访我们的星球，而他们的感官接收器只对与我们人类的不同的能量形式敏感，那么他们会体验一个与我们所体验的完全不同的世界。

⑤ The subject matter of this field is the relationship between the physical properties of stimuli and the psychological sensations they produce.

该领域的主题是刺激物的物理特性和它们产生的心理感觉的关系。

Phrases and Patterns

1. refer to 指

A key concept you will run into frequently throughout this text is stimulus, which refers to any aspect of the outside world that directly influences our behavior or conscious experience.

在这篇文章中你将频繁见到的一个关键的概念是刺激，它是指直接影响我们行为或意识体验的外部世界的任何方面。

Cognition means "knowing" and cognitive processes refer to the ways in which knowledge is gained, used and retained.

认知的意思是了解,认知过程指的是获得、使用、记忆知识的途径。

2. be defined as... 被定义成……

For this reason, absolute thresholds are defined as the magnitude of a stimulus that subjects can detect half the time.

由此,绝对阈值被定义成在一半的时间受实验者可以察觉的刺激物的量值。

Social anxiety disorder, also called social phobia, is defined as an overwhelming and disabling fear of scrutiny, embarrassment, or humiliation in everyday social situations which leads to avoidance of potentially pleasurable and meaningful activities.

社会焦虑混乱症,也叫作社会恐惧症,其定义是一种无法抵抗的、无能为力的对日常社会情境的恐惧,如被详细审查、处境尴尬或表现羞耻,这种恐惧导致人们逃避潜在的娱乐和有意义的活动。

3. Suppose... 假定……

Suppose, for example, that you are chosen to help design the instruments for a new airplane.

假如,你被选中去帮助设计一架新飞机的零件。

Suppose you have practiced it for thousands of times.

假设你已经练习过上千次了。

4.2 Perception: Interpreting Sensory Messages
知觉:解释感官讯息

Sensations that are transmitted to the brain have little "meaning" of their own. They are in the form of raw neural energy that must be organized and interpreted in the process we call perception. The process is pretty much the same in all of us. If this were not the case—if each of us were to interpret sensory input in a unique way—there would be no common "reality" in the sense of a perceived world that we all share[①]. However, some aspects of perception are unique to individuals or members of a particular culture. The specific learning experiences, memories, motives, and emotions of the individual can influence perception. For example, we all perceive the visual stimuli of a knife in pretty much the same way because of the inborn ways we organize visual information. But a knife also has unique perceptual meaning to each individual, depending on whether the person has been cut by a similar knife, has a similar favorite hunting knife, or has just been asked to carve a turkey for dinner.

In this section, we will examine the inborn organizational properties that all humans share and will briefly discuss some of the ways in which each individual's perceptions are unique. Keep in mind as we discuss perception that, although it's easy to distinguish between sensation and perception in theory, it's very difficult to do so in practice. Visual perception, for example, begins in the complex neural structures of the eye before sensory messages are transmitted to the brain[②]. The distinction between sensation and perception, then, is largely an arbitrary one, but it makes our discussion of information processing by the sense organs and brain easier to understand.

Visual Perception

In the discussion that follows, we will look at the major ways in which sensory information is interpreted into meaningful perceptions, including both those that are common to us all and those that are unique to each individual. This discussion focuses on visual perception, rather than on all of the perceptual systems, for several reasons: visual perception is a highly important sensing system; scientists understand how it works better than they do other systems; and it is representative enough of other systems to tell us something about the process of perception in general.

Raw visual sensations are like the unassembled parts of a washing machine: they must be put together in an organized way before they are useful to us. Some of the fundamental ways in which the eye and brain organize visual sensations were described about 75 years ago by Gestalt psychologists in their pioneering writings on perception[3]. These principles of perceptual organization are still worthy of our attention. The following are five of the so-called Gestalt principles of perception: figure-ground, continuity, proximity, similarity, closure. Our perceptions are actively organized according to these and other, similar inborn principles.

Perceptual Constancy

We perceive the world as a fairly constant and unchanging place. Tables, lamps, and people do not change in size, shape, or color from moment to moment. Yet, the sensations that tell us about these things do change considerably from moment to moment. The size of the image that falls on the retina changes as a person walks away from us, but we do not perceive the person as shrinking in size. The shape of a pot seen from different angles is different on the retina, but we do not believe that the pot is changing shape. This characteristic of perception is called perceptual constancy. There are several types of perceptual constancy:

Brightness constancy

A piece of white paper does not change in perceived brightness when it moves from a weakly lit room to a brightly lit room, even though the intensity of the light reaching the eye changes considerably. Fortunately for our ability to cope with the world, our perception corresponds to the unchanging physical properties of the paper, rather than to the changing sensory information about its brightness. When you stop to think about it, this is a remarkable accomplishment, but one that we take so much for granted that you may not have been aware that it was happening until you read this paragraph.

Color constancy

Colors do not appear to change much in spite of different conditions of light and surroundings that change incoming visual information.

Size constancy

A dollar bill seen from distances of 1 foot and 10 feet casts different-sized images on the retina, but we do not perceive it as changing in size. Familiar objects do not change in perceived size at different distances.

Shape constancy

A penny seen from straight ahead casts a circular image on the retina. When seen from a slight angle, however, the image it casts is oval, yet we continue to perceive it as circular.

The process of perceptual constancy means that we automatically adjust our perceptions to correspond with what we have learned about the physical world, rather than relying solely on changing stimulus input[④].

Depth Perception

The retina is a two-dimensional surface. It has an up and a down, and a left and a right, but no depth. How is it, then, that we are able to perceive a three-dimensional world using a two-dimensional retina? The eye and brain accomplish this remarkable feat by using a number of two-dimensional cues to create a perceptual distance.

The 10 major cues used in depth perception are listed here. The first 8 are known as monocular cues because they can be seen by one eye; the last 2 are known as binocular cues because they can only be perceived using both eyes. The monocular cues are as follows.

Texture gradient

The texture of objects is larger and more visible up close and smaller when far away. On curved surfaces, the elements of texture are also more slanted when they are farther away.

Linear perspective

Objects cast smaller images on the retina when they are more distant. As a result, parallel lines, such as railroad tracks, appear to grow closer together the farther away they are from us.

Superposition

Closer objects tend to be partially in front of, or partially cover up, more distant objects.

Shadowing

The shadows cast by objects suggest their depth.

Speed of movement

Objects farther away appear to move across the field of vision more slowly than do closer objects.

Aerial perspective

Water vapor and pollution in the air scatter light waves, giving distant objects a bluish, hazy appearance compared with nearby objects.

Accommodation

The shape of the lens of the eye must change to focus the visual image on the retina from stimuli that are different distances from the eye. This process is called accommodation. Kinesthetic receptors in the ciliary muscle, therefore, provide a source of information about the distance of different objects. This information is useful, however, only for short distances up to about 4 feet.

Vertical position

When objects are on the ground, the farther they appear to be below the horizon, the closer they appear to be to us. For objects in the air, however, the farther they appear to be above the horizon, the closer they appear to be to us.

The binocular cues are as follows:

Convergence

When both eyes are looking at an object in the center of the visual field, they must angle inward more sharply for a near object than for a distant object. Information from the muscles that move the eyes thus provides a clue as to the distance of an object from the viewer.

Retinal disparity

Because our two eyes are a couple of inches apart, they do not see the same view of three-dimensional objects, especially when the object is close. This disparity, or difference, between the images on the two retinas is a key factor in depth perception. Retinal disparity is the principle behind the old-fashioned stereopticon. The individual looks at two pictures of the same scene in a viewer that lets each eye see only one of the two images. The images have been photographed from two slightly different spots to duplicate the disparity between two retinal images. When seen in the stereopticon, the two images fuse into a single scene perceived in startlingly good three dimension.

Through a combination of these monocular and binocular cues, we are able to perceive our three-dimensional world using only two-dimensional information[5].

Individual and Cultural Influences on Perception

Up to this point, we have discussed factors that determine perception in the same way for all of us—characteristics of the inborn "wiring" of the human brain and sensory systems. But perception is strongly influenced by other factors as well. For example, a number of studies tell us that motivation influences perception: Hungry college students are more likely to interpret ambiguous pictures as being of food; sexually aroused males perceive females as being more physically attractive; anxious persons are more likely to interpret ambiguous sentences as being threatening; and poor children estimate the size of coins as larger than do children from higher income families.

Perception is also influenced by the different learning experiences of people living in different cultures. For example, pygmies who live in the dense rain forests of the African Congo rarely see objects at long distances. In their world, thick vegetation blocks the sight of distant objects. It is interesting, then, that, if pygmies travel to the African plains, distant buffalo are at first seen as tiny "insects". Pictures they draw are flat, two-dimensional renderings without depth cues. Even more striking evidence for the role of cultural learning experience in perception comes from studies of pain in different cultures. <u>To take an example</u> from anthropology that will be shocking to most members of Western cultures, consider the hook-swinging ceremony practiced in some remote villages in India. Each year a faithful celebrant is decked with flowers as two metal hooks are pushed through the skin and muscles of his back. He is hoisted on a primitive crane by ropes attached to the hooks and is taken from village to village, where he blesses each child and farm. The celebrant apparently experiences a sense of "exaltation"—probably due in part to the morphinelike endorphins released by the damage to the skin—rather than the excruciating pain that most of us would experience. Such evidence certainly suggests that emotional, motivational, and cultural factors are important in perception.

from: *An Introduction to Psychology*, Benjamin B. Lahey, McGraw-Hill Education, 2001

Words and Expressions

transmit	*v.*	[trænz'mit]	传输;转送
motive	*n.*	['məutiv]	动机;目的
visual	*adj.*	['vizjuəl]	视觉的
inborn	*adj.*	['in'bɔːn]	天生的;生来的

英文	词性	音标	中文
continuity	n.	[ˌkɔntiˈnju(ː)iti]	连续性;连贯性
similarity	n.	[ˌsiməˈlærəti]	相似性
proximity	n.	[prɔkˈsimiti]	邻近性
closure	n.	[ˈkləuʒə]	闭合
retina	n.	[ˈretinə]	视网膜
cue	n.	[kjuː]	暗示;线索
monocular	adj.	[mɔˈnɔkjulə]	单眼的
binocular	adj.	[baiˈnɔkjulə]	用两眼的
superposition	n.	[ˌsjuːpəpəˈziʃən]	重叠;重合
shadowing	n.	[ˈʃædəuiŋ]	阴影
cast	v.	[kɑːst]	投;抛;投射
accommodation	n.	[əˌkɔməˈdeiʃən]	眼调节
hazy	adj.	[ˈheizi]	朦胧的;烟雾弥漫的
ciliary	adj.	[ˈsiliəri]	睫状的
convergence	n.	[kənˈvəːdʒəns]	会聚
duplicate	v.	[ˈdjuːplikeit]	复写;复制
fuse	v.	[fjuːz]	熔合
stereopticon	n.	[ˌstiəriˈɔptikən]	立体感幻灯机
ambiguous	adj.	[æmˈbigjuəs]	暧昧的;不明确的
pygmy	n.	[ˈpigmi]	俾格米人
rendering	n.	[ˈrendəriŋ]	透视图
anthropology	n.	[ˌænθrəˈpɔlədʒi]	人类学
celebrant	n.	[ˈselibrənt]	(主持宗教仪式的)教士
exaltation	n.	[ˌegzɔːlˈteiʃən]	兴奋
morphinelike	adj.	[ˈmɔːfiːnlaik]	类似吗啡的
endorphin	n.	[inˈdɔːfin]	内啡肽
excruciating	adj.	[ikˈskruːʃieitiŋ]	极痛苦的;折磨人的

Gestalt principles of perception　　格式塔感知原理
visual perception　　视觉;视知觉

perceptual constancy	知觉常性
brightness constancy	明度常性
color constancy	颜色常性
size constancy	大小常性
shape constancy	形状常性
monocular cue	单眼线索
binocular cue	双眼线索
depth perception	深度知觉
texture gradient	结构级差
linear perspective	线条透视
aerial perspective	空间透视
kinesthetic receptors	运动觉感受器
vertical position	竖直[Y轴]位置
retinal disparity	网膜像差
sensory system	感觉系统

Difficult Sentences

① If this were not the case—if each of us were to interpret sensory input in a unique way—there would be no common "reality" in the sense of a perceived world that we all share.

如果事实并非如此,如果我们每个人都以独特的方式理解感官输入,那么在我们共有的感知到的世界上就不会有共同的"现实"。

② Visual perception, for example, begins in the complex neural structures of the eye before sensory messages are transmitted to the brain.

例如,视觉是感官讯息在被输送到大脑之前启动了眼部的复杂的神经结构。

③ Some of the fundamental ways in which the eye and brain organize visual sensations were described about 75 years ago by Gestalt

psychologists in their pioneering writings on perception.
一些关于眼睛和大脑组织视觉的基本途径在七十五年前格式塔派心理学家在其有关知觉的先锋作品中有所记述。

④ The process of perceptual constancy means that we automatically adjust our perceptions to correspond with what we have learned about the physical world, rather than relying solely on changing stimulus input.
知觉常性的过程意味着我们自动地调整知觉来符合我们已经认识到的物质世界,而非完全依赖于变化的刺激输入。

⑤ Through a combination of these monocular and binocular cues, we are able to perceive our three-dimensional world using only two-dimensional information.
通过单眼和双眼线索,我们可以用二维的信息认识三维的世界。

Phrases and Patterns

1. rely on 依赖
   Of all the social sciences, psychology relies most heavily on laboratory experiments and observations.
   在所有的社会科学中,心理学对实验室的实验和观察的依赖性最强。

2. as follows 如下
   The monocular cues are as follows.
   单眼线索如下所示。
   The binocular cues are as follows.
   双眼线索如下所示。

3. to take an example 举例
   To take an example from anthropology that will be shocking to most members of Western cultures.
   举一个会令大多数西方人感到震惊的人类学的例子。
   To take an example, the judgments we make about the reasons for

other people's behavior are based on the ways in which we classify their behavior.

举个例子,我们对他人行为动机的判断是以我们对他们行为分类的方法为基础。

4.3 Pain and Why It Hurts
疼痛与为什么感到疼痛

You may not like it, but we need pain. Pain acts as a warning system that protects you. Pain says, "Warning, Warning ... stop what you are doing and do something else". For example, if you have your hand on a hot stove, pain tells you to stop touching the stove and remove your hand. In this way, pain protects your body from injury (or further injury if you have already hurt yourself). Pain also helps healing, because an injury hurts, you rest.

There are some people who are born without the sense of pain. These people have a rare condition called "congenital insensitivity to pain". Their nervous systems are not equipped to detect painful information. You may think this is a good thing ... it is NOT. Without the ability to detect painful events, you would continue to cause injury to yourself. For example, if you broke a bone in your arm, you might continue using the arm because it did not hurt. You could cause further injury to your arm. People with congenital insensitivity to pain usually have many injuries like pressure sores, damaged joints and even missing or damaged fingers!

So, what kind of things in the outside world can cause pain? Events that cause reactions are called stimuli. Stimuli are painful when they damage tissues or threaten to damage tissue. Pain is nature's way of telling the brain about injury to the body. Painful stimuli can <u>be divided</u>

into several types (see Table 4.1).

Table 4.1 Painful stimuli

Energy	Example	Everyday Example	Possible result if untreated
Mechanical	Strong Pressure Pinch Squeeze Twist	Animal bite Knife cut Falling off a bike	Bruises Broken bones Cuts
Thermal (Temperature)	Hot Cold	Fire Hot chocolate Ice	Burns Frostbite
Electrical	—	Electric shock	Burns
Chemical	—	Acid Chili peppers	Chemical burns Broken skin
Visceral (Inside Your Body)	—	Heart attack Inflamed appendix	Condition gets worse

I am sure that you could add to this list... what other things can cause pain? A toothache? A broken bone?

Now we know the "stimuli" that may cause pain. How do these stimuli activate the nervous system? There are specialized "receptors" in the skin and internal organs that are sensitive to stimuli that are painful. These receptors are called "nociceptors" and are free nerve endings connected to small diameter myelinated A and unmyelinated C nerve fibers—these are the nerve fibers that are lacking in people with congenital insensitivity to pain[①]. Nociception, then, is the response of the nervous system to painful stimulation. When the nociceptors detect a nociceptive stimulus, they send a message to the spinal cord.

A famous theory concerning how pain works is called the Gate Control Theory devised by Patrick Wall and Ronald Melzack in 1965. This theory states that pain is a function of the balance between the information traveling into the spinal cord through large nerve fibers and information traveling into the spinal cord through small nerve fibers[②]. Remember, large nerve fibers carry non-nociceptive information and small nerve fibers carry nociceptive information. If the relative amount of activity is greater in large nerve fibers, there should be little or no pain. However, if there is more activity in small nerve fibers, then there will be pain. Here is what the gate control theory looks like (see Figure 4.2).

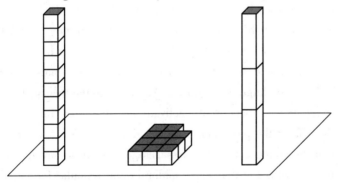

Figure 4.2 Gate Control Theory
I = "Inhibitory Interneuron"; P = "Projection Neuron"

Let's go through the theory step by step:

Without any stimulation, both large and small nerve fibers are quiet and the inhibitory interneuron (I) blocks the signal in the projection neuron (P) that connects to the brain[③]. The "gate is closed" and therefore NO PAIN.

With non-painful stimulation, large nerve fibers are activated primarily. This activates the projection neuron (P), But it also activates the inhibitory interneuron (I) which then BLOCKS the signal in the projection neuron (P) that connects to the brain. The "gate is closed" and therefore NO PAIN.

With pain stimulation, small nerve fibers become active. They activate the projection neurons (P) and block the inhibitory interneuron (I). Because activity of the inhibitory interneuron is blocked, it CANNOT block the output of the projection neuron that connects with the brain. The "gate is open", therefore, PAIN!

Although the gate control theory has support from some experiments and does explain some observations seen in pain patients during therapy, it does not explain everything. However, think of this... what is one of the first things you do after you bump your head or pinch a finger by accident? You probably rub it and it feels better, right? Could this be explained by the gate control theory? Well, rubbing your bumped head or pinched finger would activate non-nociceptive touch signals carried into the spinal cord by large nerve fibers. According to the theory, the activity in the large nerve fibers would activate the inhibitory interneuron that would then block the projection neuron and therefore block the pain④.

From the spinal cord, the messages go directly to several places in the brain including the thalamus, midbrain and reticular formation.

Some brain regions that receive nociceptive information are involved in perception and emotion. Also, some areas of the brain connect back to the spinal cord—these connections can change or modify information that is coming into the brain⑤. In fact, this is one way that the brain can reduce pain. Two areas of the brain that are involved in reducing pain are the periaqueductal gray (PAG) and the nucleus raphe magnus. Neurosurgeons have implanted electrical stimulating electrodes near the PAG of some patients with severe pain—a small electrical shock through these electrodes can relieve pain in some patients! See Table 4.2.

Table 4.2 Other ways that pain can be controlled

Method	Possible Mechanism(s)	Uses/Examples
Aspirin	Acts mostly in peripheral nervous system. Reduces inflammation	Headache Musculoskeletal pain
Morphine	Acts in central nervous system (brain and spinal cord) to block pain messages Activates pain-modulating systems in the brain that project to the spinal cord	Post-operative pain other pain conditions
Other pain reducing drugs	Act on a variety of neurotransmitter systems	Variety of pain conditions
Hypnosis	1. May activate the pain-inhibitory pathway from the brain to the spinal cord 2. May act somewhere in the brain (frontal lobe?) to shift a patient's attention away from the pain	Dental procedures Childbirth Burns Headache
Acupuncture	1. Stimulation of large diameter nerve fibers that inhibit pain ("close the gate") 2. Could be placebo effect. Causes release of endorphins ("the body's own morphine-like substances") 3. Some types of acupuncture may stimulate small diameter nerve fibers and inhibit spinal cord pain mechanisms (this would not agree with the gate control theory)	Back pain Minor surgical operations
Placebo	1. Reduces anxiety 2. Causes release of endorphins	Headache Post-operative pain

Table 4.2 (Continued)

Method	Possible Mechanism(s)	Uses/Examples
Transcutaneous Electrical Nerve Stimulation (TENS)	1. Stimulation of large diameter nerve fibers which "close the gate" and reduce pain 2. Could be placebo effect	Post-operative pain Arthritis Cancer pain
Neurosurgery	Removal or blockade of painful signals	Cancer pain
Stress	1. Activation of endogenous opiate system (endorphins) 2. Activation of non-opiate pain inhibitory system	Football player continues to play regardless of injury. Soldier continues to fight regardless of wounds

from: http://faculty.washington.edu/chudler/pain.html

Words and Expressions

congenital	adj.	[kɔn'dʒenitl]	天生的;先天的,
insensitivity	n.	[in͵sensi'tiviti]	不敏感
detect	v.	[di'tekt]	察觉
sore	n.	[sɔ, sɔə]	痛处
joint	n.	[dʒɔint]	关节
bruise	n.	[bru:z]	瘀伤;擦伤
thermal	adj.	['θə:məl]	热的;热量的
visceral	adj.	['visərəl]	内脏的
nociceptor	n.	[͵nəusi'septə]	伤害感受器
diameter	n.	[dai'æmitə]	直径
myelinated	adj.	['maiəlineitid]	有髓鞘的
unmyelinated	adj.	[͵ʌn'maiəlineitid]	无髓鞘的
thalamus	n.	['θæləməs]	丘脑

midbrain	n.	['mɪdˌbreɪn]	中脑
electrode	n	[iˈlektrəud]	电极
musculoskeletal	adj.	[ˌmʌskjuləuˈskelitəl]	肌与骨骼的
morphine	n.	['mɔːfiːn]	吗啡
lobe	n.	[ləub]	（器官的）叶
hypnosis	n.	[hipˈnəusis]	催眠
acupuncture	n.	[əˈækjupʌŋktʃə(r)]	针刺疗法
placebo	n.	[pləˈsiːbəu]	安慰剂
transcutaneous	adj.	[ˌtrænskjuː(ː)ˈteinjəs]	经过皮肤的
arthritis	n.	[ɑːˈθraitis]	关节炎
neurosurgery	n.	[njuərəuˈsəːdʒəri]	神经外科
endogenous	adj.	[enˈdɔdʒənəs]	内源性的
opiate	n.	[ˈəupiit]	鸦片制剂；麻醉剂

inflamed appendix	阑尾炎
nerve fiber	神经元；神经纤维
spinal cord	脊髓
inhibitory interneuron	抑制中间神经元
projection neuron	投射神经元
reticular formation	网状结构
periaqueductal gray	近沟区灰质
nucleus raphe	脑干缝际核

Difficult Sentences

① These receptors are called "nociceptors" and are free nerve endings connected to small diameter myelinated A and unmyelinated C nerve fibers—these are the nerve fibers that are lacking in people with congenital insensitivity to pain

这些感受器被称为"伤害感受器"。它们是不受约束的神经末梢与微小的直径有髓鞘的 A 神经元和无髓鞘的 C 神经元连在一起。这些神经元是先天对疼痛不敏感的人所缺乏的。

② This theory states that pain is a function of the balance between the information traveling into the spinal cord through large nerve fibers and information traveling into the spinal cord through small nerve fibers.

该理论说明疼痛是通过大神经元到达脊髓的信息与通过小神经元到达脊髓的信息之间平衡的一种功能。

③ Without any stimulation, both large and small nerve fibers are quiet and the inhibitory interneuron (I) blocks the signal in the projection neuron (P) that connects to the brain.

没有任何刺激时,大小神经元是安静的,抑制中间神经元(I)阻碍了与大脑相连的投射神经元(P)中的信号。

④ According to the theory, the activity in the large nerve fibers would activate the inhibitory interneuron that would then block the projection neuron and therefore block the pain.

根据该理论,大神经元中的活动刺激了抑制中间神经元,随后抑制中间神经元将阻碍投射神经元并因此阻碍疼痛。

⑤ Also, some areas of the brain connect back to the spinal cord—these connections can change or modify information that is coming into the brain.

而且,一些大脑区域连接背部与脊髓。这些连接能改变或修改即将到达大脑的信息。

Phrases and Patterns

1. be divided into... 被划分为……

Painful stimuli can be divided into several types...

疼痛刺激可以被分为几类……

The peripheral system is divided into two major parts: somatic and autonomic nervous systems.

外围系统被分为两部分:体细胞神经系统和自主神经系统。

2. according to 据(某人)所述；根据(某事物)

According to this definition, individuals who do not have needs, goals, or concerns cannot experience emotions.

根据该定义，没有需要、目标或顾虑的个体是不可能体验情感的。

3. be involved in (与某事物)有关联的

Some brain regions that receive nociceptive information are involved in perception and emotion.

一些接收疼痛信息的大脑区域与知觉和情感有关联。

The spinal cord is also involved in voluntary movements.

脊椎神经还与自觉活动有关。

Questions

1. How would life be different if human beings had a lower absolute threshold for the sense of sound? How about a higher absolute threshold for taste?
2. What is the difference between sensation and perception? Can you have a perception without a sensation?
3. What is the point of studying perceptual illusions? What can we learn from them?
4. What is the value of knowing that our perception is influenced by our emotions?
5. What is Gate Control Theory?

5

Cognition and Language
认知与语言

【本章导读】 本章介绍了认知心理学。第 1 篇文章介绍了人是如何思考的。什么是思考,思考的基本成分:心理想象与概念,演绎和推论两种推理方法和解决问题的智力捷径如:运算法则和探索法。第 2 篇文章介绍了人类最伟大的认知成果:语言。语言的生成特性,其组成成分与法则,并用沃夫假设理论说明语言与思维之间的关系。第 3 篇文章介绍了高级认知两个重要的组成部分:概念形成和问题解决,着重介绍了概念的种类和问题解决的主要步骤。

5.1 How Do We Think?
我们如何思考?

In this chapter we consider cognitive psychology, the branch of psychology that focuses on the study of cognition. Cognition encompassed the higher mental processes of humans, including how people know and understand the world, process information, make judgments and decisions and describe their knowledge and understanding to others[①].

What Is Thinking?

The mere ability to pose such a question illustrates the distinctive nature of the human ability to think. No other species can contemplate, analyze, recollect, or plan in the manner that humans can. Yet knowing that we think and understanding what thinking is are two different things. Philosophers, for example, have argued for generations about the meaning of thinking, with some placing it at the core of human beings' understanding of their own existence.

To psychologists, thinking is the manipulation to mental representations of information. The representation may be a word, a visual image, a sound, or data in any other modality. What thinking does is to transform the representation of information into a new and different form for the purpose of answering a question, solving a problem, or aiding in reaching a goal.

Although a clear sense of what specifically occurs when we think remains elusive, the nature of the fundamental elements involved in thinking is becoming increasingly well understood. We begin by considering our use of mental images and concepts, the building blocks of thought.

Mental Images: Examining the Mind's Eye

Think of your best friend. Chances are that you "see" some kind of visual image when asked to think of her or him, or any other person or object, for that matter. To some cognitive psychologists, such mental images represent a major part of thinking.

Mental images are representations in the mind that resemble the object or event being represented. They are not just visual representations; our ability to "hear" a tune in our head also represents a mental image. In fact, it may be that every sensory modality produces corresponding mental images.

Research has found that our representations of mental images have many of the properties of the actual perception of objects being represented. For examples, it takes more time to scan the mental visual representations of large objects than small ones, just as it takes more time to scan an actual large object than an actual small one. Similarly, we are ale to manipulate and rotate them in the real world.

The production of mental images has been heralded by some as a way to improve performance of various skills. For example, researcher Alvaro Pascual-Leone taught a group of people to play a five-finger exercise on the piano. One group practiced every day for five days, while a control group played without any training, just hitting the keys at random. Finally, the members of a third group were taught the exercise but were not allowed to actually try it out on the piano. Instead, they rehearsed it mentally, sitting at the piano and looking at the keys, but not actually touching them.

When brain scans of people in the groups were compared, researchers found a distinct difference between those who actually manually practiced the exercise and those who just randomly hit keys. However, the most surprising finding came from the group that mentally rehearsed. Their brain scans were virtually identical to those of the people in the group who actually practiced the exercise. Apparently, the same network of brain cells involved in carrying out the task were involved in mentally rehearsing it.

Concepts: Categorizing the World

If someone asked you what was in your kitchen cabinet, you might answer with a detailed list of every item ("a jar of Skippy peanut butter, three packages of macaroni-and-cheese mix, six unmatched dinner plates," and so forth). More likely, though, you would respond by using some broader categories, such as "food" and "dishes".

The use of such categories reflects the operation of concepts. Concepts are categorizations of objects, events, or people that share common properties. By employing concepts, we are able to organize the complex phenomena into simpler, and therefore more easily usable, cognitive categories②.

Concepts allow us to classify newly encountered objects <u>on the basis of</u> our past experience. For example, we are able to tell that a small rectangular box with buttons sitting on a chair near a television is probably a remote control—even if we have never encountered that specific brand before. Ultimately, concepts influence behavior; we would assume, for instance, that it might be appropriate to pet an animal, after determining that it is, in fact, a dog.

When cognitive psychologists first studied concepts, they focused on those that are clearly defined by a unique set of properties of features. For example, an equilateral triangle is a shape that has three sides of equal length. If an object has these characteristics, it is an equilateral triangle; if it does not, then it is not an equilateral triangle.

Other concepts—ones that often have most relevance to our everyday lives—are more ambiguous and difficult to define. For instance, concepts such as "table" or "bird" share a set of general, relatively loose characteristic features, rather than unique properties that distinguish an example of the concept from a "nonexample". When we consider these more ambiguous concepts, we usually think in terms of examples; these examples are called prototypes. Prototypes are typical, highly representative examples of a concept. For instance, a prototype of the concept "bird" is a robin; a prototype of "table" is a coffee table. Relatively high agreement exits among people about which examples of a concept are prototypes, as well as which examples are not. For instance, most people consider cars and trucks good examples of vehicles, whereas elevators and wheelbarrows are not viewed as terribly good examples. Consequently, cars and trucks are prototypes of the concept of vehicle.

Concepts enable us to think about and understand more readily the complex world in which we live. For example, the judgments we make about the reasons for other people's behavior are based on the ways in which we classify their behavior[3]. Hence, our evaluation of a person who washes her hands twenty times a day could vary, depending on whether we place her behavior within the conceptual framework of a health-care worker of a mental patient. Similarly, physicians make diagnoses by drawing upon concepts and prototypes of symptoms they learned about in medical school[4]. Finally, concepts and prototypes facilitate out efforts to draw suitable conclusions through the cognitive process we turn to next: reasoning.

Reasoning: Making up Your Mind

Although philosophers and logicians have considered the foundations of reasoning for centuries, it is relatively recently that cognitive psychologists have begun to investigate how people reason and make decisions. Together, their efforts have contributed to our understanding of formal reasoning processes as well as the mental shortcuts we routinely use—shortcuts that may sometimes lead our reasoning capabilities astray.

One approach taken by cognitive psychologists in their efforts to understand decision making is to examine how people use formal reasoning procedures. Two major forms exist: deductive reasoning and inductive reasoning.

In deductive reasoning, we draw inferences and implications from a set of assumptions and apply them to specific cases. Deductive reasoning begins with a series of assumptions or premises that are thought to be true, and then derives the implications of these assumptions[5]. If the assumptions are true, then the conclusions must also be true.

A major technique for studying deductive reasoning is through the use of asking subjects to evaluate syllogisms. A syllogism presents a series of two assumptions, or premises, that are used to derive a conclusion. By definition, the conclusion must be true if the assumptions or premises are true. For example, consider the following syllogism:

All men are mortal. [premise]
Socrates is a man. [premise]
Therefore, Socrates is mortal. [conclusion]

In this case both premises are true, and so, then, is the conclusion. On the other hand, if either or both of the premises in a syllogism are not accurate, then there is insufficient support for the accuracy of the conclusion.

The conceptual complement of deductive reasoning is inductive reasoning, in inductive reasoning, we infer a general rule from specific cases. Using our observations, knowledge, experiences, and beliefs about the world, we develop a summary conclusion. (You can recall the distinction between deductive and inductive reasoning in this way: In deductive reasoning, the conclusion is derived through the use of general rules, whereas in inductive reasoning, a conclusion is inferred from specific examples.)

Sherlock Holmes used inductive reasoning in his quest to solve mysteries. By amassing clues, he was ultimately able to determine the identity of the criminal. Similarly, we all use inductive reasoning, although typically in more ordinary situation. For instance, if the person in the apartment below you constantly plays Michael Jackson's music, you may begin to form an impression of what that individual is like, based on the sample of evidence available to you. Like Sherlock Holmes, you use pieces of evidence to draw a general conclusion.

The limitation of inductive reasoning is that any conclusions that are drawn may be biased if insufficient or invalid evidence is used.

Psychologists know this well: The various scientific methods that they may employ in the collection of data to support their hypotheses <u>are prone to</u> several sorts of biases, such as using an inappropriate sample of subjects. Similarly, we may fail to draw appropriate conclusions about our neighbor if our impressions are based only on the music he or she plays and not on a broader sample of behavior.

Algorithms and Heuristics

When faced with a decision, we often turn to various kinds of mental shortcuts, known as algorithms and heuristics, to help us. And algorithm is a rule which, if followed, guarantees a solution to a problem. We can use an algorithm even if we do not understand why it works. For example, you may know that the length of the third side of a right triangle can be found using the formula $a^2 + b^2 = c^2$. You may not have the foggiest notion of the mathematical principles behind the formula, but this algorithm is always accurate and therefore provides a solution to a particular problem.

For many problems and decisions, however, no algorithm is available. In those instances, we may be able to use heuristics to help us. A heuristic is a rule of thumb or mental shortcut that may lead to a solution. Unlike algorithms, heuristics enhance the likelihood of success in coming to a solution but cannot ensure it. For example, chess players often follow the heuristic of attempting to gain control of the center of the board in determining what move to make. This tactic doesn't guarantee that they will win, but it does increase their chances of success. Similarly, some students follow the heuristic of preparing for a test by ignoring the assigned textbook reading and only studying their lecture notes—a strategy that may or may not pay off.

Although they may help people solve problems and make decisions, the use of certain kinds of heuristics may backfire. For example, we sometimes use the representativeness heuristic, a rule we apply when we judge people by the degree to which they represent a certain category or group of people. Suppose, for instance, you are the owner of a fast-food store and have been robbed many times by teenagers. The representativeness heuristic would lead you to raise your guard each time someone of this age group enters your store (even though, statistically, it is unlikely that any given teenager will rob you).

The availability heuristic involves judging the probability of an event by how easily the event can be recalled from memory. According to this heuristic, we assume that events we remember easily are likely to have occurred more frequently in the past than those that are harder to remember. Furthermore, we assume that the same sort of event is more likely to occur in the future. For example many people are more afraid of dying in a plane crash than in an auto accident—despite statistics showing that airplane travel is much safer than auto travel. The reason is that plane crashes receive far more publicity than auto wrecks, and are therefore more easily remembered. And so it is the availability heuristic that leads people to conclude that they are in greater jeopardy in an airplane than a car.

from: *Essentials of Understanding Psychology*, Robert S. Feldman, 1997

Words and Expressions

cognition	n.	[kɔgˈniʃən]	认知
contemplate	v.	[ˈkɔntempleit]	沉思
recollect	v.	[ˌrekəˈlekt]	回忆
manipulation	n.	[məˌnipjuˈleiʃən]	处理;操作
elusive	adj.	[iˈljuːsiv]	难懂的;难捉摸的
modality	n.	[məuˈdæliti]	形式;形态
imagery	n.	[ˈimidʒəri]	意象;形象化的描述

categorization	n.	[kæˌtigərˈzeiʃən]	类别
rectangular	adj.	[rekˈtæŋgjulə]	矩形的
equilateral	adj.	[ˌi:kwiˈlætərəl]	等边的
prototype	n.	[ˈprəutətaip]	典型事例
shortcut	n.	[ˈʃɔ:tkʌt]	捷径
inference	n.	[ˈinfərəns]	推论
implication	n.	[ˌimpliˈkeiʃən]	暗示
premise	n.	[ˈpremis]	前提
syllogism	n.	[ˈsilədʒizəm]	三段论
algorithm	n.	[ˈælgəriðəm]	运算法则
heuristic	n.	[hjuəˈristik]	探索法；启发法

to lead ... astray			引入歧途
mental image			心理想象
deductive reasoning			演绎推理
inductive reasoning			归纳推理
a rule of thumb			单凭经验的方法

Difficult Sentences

① Cognition encompassed the higher mental processes of humans, including how people know and understand the world, process information, make judgments and decisions and describe their knowledge and understanding to others.
认知由人类更高一级的心理过程构成,包括人们如何认识和了解世界,加工信息,做出判断的决定,以及向他人描述自己的知识和见解。

② By employing concepts, we are able to organize the complex phenomena into simpler, and therefore more easily usable, cognitive categories.
通过使用概念,我们能够把复杂的现象组织成简单又便于使用

的认知范畴。
③ For example, the judgments we make about the reasons for other people's behavior are based on the ways in which we classify their behavior.
例如,我们对他人行为动机的判断是以我们对他们行为分类的方法为基础。
④ Similarly, physicians make diagnoses by drawing upon concepts and prototypes of symptoms they learned about in medical school.
同样地,医生通过利用概念和他们在医学院学到的症状典型事例做出诊断。
⑤ Deductive reasoning begins with a series of assumptions or premises that are thought to be true, and then derives the implications of these assumptions.
演绎推理以一系列的被认为是真实的假设或前提开始,然后从这些假设中推导出含意。

Phrases and Patterns

1. transform ... into 改变

   What thinking does is to transform the representation of information into a new and different form for the purpose of answering a question, solving a problem, or aiding in reaching a goal.

   思维所做的就是把信息的表现形式转变成一种崭新又不同的形式,目的是回答一个疑问,解决一个问题或帮忙达到一个目标。

2. on the basis of 构成某事物的基础

   Concepts allow us to classify newly encountered objects on the basis of our past experience.

   概念使我们在我们过去经验基础上分类新遇到的事物。

   Consequently, we simplify matters by forming mental representations of types of people on the basis of important or noticeable similarities and differences between them.

结果,我们基于一些重要显著的异同点来形成对不同类型的人的心理表征,从而简化事情。

3. contribute to 贡献

Together, their efforts have contributed to our understanding of formal reasoning processes as well as the mental shortcuts we routinely use—shortcuts that may sometimes lead our reasoning capabilities astray.

总的来说,他们的努力有助于对我们理解正式的推理过程以及我们常用的心理捷径,但这些捷径会把我们的推理能力引入歧途。

Her work has contributed enormously to our understanding of this difficult subject.

她的著作极有助于我们对这个困难问题的了解。

4. be prone to 有……趋向的;倾向的

The various scientific methods that they may employ in the collection of data to support their hypotheses are prone to several sorts of biases, such as using an inappropriate sample of subjects.

他们收集数据来支持他们的假设所使用的不同科学方法会有某种偏差,例如,使用不恰当的抽样对象。

And beholders, they argue, are prone to many perceptual biases.

他们主张旁观者易受到知觉偏见的影响。

5.2 Language: Symbolic Communication
语言:符号的交际

Language is one of the most significant cognitive achievements of the human species. Without language, human beings and human civilization would be a pale shadow of what they are. Language is a symbolic code used in communication. Without an efficient means of communication, it would not be possible to coordinate the efforts of many people in a division of labor, to regulate their behavior for the common good through laws, or to amass the wisdom learned through experience by previous generations and pass it on through education①. And perhaps the most keenly felt loss of all is that psychology textbooks could be neither written nor read!

Semantics: The Meaning of What Is Said

The function of language is to say something to someone. The "something" is the meaning (the semantic content) that is communicated through language. Suppose you want to communicate to your child that the bananas are on the top shelf. That idea must be translated into the language code and expressed to your child, who must receive and comprehend it by translating it back into the same idea. Thus, meaningful ideas are sent from person to person via the system of symbols that we call language.

The fact that semantic content and language codes are not the same thing can easily be seen in a number of ways. For example, it is possible to express the same meaning in more than one way. *The bananas are on the top shelf* and *it's on the top shelf that the bananas are located* are physically very different patterns of sounds, but they express exactly the same meaning. Furthermore, it would be possible to express the same proposition in Chinese, Latin, French, or sign language. This distinction was made by linguist Noam Chomsky, who called the superficial spoken or written structure of a statement its surface structure and the underlying structure that holds the statement's meaning its deep structure.

Generative Property of Language: Elements and Rules

Human language is a highly efficient system. It's particularly efficient in accomplishing so much while putting so little demand on our memories. Stop for a second and think about the sheer magnitude of language. Consider how many different things you have said in your lifetime. If we could accurately estimate the number, it would be staggering. Now let's imagine that human language were not an efficient system. Imagine that we had to learn and remember a different utterance for everything we wanted to say. Although it would be theoretically possible to store that many utterances in long-term memory, we would have to spend every waking hour of our lives doing nothing but memorizing utterances[②]. Obviously, we do not spend anywhere near that amount of time learning language. More important, humans do not speak using a fixed stock of utterances. We could get by in a crude and uninteresting way if we talked like that, but fortunately we do not. Every day you say utterances that no one has ever said before.

If we do not memorize our utterances, where do they come from? We make them up as we go along. In more precise terms, we "generate" language from a set of elements and a set of rules for combining them into speech. When we say that language is generative, we mean that an infinite set of utterances can be made using a finite set of elements and rules. What are these elements and rules?

Phonemes

One way of looking at the elements of language is to consider its individual sounds. Phonemes are the smallest units of sound in a language. In English, everything we say, and everything that we will ever say, is made up of only 44 phonemes (there are more phonemes than letters of the alphabet in English, because some letter combinations such as *ch* and *th* stand for separate phonemes). Different languages have different numbers of phonemes, but the principle is the same in every language: Every utterance is generated from a surprisingly small number of sounds.

Morphemes

When most people think about the individual building blocks of language, they have in mind something like morphemes. The morphemes are the smallest units of meaning in a language. Morphemes are closely related to but are not the same as words. Some morphemes stand alone as words. *Word*, *stand*, and *fast* are each single freestanding morphemes. Other morphemes can exist only if they are bound to other morphemes. Examples are the morpheme for past tense in push*ed*, the plural morpheme in car*s*, and the prefix morpheme *anti* meaning "against" in the word *antibiotic*. The average person knows thousands of morphemes but can speak an infinite number of utterances using a finite set of morphemes and rules for combining them.

Syntax

The rules of a language that allow an infinite number of understandable utterances to be generated are called syntax. There are rules for the ways in which phonemic sounds can be combined in morphemes and rules for how morphemes can be combined in utterances. For instance, in English, we learn that the suffix-*ed* communicates past tense and that the suffix-*s* denotes a plural. We learn the importance of word order. For example, we wouldn't say "this an interesting class is." These rules of syntax are the heart of generative language, for, without them, only a finite number of things could be said with the finite set of morphemes. These rules allow us to make new sentences that will immediately and effortlessly be understood by all speakers who speak normally in the same language.

It is interesting to consider, however, the differences between rules of syntax and the *prescriptive rules* of grammar that are usually taught by authorities, such as parents and teachers. Everyone who speaks a language in a way that can be understood by others knows the syntax of that language, but not everyone uses "proper" grammar. Winston Churchill, an undisputed master of the English language, provided a humorous example of the artificiality of prescriptive rules when he wrote the awkward but grammatically correct "this is the kind of language up with which I will not put."③ It is also interesting to note that few cultures emphasize prescriptive rules of syntax as much as Western European cultures. Other cultures feel that speaking in an understandable way is all that matters.

It's interesting to note that children develop language by learning phonemes first, then morphemes, and then syntax. Children first learn to babble in the speech sounds of their language, then they use some freestanding morphemes by themselves (*mamma*, *milk*, *bye-bye*), and then they begin to acquire syntactic rules for combining morphemes into longer and more complex utterances.

Language and thinking are closely related phenomena. Although we often think in visual images, sounds, and images of movements—and some thought may involve no conscious images at all—much of our thinking takes place in the form of silent conversations with ourselves. If this is true, does language exert any influence on our thinking? If so, it is possible that people who speak different languages might think somewhat differently.

This hypothesis was stated by Benjamin Whorf and is known as the Whorfian hypothesis, or linguistic relativity hypothesis. Although Whorf was most concerned with the impact of different languages on the thinking of people from different cultures, his concrete examples of how this might happen generally concerned the relationship between language and perception. For example, Eskimos have several words for *snow* and can discriminate among different kinds of snow better than, say, lifelong residents of Florida. Does the fact that Eskimos have more words to describe different kinds of snow—and can notice small differences among different kinds of snow—mean that their additional words improve their perception of snow? Whorf proposed that the presence of these words in the Eskimo vocabulary improved visual perception. It seems at least as plausible to assume that the Eskimos first learned to perceive slight differences among different kinds of snow and *then* invented a vocabulary for talking about them to others.

A test of the Whorfian, or linguistic relativity, hypothesis was performed by researchers at the University of Alberta. Their experiment was based on the fact that each language contains terms referring to "personality types" that are important in each culture. For example, most of us understand that the "artistic type" is a person who is interested in the arts, imaginative, intense, moody, and unconventional. Each language contains such terms, but not every language has terms to describe the same personality types. For example, the Chinese language does not have a term for the artistic type, but it contains labels for other personality types that are not found in the English language. For example, the "shen cáng bu lòu" type is recognized by speakers of Chinese to be a very knowledgeable person but one so shy that he or she is reluctant to reveal knowledge and skills unless it is absolutely necessary.

The Whorfian hypothesis suggests that these labels for personality types influence how we think about people. Do they? Fluent speakers of English were compared in their memories for, and reasoning about, hypothetical persons whose personality types were described by the experimenters[4]. Individuals whose language contained a label for the particular personality type described by the experimenter were able to recall the hypothetical people more easily and thought about them in ways that were more consistent with the personality type[5]. For example, English-speaking research participants recalled the characteristics of the hypothetical person described as artistic more often and reasoned about the artistic type in ways that reflected the description of his or her personality more accurately than Chinese-speaking participants. The opposite was true of the shen cáng bu lòu type. In this sense, the words in our language do seem to influence our cognition.

However, another test of the Whorfian hypothesis that reached a different conclusion was conducted by Eleanor Rosch with the same Dani tribe from New Guinea used in her research on learning natural color concepts. She compared the memories of the Dani for colors, whose language uses only two color names, with that of American college students whose language contains many color names. The participants were briefly shown single-color chips and asked to find the same color 30 seconds later among 40 color chips. According to the Whorfian hypothesis, a person's language should influence memory for colors. Specifically, colors with the same name should be confused in memory more easily than colors with different names, so the Dani were expected to remember less than the English speakers. The results did not support Whorf's theory. Neither the Dani nor the American individuals confused colors equally different in wavelength any more often when they had the same color names than different color names, in spite of the large differences in the number of color names in the two languages. Perhaps the Whorfian hypothesis is correct only for some aspects of cognition.

Linguistic relativity has led us to reexamine some of our common language usage. Persons concerned about gender equity have lobbied for the substitution of gender-neutral terms for unnecessarily masculine terms, as in the case of changing *chairman* to *chairperson*. If Whorf is correct, using *chairman* might subtly affect the way we think about the capabilities of females to serve in leadership roles. Although some of the changes seem initially odd to some people (*server* instead of *waiter* or *waitress*), they seem to be rapidly taking over common usage. Producers of *Star Trek, the Next Generation* took this trend one step further when the original "where no *man* has gone before" was changed to "where no *one* has gone before." Neither females nor nonhumans are now excluded.

from: Psychology, Camille B. Wortman & Elizabeth F. Loftus, Alfred A. Knopf. Inc., 1988

Words and Expressions

symbolic	adj.	[sim'bɔlik]	象征的
communication	n.	[kə‚mjuːni'keiʃn]	交流;沟通
coordinate	v.	[kəu'ɔːdinit]	调整;整理
division	n.	[di'viʒən]	分割;区分
regulate	v.	['regjuleit]	控制;调节
semantics	n.	[si'mæntiks]	语义学
proposition	n.	[‚prɔpə'ziʃən]	命题
superficial	adj.	[sjuːpə'fiʃəl]	表面的
underlying	adj.	[‚ʌndə'laiiŋ]	在下面的
generative	adj.	['dʒenərətiv]	生成的
utterance	n.	['ʌtərəns]	言辞;言论
phoneme	n.	['fəuniːm]	音位;音素
morpheme	n.	['mɔːfiːm]	词素
artificiality	n.	[‚ɑːtifiʃ'æliti]	人工
freestanding	adj.	['friːstændIŋ]	独立的
syntax	n.	['sintæks]	句法
hypothesis	n.	[hai'pɔθisis]	假设
plausible	adj.	['plɔːzəbl]	似是而非的
wavelength	n.	['weivleŋθ]	波长
substitution	n.	[‚sʌbsti'tjuːʃən]	代替;置换

surface structure	表层结构
deep structure	深层结构
prescriptive rules	法定规则
Whorfian hypothesis	沃夫假说
linguistic relativity hypothesis	语言相对性假说

Difficult Sentences

① Without an efficient means of communication, it would not be possible to coordinate the efforts of many people in a division of labor, to regulate their behavior for the common good through laws, or to amass the wisdom learned through experience by previous generations and pass it on through education.

如没有有效的交流手段,便不可能协调众人工作分工,也不可能用法律来规范为了共同利益的行为,更不可能积累从前人那学到的智慧并把它通过教育传下去。

② Although it would be theoretically possible to store that many utterances in long-term memory, we would have to spend every waking hour of our lives doing nothing but memorizing utterances.

尽管理论上储存大量的话语在长时记忆中是有可能的,但我们不得不在我们生命中的每一个清醒时刻来记忆话语。

③ Winston Churchill, an undisputed master of the English language, provided a humorous example of the artificiality of prescriptive rules when he wrote the awkward but grammatically correct "this is the kind of language up with which I will not put."

温斯顿·丘吉尔无疑是英语语言大师,他提供了一个有趣的人造法定规则的例子,写出来很别扭但语法正确"这是我不能忍受的语言。"

④ Fluent speakers of English were compared in their memories for, and reasoning about, hypothetical persons whose personality types were described by the experimenters.

对英语说得流利的人的记忆进行比较,并推断出假定的人,这些假定的人的人格类型由实验者向他们描述。

⑤ Individuals whose language contained a label for the particular personality type described by the experimenter were able to recall the hypothetical people more easily and thought about them in ways

that were more consistent with the personality type.
实验者把语言带有独特人格类型标签的人描述成能够很容易回想起假定的人,以与个性特征相一致的方式想起他们。

Phrases and Patterns

1. exert influence on 施加影响
   If this is true, does language exert any influence on our thinking?
   如果这是事实,语言会对我们的思想产生影响吗?
   So persuasive were their arguments at the time they were proposed that many psychologists came to accept the view that situations generally exert a more powerful influence on human behavior than do inner dispositions.
   他们提出的论点在当时是如此的有说服力以至于许多心理学家接受情景通常比内在性情对人类行为的影响更大这一观点。

2. refer to... 与……有关;涉及;关于
   Their experiment was based on the fact that each language contains terms referring to "personality types" that are important in each culture.
   每种语言都含有涉及个性特征并对其文化很重要的词语,他们的研究正基于此事实之上。

3. compare ... with ... 对……与……进行比较
   She compared the memories of the Dani for colors, whose language uses only two color names, with that of American college students whose language contains many color names.
   她对只使用两种颜色名称的丹尼部落的人和使用的语言包含许多颜色名称的美国大学生进行记忆颜色的比较。
   One of its duties seems to be to compare sensory messages with what the brain has learned about the world.
   它的一个任务似乎是把感官信息与大脑学习到关于世界的知识进行比较。

5.3 Concept Formation and Problem Solving: Understanding and Managing Two Key Components of Higher Order Cognition
概念形成与问题解决:理解和使用两个关键的高级认知组成部分

A high school biology begins a unit on photosynthesis by using a picture to illustrate the complex process. A middle school social studies teacher asks students to read a chapter in the text about how a bill becomes law. A student attempts to work her way out of a minor conflict with her two best friends.

Each day teachers ask students to engage sophisticated brain functions that comprise higher order cognition. This is thinking beyond the basic processing and production of information (e. g. yes, no questions; listing information). Dr. Levine stated: "Higher order cognition is the pathway to complex thinking. It enables students to grapple with intellectually sophisticated challenges, integrate multiple ideas and facts, undertake difficult problems, and find effective and creative solutions to dilemmas whose answers are not immediately obvious[①]."

This description makes it apparent that higher order cognition is not a single entity but a multi-faceted and complex area of thinking. Higher order cognition is composed of seven interrelated processes: concept formation, problem solving, rule use, reasoning/logical thinking, critical thinking, creativity/brainstorming, and mental representation. This article will focus on concept formation and problem solving. Excellent sources on the other areas of higher order include Dr. Levine's books *Developmental Variations and Learning Disorders* and *a Mind a Time*.

Concept Formation

A single concept (e. g. dog, table, democracy, due process, energy) is a grouping of facts, attributes, or steps in a process. For example, the following critical attributes group together to define the concept bird: (a) Has feathers, (b) flies, (c) small, (d) eats insects, (e) perches in trees. Every concept possesses critical attributes.

Concept formation is the process of integrating a series of features that group together to form a class of ideas or objects. Developmentally, a younger child might define a bird as any object that flies in the air. The first time this child sees an airplane in flight may point to the sky and say, "Bird!" The observant parent or caregiver might correct the child by saying, "No, that's an airplane. Birds fly but they have feathers. Airplanes fly but they don't have feathers."

Possibly the most important role of concepts is cognitive economy. Imagine if there were no concepts we would have to learn and recall the word that represents each individual entity in our world. For example, each type of table, automobile, or tree would need its own name in order for us to learn and communicate about it in any meaningful way. The size of our mental vocabulary would be so large that communication would be nearly, if not outright, impossible[②].

Types of Concepts

Concepts come in at least five forms: concrete concepts, abstract concepts, verbal concepts and non-verbal concepts. Concrete concepts can be seen, touched, or heard. In other words they have some direct sensory input. Examples of concrete concepts include furniture, transportation, and dog. In contrast, abstract concepts are thought to have no direct sensory input unless by metaphor or analogy. The concepts of metaphor and analogy can be thought of abstract concepts. Verbal concepts are often thought of as classes of ideas or objects that are best understood and used using language. Examples include friendship and irony. These examples may also be classified as abstract concepts. Therefore, types of concepts may overlap.

Nonverbal concepts are often thought to be best understood making mental pictures to represent their critical attributes. The process of painting mental pictures to aid learning and production is often referred to as visualization. Examples of nonverbal concepts include perimeter, area, volume, and mass.

A final type of concept is a process concept. Process concepts represent mechanisms such as photosynthesis or an atomic reaction.

An initial step to promote concept formation is to preview the different concepts students will encounter during the school year or school day or a lesson. Present them with the definition of the different types of concepts listed above telling them which type they will see most and least often in class. Then provide them with examples of important concepts of each type taken directly from their textbooks, class syllabi, and/or outlines. Another important step requires helping students to develop a firm sense of the critical attributes that define individual concept making clear that each concept (i. e. , separate) may share some critical attributes with other concepts. Writing the critical attributes on one side of a flash card and the concept on the other side may help them to collaborate with others or go off by themselves to learn the attributes. The concept flashcards may also help students automatize the retrieval of the concept from memory.

Concept maps may also prove to be an invaluable aid in concept formation. Concept maps (sometimes referred to as concept webs or semantic maps) are diagrams that illustrate the critical attributes of concepts. For example, the name of a concept could be written in the center of a blank page with a circle around it. The five critical attributes of that concept could each be written in smaller circles around the concept, connected by a line. Students would then have a mental image that concept to carry into any discussion or test. Other strategies for enhancing concept formation include: providing students with concrete experiences, using metaphors or analogies, or multiple pathways to learn concepts such as videos, audiotapes, hands-on experiences.

Problem Solving

Each day students face a wide range of problems to be solved and not all problems are found in the mathematics textbook. Younger children face word decoding and math calculation problems, early adolescents stare down growing time and materials management problems, and adolescents confront complex social situations and important decisions about what to do after high school. Solving problems such as these will require using the products of other areas of higher order cognition such as concepts, creativity, and critical thinking. But, problem solving represents a process that is separate from other components of higher order cognition.

Problem solving is the systematic use of a stepwise approach to answering complex questions or addressing difficult issues[3]. Dr. Levine listed the following as the critical steps in problem solving: (a) Recognizing a problem when you see a problem (b) Stating exactly what the problem is (c) Searching memory to see if a similar problem has been dealt with in the past (d) Searching and using prior knowledge and experience to solve the problem (e) Preview the desired outcome (f) Decide if the problem can be solved (g) Break the process of attaining the desired outcome into a series of steps (h) Conduct research (i) Consider alternative strategies for solving the problem (j) Select the best strategy (k) Talk oneself through the task (l) Pace yourself (m)

Monitor progress (n) Manage difficulties (o) Stop when the problem is solved and (p) Reflect on the effectiveness of the problem solving process and store it away in long term memory for later use.

Everyone can be helped by being explicitly taught the steps in the problem solving process. Of course, younger students would not be exposed to all 16 steps but they should be made aware of the steps that are relevant to meeting the problem solving demands of their setting. Older students will benefit from a more comprehensive presentation of stepwisdom represented in the aforementioned list[④]. Some students may also need to be provided with specific strategies to solve problems which pose a great deal of problems for them. Adults and other students may need to model how the strategies are used. The models will need to think aloud as they use the strategy so that the students can experience the decision making that goes along with using any strategy. Then students who were taught the strategy will need to practice its use on low risk tasks (i. e. , not graded). The anxiety of using a new strategy on graded activities may cause the students to not use the best strategy. Therefore, allow students to practice stepwisdom on activities that will not be graded and possibly with assistance from adults or peers. Finally, students need to develop their own personal cognitive toolbox full of problem solving strategies that work for them. The development of the cognitive toolbox may begin by asking students to reflect on the effectiveness of the strategies and how they might improve them or adapt them to other problem solving tasks.

Summary

Higher order cognition represents a multi-faceted and complex network of processes that enhance the processing and production of information. Two important components of higher order cognition are concept formation and problem solving. Although presented separate from each other these areas are interrelated and interdependent. Fortunately, the formation of concepts and problem solving may be enhanced by a thoughtful mix of demystification of these functions, direct instruction in strategies that promote concept formation and problem solving, modeling, and use of accommodations such as concept maps⑤.

from: www. allkindsofminds. org. com, written by Carl W. Swartz.

Words and Expressions

photosynthesis	n.	[ˌfəutəu'sinθəsis]	光合作用
dilemma	n.	[di'lemə]	进退两难的局面
entity	n.	['entiti]	实体
multi-faceted	n.	[ˌmʌlti'fæsitid]	多面的
creativity	n.	[ˌkriːei'tivəti]	创造力
brainstorming	n.	['breinˌstɔːmiŋ]	脑力激荡
attribute	n.	[ə'tribju(ː)t]	属性
perch	v.	[pəːtʃ]	栖息
metaphor	n.	['metəfə]	暗喻
analogy	n.	[ə'nælədʒi]	类比
overlap	v.	['əuvə'læp]	重叠
visualization	n.	[ˌvizjuəlai'zeiʃən]	形象化；可视化
perimeter	n.	[pə'rimitə]	周界
automatize	v.	[ɔː'tɔmətaiz]	使自动化
stepwise	adj.	['stepˌwaiz]	逐步的
demystification	n.	[diːˌmistifi'keiʃən]	非神秘化启蒙

critical attribute	重要属性
concrete concept	具体概念
abstract concept	抽象概念
verbal concept	言语概念
non-verbal concept	非言语概念

atomic reaction 原子反应

Difficult Sentences

① Higher order cognition is the pathway to complex thinking. It enables students to grapple with intellectually sophisticated challenges, integrate multiple ideas and facts, undertake difficult problems, and find effective and creative solutions to dilemmas whose answers are not immediately obvious.
高级认知是复杂思想的途径。它能使学生努力地应对复杂的智力挑战,融合多种思想与事实,着手解决难题,找出既有效又有创造性的解决方法来摆脱困境,尽管这些困境的解决方法并不直观明显。

② The size of our mental vocabulary would be so large that communication would be nearly, if not outright, impossible.
脑子里的词汇量太多以至于若不是在当场,交际几乎成为不可能。

③ Problem solving is the systematic use of a stepwise approach to answering complex questions or addressing difficult issues.
问题解决是系统地使用逐步的方法来回答复杂的问题或处理难题。

④ Older students will benefit from a more comprehensive presentation of stepwisdom represented in the aforementioned list.
年龄大一些的学生将得益于上述清单中陈述的逐级步骤的更全面的展现。

⑤ Fortunately, the formation of concepts and problem solving may be enhanced by a thoughtful mix of demystification of these functions, direct instruction in strategies that promote concept formation and problem solving, modeling, and use of accommodations such as concept maps.
很幸运,这些功能的启示、具有促进作用的策略直接指导、建模

和方便设施的使用,如:概念图的使用,把上述几方面细心地结合能够促进概念形成和问题解决。

Phrases and Patterns

1. be composed of (由某事物)组成或构成

   Higher order cognition is composed of seven interrelated processes...
   高级认知由七种相关联的过程组成……

   The library mangement system is composed of two parts, the human, and the computer. It can be used for collecting, transmitting, and processing information.
   图书管理系统由两部分构成,即人与计算机。它可以用来进行信息的收集、传递与加工。

2. focus on 集中于;为焦点

   This article will focus on concept formation and problem solving.
   本文将以概念形成和问题解决为焦点。

   This means that from the primary early focus on animal behaviors, motivation research has shifted to a primary concern with what we think of as uniquely human behaviors, such as achievement striving and seeking self-esteem.
   这意味着从最早研究动物行为以来,动机研究已经转向主要研究我们自认为的独特的人类行为了,比如获取成就的奋斗和追求自尊的行为。

3. be relevant to 有关的

   Of course, younger students would not be exposed to all 16 steps but they should be made aware of the steps that are relevant to meeting the problem solving demands of their setting.
   当然,年龄小一些的学生将不会受到所有十六个步骤的影响,但是他们应当了解这些步骤,这些步骤与满足他们所处环境的问题解决需要有关。

   We can say that an emotion is a pattern of responses to an event that is

relevant to the goals or needs of the organism.
我们会说情感是对与生物体的目标和需要相关的事件的一种反应模式。

Questions

1. How do we think?
2. What processes underlie reasoning and decision making?
3. What is semantics?
4. How does culture influence language?

6

Motivation and Emotion
动机与情感

【本章导读】 本章第 1 篇文章给出了情感和动机的定义和基本理论。激励理论是动机与情感篇章中主要理论之一。第 2 篇文章阐述了激励理论的理论基础。第 3 篇文章具体就员工激励这个话题阐释了情感与动机中激励理论的运用。

6.1 An Overview of Emotion and Motivational Concept
情感与动机综述

What Is Emotion?

It is difficult to define an emotion, in part because our emotional experience is varied and complex. There are hundreds of emotion words in the English language, from "abashed" to "xenophobic". Do all these terms mean that there are actually hundreds of emotions? Psychologists have tried to sort out this profusion of emotion terms by identifying a few underlying dimensions of emotional experience. Virtually all accounts of emotion agree that emotions can be classified also two broad dimensions: degree of pleasantness and degree of physical excitement or arousal. Some emotions, such as fear, are clearly negative or not pleasant, and others, such as joy, are just as clearly positive or pleasant. Some emotions, such as anger and joy, involve high levels of activity, excitement, physiological arousal, whereas others, such as sadness, involve decreased energy and low levels of arousal.

Although researchers agree that pleasantness and arousal are two important dimensions of the emotional experience, they have not agreed about other dimensions. Yet it is clear that emotions are more common than a two-dimensional model suggests. Consider, for example, anger and fear. Both of these emotions are negative and both are high in arousal, yet they are quite distinct emotional experiences.

Another way to make sense of the variety of emotion terms is to identify which emotions are basic, in the sense that they share some kind of underlying biological foundation or are universal, and which are subordinate, or variations on the basic emotions[①]. The majority of emotion researchers agree that the list of basic emotions is limited to five or six: the positive emotions of love, joy, and possibly, surprise; and the negative emotions of anger, fear, and sadness. These emotions appear in most scientific theories of emotions, and they also seem to organize the way all people talk and think about emotions. Yet even here, there is some disagreement. Some researchers consider disgust a basic negative emotion; some think surprise is a reflex rather than an emotion; and others strike love from the list.

Given this lack of agreement and the complexity of the issue, how are we to define emotion, which we must do, at least provisionally, in order to study it? We can say that an emotion is a pattern of responses to an event that is relevant to the goals or needs of the organism. The responses include physiological arousal, impulses to action, thoughts and expression of all these. According to this definition, individuals who do not have needs, goals, or concerns cannot experience emotions. The needs or goals may be as fundamental as food, shelter, and survival, or they may be as complex as the yearning for love, an ambition to win a Nobel Prize, or a will to build self-respect. As we shall see, each component of an emotion plays an important role in our subjective experience of it. We will also see that different theorists have rather different ideas about the relative importance of the three components.

An Overview of Motivational Concepts

Instinct Theories

Darwin's theory of evolution, which emphasized the continuity between people and other species, had a powerful impact on early theorizing about motivation. Much of the behavior of lower animals, such as web spinning by spiders, see be the result of instincts—innate, fixed responses characteristic of a species propel it toward some end state. Instinctive behavior is fixed, rather than flexible, because it does not depend on the state of the organism at the time of the behavior. Instincts are also irrational in that they are not under the conscious control of individual. If instincts are the primary motivational force initiating the behavior so-called lower animals, then, ran Darwin's argument, instincts may also motivate human behavior. Researchers began to propose instinct explanations for a variety of human behavior, including conformity (the "herd instinct"), isolation (the "antisocial instinct"), and many others. The proliferation of instincts (a point more than 2,500 instincts had been proposed) made it clear that the territory not particularly useful for explaining human behavior, because any behavior be "explained" by proposing an instinct for that behavior. Psychologists replaced the term "instinct" with "fixed action pattern", which has a more profound meaning. A fixed action pattern is a stereotyped and often-repeated pattern movement, which is not altered by experience. Most human behavior is too possible to be caused by fixed action patterns.

Drive-Reduction Theories

In contrast to instinct theories, drive-reduction theories, the origins of which are largely credited to Clark Hull, propose that the behavior of the individual depends on its physical state[②]. In particular, drives are motivational states that result from physiological deficits or needs and instigate behaviors to reduce those needs. For example, an organism in a state of water deprivation is motivated by the hunger drive, and an organism in a state of water deprivation is motivated by the drive of thirst. Drive-reduction theories allow greater flexibility in behavior than theories of instincts of fixed action patterns because many different behaviors might satisfy the same drive. For example, a person who is hunger might go grocery shopping and cook dinner, reheat leftovers, order a pizza, or go out to a restaurant, all of which would result in a reduction of the hunger drive.

Biologically, the goal of drive reduction is homeostasis—maintaining a balanced or constant physiological state. For example, drinking to reduce thirst has the goal of maintaining a constant fluid concentration in the body's cells. The human body achieves homeostasis in much the same way a thermostat maintains a constant temperature. When the room temperature drops below the "set" or desire temperature, the furnace is turned on, and when the temperature reaches the desired level, the furnace is turned off.

Of course, with a moment's reflection it becomes obvious that much human behavior is not motivated by physiological drives such as hunger and thirst. There are no known biological needs that impel us to go to the movies, write novels, or study psychology. To accommodate such behaviors into their analysis, drive-reduction theorists proposed two types of drives—primary and secondary. Primary drives are based on physiological need states, and secondary drives are acquired or learned through their association with primary drives[3]. For example, wanting money when you <u>are short of</u> cash might become a secondary drive; the need for money is not a physiological need, but it is associated with the reduction of hunger: money buys food.

Drive-reduction theories have evolved to acknowledge that behavior is controlled not only by internal states but also by external conditions, or stimuli. You might continue to study even if you were getting hungry, but if a friend set a milkshake on your desk, you would probably stop studying and drink the shake; the milkshake would reduce your hunger drive if you drank it. Such external stimuli that serve as anticipated rewards for certain behaviors are called incentives.

Drive-reduction theories have had a major impact on psychological theorizing about motivation and they continue to explain some types of behavior quite well.

Cognitive Theories

Expectancy-value theories are one type of theory that includes cognitive activity in motivational processes. These theories propose that behavior is the result of two types of cognitions—the individual's expectation that a behavior will result in achieving some goal, plus the value of that goal to the individual[4]. For example, if you have a low expectation that studying will improve your performance in class, you will not study, according to expectancy value theories, even if you value good performance very highly. Similarly, if you do not value good performance at tennis, you will be unlikely to practice, even if you have a strong expectation that practice improves performance.

Expectancy-value theories represent a significant shift in motivational theories because they place importance on cognitive determinants of behavior. The types of cognitions these theories stress, however, are limited to just two—expectancies and values, and some researchers have argued that this is too limited a role. For example, as we shall see, Bernald Weiner has developed a theory of achievement motivation that emphasized how we explain our own successes and failures to ourselves.

Nevertheless, this transition in motivation research from mechanistic and physiologically based theories to more cognitive theories is a significant one. Indeed, it parallels the development of theoretical approaches to the study of emotion. This means that from the primary early focus on animal behaviors, motivation research has shifted to a primary concern with what we think of as uniquely human behaviors, such as achievement striving and seeking self-esteem⑤.

from: *Psychology Today: An Introduction* Richard R. Bootzin, Gordon H. Bower, Jennifer Crocker, Elizabeth Hall, Von Hoffmann Press, 1991

Words and Expressions

abashed	adj.	[əˈbæʃt]	不安的;窘迫的
xenophobic	adj.	[ˌzenəuˈfəubik]	恐惧(或憎恨)外国人的;恐外的
profusion	n.	[prəˈfjuːʒən]	丰富
provisional	adj.	[prəˈviʒənl]	临时的
organism	n.	[ˈɔːgənizəm]	生物体;有机体
yearning	n.	[ˈjəːniŋ]	向往
species	n.	[ˈspiːʃiz]	种类;(原)核素
spinning	n.	[ˈspiniŋ]	[纺]纺纱
innate	adj.	[ˈineit]	先天的;天生的
propel	vt.	[prəˈpel]	推进;驱使
propose	v.	[prəˈpəuz]	计划;建议;向……提议;求(婚)
proliferation	n.	[prəuˌlifəˈreiʃən]	增殖;分芽繁殖
credit	vt.	[ˈkredit]	相信;信任;把……归给

deficit	n.	[ˈdefisit]	赤字;不足额
instigate	v.	[ˈinstigeit]	鼓动
deprivation	n.	[ˌdepriˈveiʃən]	剥夺
grocery	n.	[ˈgrəusəri]	<美>食品杂货店;食品;杂货
homeostasis	n.	[ˌhəumiəuˈsteisis]	(社会群体的)自我平衡;原状稳定
thermostat	n.	[ˈθəːməstæt]	自动调温器;温度调节装置
incentive	n.	[inˈsentiv]	动机
parallel	v.	[ˈpærəlel]	相应;平行

physiological arousal	生理激励
instinct theories	本能理论
fixed action pattern	固定行为模式
drive-reduction theories	动机减少理论
physiological state	生理状态
physiological drives	生理动机
biological needs	生物需求
physiological needs	生理需求
cognitive activity	认知活动

Difficult Sentences

① Another way to make sense of the variety of emotion terms is to identify which emotions are basic, in the sense that they share some kind of underlying biological foundation or are universal, and which are subordinate, or variations on the basic emotions.
另一种理解各种情感术语的方法是确定哪些情感是基本的,它们享有根本的或者是普遍的生物基础;哪些是基本情感的下级情感或变形情感。

② In contrast to instinct theories, drive-reduction theories, the origins of which are largely credited to Clark Hull, propose that the behavior of the individual depends on its physical state.

与本能理论不同,主要源于克拉克·哈尔的动机减少理论认为个人行为取决于其身体状态。

③ Primary drives are based on physiological need states, and secondary drives are acquired or learned through their association with primary drives.

主要动机是以生理需求状态为基础的,而次要动机是通过它们与主要动机相关联来获取或学会的。

④ These theories propose that behavior is the result of two types of cognitions—the individual's expectation that a behavior will result in achieving some goal, plus the value of that goal to the individual.

这些理论认为行为是两种认知的结果,这两种认知是个人期望,即一种行为即将达成的目标,加上个人的目标价值。

⑤ This means that from the primary early focus on animal behaviors, motivation research has shifted to a primary concern with what we think of as uniquely human behaviors, such as achievement striving and seeking self-esteem.

这意味着从最早研究动物行为以来,动机研究已经转向主要研究我们自认为独特的人类行为了,比如获取成就的奋斗和追求自尊的行为等。

Phrases and Patterns

1. sort out 挑选出

Psychologists have tried to sort out this profusion of emotion terms by identifying a few underlying dimensions of emotional experience.

心理学家努力通过确定一些情感经历的根本性纬度来挑选丰富的情感术语。

2. all accounts of 各种各样的

Virtually all accounts of emotion agree that emotions can be classified also two broad dimensions: degree of pleasantness and degree of physical excitement or arousal.

最终各种各样的情感统一被分为两大维度：一是快乐程度，二是身体激动或激励程度。

3. have an impact on... 对……有影响；对……起作用；产生效果

   Darwin's theory of evolution, which emphasized the continuity between people and other species, had a powerful impact on early theorizing about motivation.

   达尔文的进化论强调人类和其他物种的连续性，该理论对早期动机理论有巨大的影响。

   Freud's psychoanalytic approach had a great impact on psychology and psychiatry.

   弗洛伊德的心理分析的研究方法对心理学和精神病学有很大的影响。

4. depend on 依靠；依赖

   Ability in turn depends on education, experience and training and its improvement is a slow and long process.

   同样，能力依靠教育、经验和培训，能力的提高是缓慢又漫长的过程。

5. be short of

   For example, wanting money when you are short of cash might become a secondary drive; the need for money is not a physiological need, but it is associated with the reduction of hunger: money buys food.

   例如，当你缺现金时想要钱可能成为次要动机，因为对钱的需要不是生理需求，但是它能帮助填饱肚子：钱能买食物。

6.2 Arousal Theory
激励理论

The arousal approach tends to emphasize the organism as a whole and argues that we can best understand behavior by understanding how the organism becomes activated.

The basic idea underlying arousal theory is that we can understand emotion and motivation by viewing them on a continuum of behavioral activation. This continuum ranges from low levels of arousal (e.g. coma or sleep) to very high levels (e.g. rage). Basically arousal theory regards emotion as the result of the individual's arousal level.

Arousal theory assumes that behavior will change as we become more aroused. Some changes in arousal, as from sleep to alert wakefulness, will result in increased efficiency of performance, but other arousal changes, as from alert wakefulness to extreme emotional arousal, will interfere with efficient responding[①]. This reasoning suggests that an optimal level of arousal exists at which behavior will be most efficient, as depicted in Figure 6.1.

The curve in Figure 6.1 is called an inverted U function and indicates that increasing arousal improves performance only up to a point, after which continued increases in arousal actually begin to interfere with responding. This arousal-performance relationship, sometimes called the Yerkes-Dodson law, is easily seen. In order to study objectively for an exam, we must be sufficiently aroused; on the other hand, if we become "too emotional" about the exam, our anxiety may interfere with our studying to the point that we cannot learn the material.

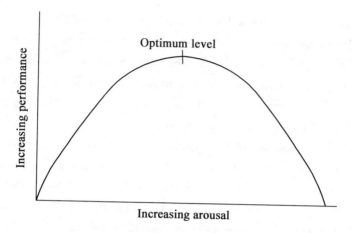

Figure 6.1 Yerkes-Dodson law

Hokanson noted that the proposed relationship between arousal and performance holds for some types of tasks but not for others. For example, Freeman obtained an inverted U function between arousal (as measured by skin conductance) and reaction time, but Hokanson did not obtain inverted U functions for tasks such as symbol matching and concept formation. Thus the relationship between arousal and behavior is apparently more complex and task specific than arousal theory has indicated.

If emotion and motivation result from activation of the nervous system, as arousal theory suggests, there should be structures in the nervous system that trigger this activation[2]. Bremer has shown that if we cut through the brainstem of an animal between the medulla and the spinal cord, the animal continues to go through its normal sleep-wake cycle even though the body has been deprived of all its higher cortical brain tissue (Bremer called this preparation encephale isolé). On the other hand, if we cut higher up the brainstem at the level of the colliculi, the sleep-wake cycle is abolished and the animal sleeps constantly, showing no spontaneous waking (called the cerveau isolé).

Taken together, the results of Bremer's two cuts suggest that some brain structure (or structures) located between the two cuts may control changes in the arousal level involved in moving from sleeping to waking. Further, such a structure is probably located in the vicinity of the pons.

Arousal theory received a big boost with the discovery by Moruzzi and Magoun of the role of the reticular activating system in arousal. The reticular activating system (RAS) is a group of neurons (i.e., nerve cells) located in the brainstem's central core, which runs from the level of the medulla through the thalamus. Moruzzi and Magoun found that electrical stimulation of the RAS led to changes in the electrical activity of the cortex (recorded by the electroencephalogram or EEG) that were indistinguishable from changes seen when external stimuli (e.g. a loud noise) were being paid attention to. In order to understand the role of the RAS in arousal, we must briefly examine what is shown by an EEG.

An individual resting quietly shows a regular pattern of cortical electrical activity that can be measured by means of the EEG. The electrical activity of the cells in this relaxed state tends to occur simultaneously (i.e., they are synchronous) and leads to a pattern of electrical activity known as alpha waves. If we make a loud sound, however, the individual will open the eyes and look around in an alert manner, and the pattern of the EEG during this alert behavior is very different. The cells of the cortex tend now to be active independently of one another (i.e., they are desynchronized), which leads to a new EEG pattern sometimes called alpha blocking. Alpha blocking is associated with alert, attentive, and aroused individuals ready to deal with changes in their environment.

Moruzzi and Magoun found that stimulation of the RAS leads to alpha blocking just as environmental stimuli do. Therefore it seemed reasonable that the RAS is responsible for the activation of the organism to begin with. Support for this idea was provided in a number of different ways. First, the RAS receives sensory input from the external sensory systems as well as from the muscles and internal organs; thus it has the necessary inputs to trigger arousal. Second, Lindsley cut all the brain structures surrounding the RAS in experimental animals and found that the animals still displayed normal sleep-wake cycles. But when he cut the RAS, leaving everything else intact, the result was a permanently sleeping animal, just as in Bremer's cerveau isolé preparation. Finally, the RAS is known to send fibers diffusely to the whole cortex. Apparently, therefore, the RAS is the brain structure that serves to arouse the organism from sleep to wakefulness. Thus the RAS most likely determines where on the arousal continuum we find ourselves.

The discovery of the role of the RAS in arousal led activation were equivalent to cortical arousal.

Arousal theory is based on the assumption that one can measure arousal by monitoring the activity of the brain or changes in the autonomic nervous system and correlating these with changes in behavior[3]. As researchers soon discovered, however, these correlations were often minimal (although usually positive). The lack of substantial correlations between different indexes of arousal has created problems for arousal theory and led Lacey to propose that more than one type of arousal exists. Thus we may see behavioral arousal as indicated by a responding organism, autonomic arousal as shown by changes in bodily functions, or cortical arousal as evidenced by desynchronized, fast brain waves[4]. Lacey proposed that although these three arousals often occur together, they do not have to and are in fact independent. He noted, for example, that certain chemicals (e.g. atropine) produce EEG activity akin to sleep in cats and dogs, which nevertheless respond behaviorally in a normal, awake manner. Other chemicals (e.g. physostigmine) produce

EEG activity like that of an alert animal, but the animal behaves as if drowsy. Comatose patients sometimes show "normal" EEGs, and normal responding is sometimes observed in individuals with sleeplike EEGs. Lacey also reported several studies indicating that sometimes little relationship exists between central nervous system activity and autonomic changes. As a result of these problems, he proposed that arousal is multidimensional. He believed that different situations produce different patterns of somatic responses (e. g. heart rate).

Feedback from the periphery of the body is also important in Lacey's model of arousal. For example, he reported research showing that distention of the carotid sinus (a mechanism in the carotid artery) causes EEG activity to change from alert, high-frequency activity to low-frequency activity generally associated with sleep. This change indicates that feedback from various systems of the body can directly influence the arousal system and suggests that bodily systems may also play a role in the length of arousal episodes[⑤].

To summarize, RAS research indicates a physiological mechanism that is involved with arousal of the organism, the sleep-wake cycle, and alert attention to the environment. These conclusions fit nicely with arousal theory's concept of motivation and emotion as equivalent to arousal.

form: *Motivation*: *Theory*, *Research*, *and Applications*, Herbert L. Petri, *Washington Publishing Company*, 1990

Words and Expressions

arousal	*n.*	[ə'rauzəl]	觉醒;激励
continuum	*n.*	[kən'tinjuəm]	连续统一体
conductance	*n.*	[kən'dʌktəns]	电导;导率;电导系数
cortical	*adj.*	['kɔ:tikəl]	皮层的;皮质的;有关脑皮层的
colliculus	*n.*	[kɔ'likjuləs]	[解]丘

vicinity	n.	[vi'siniti]	邻近;附近;接近
thalamus	n.	['θæləməs]	丘脑;室;花托
cortex	n.	['kɔ:teks]	(植物的)皮层;树皮;(脑或肾的)皮层,皮质
desynchronize	vt.	[di:'siŋkrənaiz]	使去同步;使失同步
intact	adj.	[in'tækt]	完整无缺的;尚未被人碰过的;(家畜)未经阉割的
index	n.	['indeks]	索引;[数学]指数;指标;(刻度盘上)指针
atropine	n.	[ætrə'pin]	[药]阿托品(含颠茄碱)
akin	adj.	[ə'kin]	同族的;类似的
physostigmine	n.	[ˌfaisəu'stigmi:n]	[药]毒扁豆碱(一种眼科缩瞳药)
drowsy	adj.	['drauzi]	昏昏欲睡的;催眠的;(街、市等)沉寂的
comatose	adj.	['kəumətəus]	昏睡的;昏睡状态的
somatic	adj.	[səu'mætik]	肉体的
periphery	n.	[pə'rifəri]	外围
carotid	adj.	[kə'rifɔriə]	颈动脉的
sinus	n.	['sainəs]	窦;穴;湾;凹处
artery	n.	['ɑ:təri]	动脉;要道
episode	n.	['episəud]	一段情节;[音]插曲,插话
equivalent	adj.	[i'kwivələnt]	相等的;相当的;同意义的

an inverted U function	反向 U 功能(曲线)
nervous system	神经系统
reticular activating system (RAS)	网状活动系统
sensory input	感觉输入
arousal continuum	激励序列
physiological mechanism	生理机制

Difficult Sentences

① Some changes in arousal, as from sleep to alert wakefulness, will result in increased efficiency of performance, but other arousal changes, as from alert wakefulness to extreme emotional arousal, will interfere with efficient responding.
例如,从睡眠到清醒的一些激励变化将导致行为效率的提高,但是其他的一些激励变化,如从清醒到极端的情感刺激,将干涉有效的反应行为。

② If emotion and motivation result from activation of the nervous system, as arousal theory suggests, there should be structures in the nervous system that trigger this activation.
如果情感和动机是来源于神经系统活动,那么激励理论认为神经系统内应该有专门的结构刺激这种活动。

③ Arousal theory is based on the assumption that one can measure arousal by monitoring the activity of the brain or changes in the autonomic nervous system and correlating these with changes in behavior.
激励理论基于这一假设:人能通过监测大脑活动或者自主神经系统本身的变化,并将这些与行为变化相联系,从而测量激励。

④ Thus we may see behavioral arousal as indicated by a responding organism, autonomic arousal as shown by changes in bodily functions, or cortical arousal as evidenced by desynchronized, fast brain waves.
因此我们可以了解反应物来说明行为激励,身体功能的变化表现自动激励,同步快速脑波证明脑皮层激励。

⑤ This change indicates that feedback from various systems of the body can directly influence the arousal system and suggests that bodily systems may also play a role in the length of arousal episodes.
这个变化说明身体各系统的反应能直接影响激励系统,也说明

身体系统在激励长度上也起到了重要作用。

Phrases and Patterns

1. cut through 刺穿

    Bremer has shown that if we cut through the brainstem of an animal between the medulla and the spinal cord, the animal continues to go through its normal sleep – wake cycle even though the body has been deprived of all its higher cortical brain tissue

    布莱默指出如果我们刺穿动物骨髓和脊髓之间的脑干，即便它的高级脑组织已经剥离了它的身体，它仍能继续正常的睡眠—清醒循环活动。

2. deprive of 剥夺

    The animal continues to go through its normal sleep – wake cycle even though the body has been deprived of all its higher cortical brain tissue.

    即便它的高级脑组织剥离了身体，动物仍然可以继续它的睡眠—清醒循环活动。

3. pay attention to 注意

    Theorists paid attention to external stimuli as examining arousal systems.

    理论家研究激励系统时很关注外在刺激。

    Freud paid attention to the unconscious.

    弗洛伊德注重潜意识。

4. in order to 为了

    In order to understand the role of the RAS in arousal, we must briefly examine what is shown by an EEG.

    为了理解激励理论中的网状活动系统的作用，我们必须简单地解释一下脑电图显示情况。

    Some, for instance, planned to strive hard in order to succeed in college.

例如，一些人打算努力奋斗为了在大学中获得成功。

6.3 Employee Motivation: Theory and Practice
员工动机的理论与实践

The job of a manager in the workplace is to get things done through employees. To do this the manager should be able to motivate employees. But that's easier said than done! Motivation practice and theory are difficult subjects, touching on several disciplines.

In spite of enormous research, basic as well as applied, the subject of motivation is not clearly understood and more often than not poorly practiced[①]. To understand motivation one must understand human nature itself. And there lies the problem!

Human nature can be very simple, yet very complex too. An understanding and appreciation of this is a prerequisite to effective employee motivation in the workplace and therefore effective management and leadership.

These articles on motivation theory and practice concentrate on various theories regarding human nature in general and motivation in particular. Included are articles on the practical aspects of motivation in the workplace and the research that has been undertaken in this field, notably by Douglas McGregor (theory y), Frederick Herzberg (two factor motivation hygiene theory), Abraham Maslow (theory a, hierarchy of needs), Elton Mayo (Hawthorne Experiments), Chris Argyris, Rensis Likert and David McClelland (achievement motivation).

Why study and apply employee motivation principles?

Quite apart from the benefit and moral value of an altruistic approach to treating colleagues as human beings and respecting human dignity in all its forms, research and observations show that well motivated employees are more productive and creative. The inverse also holds true. The schematic below indicates the potential contribution the practical application of the principles this paper has on reducing work content in the organization.

Motivation is the key to performance improvement.

There is an old saying you can take a horse to the water but you cannot force it to drink; it will drink only if it's thirsty—so with people[2]. They will do what they want to do or otherwise motivated to do. Whether it is to excel on the workshop floor or in the "ivory tower" they must be motivated or driven to it, either by themselves or through external stimulus.

Are they born with the self-motivation or drive? Yes and no. if no, they can be motivated, for motivation is a skill which can and must be learnt. This is essential for any business to survive and succeed.

Performance is considered to be a function of ability and motivation, thus:

· Job performance $=f$ (ability) (motivation)

Ability in turn depends on education, experience and training and its improvement is a slow and long process. <u>On the other hand</u> motivation can be improved quickly. There are many options and an uninitiated manager may not even know where to start. As a guideline, there are broadly seven strategies for motivation.

· Positive reinforcement/high expectations.
· Effective discipline and punishment.
· Treating people fairly.
· Satisfying employees needs.
· Setting work related goals.
· Restructuring jobs.

· Base rewards on job performance.

These are the basic strategies, though the mix in the final "recipe" will vary from workplace situation to situation③. Essentially, there is a gap between an individual's actual state and some desired state and the manager tries to reduce this gap④.

Motivation is, in effect, a means to reduce and manipulate this gap. It is inducing others in a specific way towards goals specifically stated by the motivator. Naturally, these goals as also the motivation system must conform to the corporate policy of the organization. The motivational system must be tailored to the situation and to the organization.

In one of the most elaborate studies on employee motivation, involving 31 000 men and 13 000 women, the Minneapolis Gas Company sought to determine what their potential employees desire most from a job. This study was carried out during a 20 year period from 1945 to 1965 and was quite revealing. The ratings for various factors differed only slightly between men and women, but both groups considered security as the highest rated factor. The next three factors were:

· Advancement.

· Type of work.

· Company—proud to work for.

Surprisingly, factors such as pay, benefits and working conditions were given a low rating by both groups⑤. So after all, and contrary to common belief, money is not the prime motivator, though this should not be regarded as a signal to reward employees poorly or unfairly.

from: http://www.accel-team.com/index.html

Words and Expressions

enormous	adj.	[i'nɔ:məs]	巨大的;庞大的
appreciation	n.	[ə͵pri:ʃi'eiʃən]	感谢;感激;正确评价;

			欣赏;增值
prerequisite	n.	['priː'rekwizit]	先决条件
altruistic	adj.	[,æltru'istik]	利他的;无私心的
dignity	n.	['digniti]	尊严;高贵
inverse	n.	['in'vəːs]	反面
schematic	adj.	[ski'mætik]	示意性的
stimulus	n.	['stimjuləs]	刺激物;促进因素;刺激
essential	adj.	[i'senʃəl]	本质的;实质的;基本的; 精华的
initiate	v.	[i'niʃieit]	开始;发动;传授
recipe	n.	['resipi]	处方
manipulate	v.	[mə'nipjuleit]	(熟练地)操作;巧妙地处理

employee motivation	员工激励
human nature	人性
self-motivation	自我激励
job performance	工作表现
Minneapolis Gas Company	明尼阿波利斯天然气公司
working conditions	工作环境

Difficult Sentences

① In spite of enormous research, basic as well as applied, the subject of motivation is not clearly understood and more often than not poorly practiced.

尽管有大量的基础的和应用的调查研究,激励理论还是不能清楚地被认识,激励实践也很少。

② There is an old saying you can take a horse to the water but you cannot force it to drink; it will drink only if it's thirsty—so with people.

有一句古谚语说,你能牵马去水边,但是不能强迫它喝水;它只有渴了才会喝。人也一样。

③ These are the basic strategies, though the mix in the final "recipe" will vary from workplace situation to situation.

以上这些就是基本策略,尽管最后一条的综合会根据工作环境的不同而变化。

④ Essentially, there is a gap between an individual's actual state and some desired state and the manager tries to reduce this gap.

本来,个人实际状态和一些渴望状态之间存在差距,因此经理努力想减小这个差距。

⑤ Surprisingly, factors such as pay, benefits and working conditions were given a low rating by both groups.

令人惊讶的是两组人都把工资、福利和工作环境等因素列在较低的等级。

Phrases and Patterns

1. concentrate on 集中;全神贯注于

These articles on motivation theory and practice concentrate on various theories regarding human nature in general and motivation in particular.

这些关于激励理论和实践的文章主要讲各种关于一般人性的理论,特别是激励理论。

The advantage of maladaptive behavior as a standard is that it concentrates on a person's behavior in relation to the behavior of others.

把不利于适应的行为作为标准的优点是它关注了一个人的行为和其他人的行为的对比。

2. apart from 远离;除……之外

Quite apart from the benefit and moral value of an altruistic approach to treating colleagues as human beings and respecting human dignity in all its forms, research and observations show that well motivated employees are more productive and creative.

除了像对待人类一般对待同事、尊重他人的各种尊严等利他主义的方法有许多好处和道德价值外,研究和观察表明被适当激励的员工们生产力更强,创造性更大。

Apart form interfering with normal activities, compulsions can have other serious effects.

除了妨碍正常的行为,冲动还会有其他严重的影响。

3. on the other hand 另一方面

On the other hand motivation can be improved quickly.

另一方面,激励能得到迅速改善。

On the other hand, if either or both of the premises in a syllogism are not accurate, then there is insufficient support for the accuracy of the conclusion.

另一方面,一个推论中两个前提中的任意一个或两个都不是正确的,那么结论的正确性就不会有充足的支持。

4. regard as 把……认作

So after all, and contrary to common belief, money is not the prime motivator, though this should not be regarded as a signal to reward employees poorly or unfairly.

与共同信仰相反,金钱毕竟不是主要激励因素,虽然这不能被看作是回报员工的金钱不能太少或者不公平的一个信号。

Basically arousal theory regards emotion as the result of the individual's arousal level.

激励理论基本上把情感视作个人激励的结果。

Questions

1. What is emotion?
2. Can you give the definition of motivation by each of the three theories: instinct theory, drive-reduction theory, and cognitive theory?
3. What is arousal and what does arousal theory state?
4. What are the three types of arousal by Lacey? And can you explain them with examples?

Personality
人格

【本章导读】 本章主要介绍人格。第 1 篇文章介绍了关于人格的主要观点,包括心理分析的观点、特性的观点、人本主义的观点和社会认知观点。第 2 篇文章介绍了不同心理学家对人类的行为是否保持一致有不同的观点,以及目前的研究成果。第 3 篇文章介绍了四个有价值的、未来的人格研究的领域,包括建构和预测有效性的研究、结合传统的和细微的评估程序的研究、人格中个体内部可变性的前因和结果的研究以及在不同背景下同化或对比效果的研究。

7.1 Major Perspectives on Personality
关于人格的主要观点

The novelist William Faulkner was a master at creating characters with vivid personalities, personalities so real they seem to cast shadows. Faulkner's characters, as they appear and reappear throughout his fiction, exhibit the kinds of distinctiveness and consistency that define personality. Having emphasized in the preceding chapters of this book how we are similar—how we develop, perceive, learn, remember, think, and feel—we now acknowledge that each of us is in some ways unique. This distinctiveness helps define our individual personalities. Personality consists of "an individual's enduring response patterns". Thus, your personality is defined as you relatively distinctive and consistent ways of thinking, feeling and acting. If your response patterns are unusually distinctive and consistent—if, say, you are strikingly outgoing, whether at a party or in a classroom—people are likely to say that you have a "strong" personality. We will examine four major perspectives on personality, each valuable for the light it sheds on our complex workings.

The Psychoanalytic Perspective

Exploring the Unconscious

Sigmund Freud's treatment of emotional disorders led him to believe they resulted from the unconscious dynamics of personality, dynamics which he sought to analyze through his own and his patients' free associations and dreams①. Freud saw personality as composed of a reservoir of pleasure-seeking psychic impulses (the id), a reality-oriented executive (the ego), and an internalized set of ideals (the superego)②.

Freud believed that children develop through several formative psychosexual stages, which he labeled the oral, anal, phallic, latency, and genital stages. He suggested that people's later personalities were influenced by how they resolved conflicts associated with these stages and whether they remained fixated at any stage.

To cope with anxiety caused by the tensions between the demands of id and superego, the ego has protective defense mechanisms, of which repression is the most basic. New-Freudians Alfred Adler, Karen Horney, Erich Fromm, and Erik Erikson accepted many of Freud's ideas, as did Carl Jung, but argued that we have more positive motives than sex and aggression.

Assessing the Unconscious

Psychoanalytic assessment techniques attempt to reveal aspects of personality that are thought to be hidden in the unconscious. However, some projective tests such as the Rorschach inkblots have been criticized for their minimal reliability and validity.

Evaluating the Psychoanalytic Perspective

Many of Freud's specific ideas have been criticized as implausible or have not been validated. His theory has also been faulted for offering after-the-fact explanations. Nevertheless, Freud drew psychology's attention to the unconscious, to the struggle to cope with anxiety and sexuality, and to the conflict between biological impulses and social restraints. Moreover, his cultural impact has been enormous.

The Trait Perspective

Describing Traits

Rather than explain the hidden aspects of personality, trait theorists have described the predispositions that underlie our actions. For example, through factor analysis, these theorists have isolated distinct dimensions of personality.

Assessing Traits

To assess traits, psychologists have devised objective personality inventories such as the empirically derived MMPI (Minnesota Multiphasic Personality Inventory). Computerized testing has made these inventories widely available; however, they are still most helpful when used to assess those who are emotionally troubled.

Evaluating the Trait Perspective: How Consistent Are We?

Critics of trait theory question the consistency with which traits are expressed. Although people's traits do seem to persist through time, human behavior varies widely form situation to situation. Despite these variations, people's average behavior across different situations is fairly consistent.

The Humanistic Perspective

Humanistic psychologists have sought to turn psychology's attention to the growth potential of healthy people, as seen through the individual's own experiences.

Exploring the Self

Abraham Maslow believed that if more basic human needs are fulfilled, people will strive to actualize their highest potential. To describe self-actualization, he studied some exemplary personalities and summarized his impressions of their qualities. To nurture growth in others, Carl Rogers advised being genuine, accepting, and empathic. In such a climate, people can develop a deeper self-awareness and a more realistic and positive self-concept

Assessing the Self

Humanistic psychologists assess personality through questionnaires that rate self-concept and by seeking to understand others' subjective personal experiences in therapy[3].

Evaluating the Humanistic perspective

Humanistic psychology's critics complain that its concepts are vague and subjective, its values self-centered, and its assumptions naively optimistic. Nevertheless, humanistic psychology has helped to renew psychology's interest in the concept of self, which is now being vigorously researched through studies of phenomena such as self-esteem and self-serving bias[4].

The Social-Cognitive Perspective

The social-cognitive perspective applies principles of social learning and cognition to personality, with particular emphasis on the ways in which our personalities are influenced by our interaction with the environment.

Exploring Behavior in situations

This perspective deals with reciprocal determinism—how personal-cognitive factors combine with the environment to influence people's expectations regarding their situations. By studying variations among people in their perceived locus of control and in their experiences of learned helplessness or self-efficacy, researchers have found that an inner locus of control helps people to cope with life⑤.

Assessing behavior in situations

Social-cognitive researchers study how people's behaviors and beliefs both affect and are affected by their situations. They have found that the best way to predict someone's behavior in a given situation is to observe that person's behavior in similar situations.

Evaluation the social-cognitive perspective Though faulted for underemphasizing the importance of unconscious dynamics and inner traits, the social-cognitive perspective builds on psychology's well-established concepts of learning and cognition and reminds us of the power of social situations.

from: *Psychology* (second edition), David G. Myers, Worth Publishers. Inc. , 1989

Words and Expressions

distinctiveness	n.	[dis'tiŋktivnis]	特殊性;独特性
consistency	n.	[kən'sistənsi]	一致性;连贯性
enduring	adj.	[in'djuəriŋ]	持久的;不朽的
psychoanalytic	adj.	['saikəuˌænə'litik]	心理分析的
dynamics	n.	[dai'næmiks]	动态
psychic	adj.	['saikik]	精神的
id	n.	[id]	本我

ego	n.	['igəu]	自我
internalized	v.	[in'tə:nə,laiz]	使内在化
formative	adj.	['fɔ:mətiv]	格式化的
psychosexual	adj.	[,saikəu'sekʃuəl]	性心理的
oral	adj.	['ɔ:rəl]	口部快感
anal	adj.	['einəl]	肛门的
phallic	adj.	['fælik]	生殖器的
latency	n.	['leitənsi]	潜伏期
genital	adj.	['dʒenitl]	性心理发育早期的
fixated	adj.	[fik'seitid]	异常依恋
mechanism	n.	['mekənizəm]	机制
repression	n.	[ri'preʃən]	压抑作用
reliability	n.	[ri,laiə'biliti]	信度
validity	n.	[və'lidti]	效度
predisposition	n.	[pri:,dispə'ziən]	性向;倾向;易患病体质
trait	n.	[treit]	特性
humanistic	adj.	[,hju:mə'nistik]	人文主义的
empathic	adj.	[em'pæθik]	移情作用的
reciprocal	adj.	[ri'siprəkəl]	相互的
determinism	n.	[di'tə:minizəm]	决定论

psychoanalytic perspective	心理分析的观点
psychosexual stage	性心理阶段
defense mechanism	自卫机能
Rorschach inkblots test	罗夏墨迹测验
trait perspective	特性的观点
Minnesota Multiphasic Personality Inventory	明尼苏达多项个性检查表
humanistic perspective	人本主义的观点
social-cognitive perspective	社会认知观点
reciprocal determinism	相互决定论

lotus of control　　　　　　　　　　控制点

Difficult Sentences

① Sigmund Freud's treatment of emotional disorders led him to believe they resulted from the unconscious dynamics of personality, dynamics which he sought to analyze through his own and his patients' free associations and dreams.
西蒙·弗洛伊德对情绪失调的治疗使他相信这种失调是由个性的无意识动态产生的,这是他试图通过自己和病人的自由联想和梦分析出来的。

② Freud saw personality as composed of a reservoir of pleasure-seeking psychic impulses (the id), a reality-oriented executive (the ego), and an internalized set of ideals (the superego).
弗洛伊德认为个性包括丰富的享乐主义的精神动力(本我),现实导向的执行者(自我)和藏在心底的理想(超我)。

③ Humanistic psychologists assess personality through questionnaires that rate self-concept and by seeking to understand others' subjective personal experiences in therapy.
人本主义心理学家用调查表进行人格测评。调查表通过试图了解他人在治疗中的主观个人经历来评定自我观念。

④ Nevertheless, humanistic psychology has helped to renew psychology's interest in the concept of self, which is now being vigorously researched through studies of phenomena such as self-esteem and self-serving bias.
然而,人文主义心理学帮助心理学恢复了对自我观念的兴趣,目前通过对自尊和自私偏见等现象的研究自我观念的研究正在积极地进行。

⑤ By studying variations among people in their perceived locus of control and in their experiences of learned helplessness or self-efficacy, researchers have found that an inner locus of control helps people to cope with life.

通过研究人们感知到的控制点的变化以及学习到的无助或自我效验的经历的变化,研究者发现内部的控制点能帮助人们应付生活。

Phrases and Patterns

1. result from 由……产生

   If emotion and motivation result from activation of the nervous system, as arousal theory suggests, there should be structures in the nervous system that trigger this activation.

   如果情感和动机是来源于神经系统活动,那么激励理论认为神经系统内应该有专门的结构刺激这种活动。

2. be composed of 由……组成或构成

   Higher order cognition is composed of seven interrelated processes.

   高级认知由七种相关联的过程组成。

3. associate with 关联

   He suggested that people's later personalities were influenced by how they resolved conflicts associated with these stages and whether they remained fixated at any stage.

   他提出人们后来的个性受到他们如何解决与这些阶段相关联的矛盾以及在任何阶段是否保持异常依恋的影响。

   Because the anxiety is general and not associated with a particular object, the individual does not know from where the threat and doom will come and must therefore be exceptionally vigilant and must continually scan the surroundings for the threat.

   因为这种焦虑是综合性的而不与任何一个具体的物体相联系,个人不知道威胁和厄运从哪里来,所以个人必须特别警惕而且必须不断地审视周围的威胁。

7.2 Is Behavior Really Consistent
行为真的是前后一致的吗

The trait approach to studying personality makes several important assumptions about human behavior. For one thing, it assumes that personality characteristics are relatively stable over time. The person who is shy at parties at age twenty, trait theorists say, is likely still to be shy at parties, five, ten, even fifteen years later. There is a good deal of evidence to support this assumption. For example, Alexander Thomas and his colleagues have discovered that from birth through adolescence, children can be remarkably stable in certain basic traits, such as activity level, attention span, adaptability to new situations, and general quality of mood. Other researchers have found similar stability throughout the adult years. For instance, when James Conley measured the traits of several hundred adults at three different times in their lives, he discovered that extraversion, neuroticism, and impulse control in particular remained remarkable stable even over a forty-five-year period[①].

Another assumption of trait theory is that people are relatively consistent in the ways they act. That is to say, the same basic traits emerge time and again in many different kinds of situations. Granted, situational pressures can encourage or discourage the expression of a given trait. An aggressive person, for example, is more likely to display aggressiveness on a tennis court than in church. But in general, people's central traits, according to trait theorists, incline them to behave similarly in many different contexts. This view of relative consistency in human behavior conforms to our intuitive perceptions, and a large number of psychologists accepted it for many years. But in the late 1960s, the social learning theorist Walter Mischel made a startlingly contradictory assertion in his book *Personality and Assessment* . Mischel's view triggered such and important debate, that we will examine this controversy in depth.

The Initial Studies

Reviewing study after study, Mischel gathered evidence to show that there is actually very little correlation among different behaviors thought of as reflecting the same underlying trait. In one study, for instance, children were given a variety of opportunities to be dishonest, including lying to save face, cheating on a test, and stealing money. These opportunities were also presented in a variety of contexts. The researchers found that only rarely did a child's degree of honesty in the face of one temptation in one context correspond with his or her degree of honesty in all other situations. A child who lied to save face when interacting with peers might refuse to steal money form one of the experimenters, and yet later steal money that belonged to a brother or sister. Mischel also found that there is often a low correlation between a person's score for a certain trait, as measured by a questionnaire, and that person's actual performance of behaviors related to the trait. Thus people who score high on a scale measuring generosity are often only slightly more willing than other people to give money to charity, to donate blood, or to perform other acts typically considered signs of a generous nature[2]. If a person's behavior is so variable, Mischel argued, the concept of enduring personality traits may be of little practical value. Instead, it may be largely the context or situation, not an underlying disposition that determines how we act.

But if behavior is not very consistent form one situation to the next, why do most of us believe that it is? Why are we convinced that fairly stable personality traits do indeed exist? The answer, Mischel and others say, is that the traits a particular person possesses lie as much in the eye of the beholder as in the psyche of the beheld[3]. And beholders, they argue, are prone to many perceptual biases. One such bias is the so-called primary effect—the tendency to maintain our first impression of a person even if her or she acts quite differently later. Thus, if your first impression of particular woman is that she is selfish and cruel, it will be difficult for you to view her otherwise even after you see her perform several acts of kindness. Because we tend to want consistency in our beliefs and perceptions, we often discount information that doesn't fit our initial view. Another reason why we may see more consistency in behavior than actually exists is that we tend to see most people in only one role. If you see the head librarian only when she is sitting quietly at her desk, you may assume that she is in fact a very reticent person. What you fail to consider is that this demeanor is required by her job. In other contexts she may behave quite differently, but you never have a chance to see her do so. Adding to these perceptual biases is the fact that our own behavior may conspire to produce the illusion of consistency in others. If you believe that a person is hostile, you may, by subtle cues of speech and body language (such as acting cold or unfriendly when he asks you something) elicit the very acts of hostility you expect to see. To the extent that our behavior toward another person consistently elicits the same responses, we may attribute to that person very stable traits that in reality are not so stable.

    Mischel and others have pointed to a number of other factors—all supported by experimental data—that could cause us to see behavior as more consistent than it actually is. So persuasive were their arguments at the time they were proposed that many psychologists came to accept the view that situations generally exert a more powerful influence on human behavior than do inner dispositions[4]. This view also made a great deal of sense in terms of human coping. The tendency to modify behavior according to situational demands seemed to offer a decided advantage in dealing with life's problems.

Criticisms, Alternatives, and Further Research

Other psychologists, however, viewed Mischel's perspective as a broadside attack on the concept of personality itself. How can personality have any real meaning, they asked, if inner dispositions are so weak? Some researchers therefore proposed an alternative possibility. Perhaps, they argued, Mischel was simply not assessing behavioral consistency in the right way. This possibility generated a number of efforts designed to see if different measurement techniques might reveal more behavioral consistency.

On such effort was carried out by Daryl Bem and Andrea Allen. While acknowledging the validity of some of what Mischel said, they believed that our intuitions about the consistency of people's behavior are not entirely wrong. Although no one is consistent in all areas of behavior, most people are relatively consistent in at least some areas. To demonstrate this fact, Bem and Allen asked students to rate their own consistency regarding "friendliness" and "conscientiousness". As predicted, those who described themselves as being quite consistent on one or the other of these traits did tend to show a high degree of consistency in behaviors related to that trait. Bem and Allen concluded that most of us do have some traits that we display fairly consistently, but those traits differ among people. As a result, when researchers study a large group of randomly selected people regarding an arbitrarily chosen trait, the behavior on average <u>is bound to</u> appear only slightly consistent.

Recently, psychologist Nancy Cantor and her colleagues have found substantial consistency in the strategies people use to accomplish important life tasks that they set for themselves. These researchers asked freshmen at the University of Michigan both to list the goals they expected to work toward in the remainder of the year and to describe some of the ways they planned to achieve those goals. While many similarities existed in the aims that students had (making new friends, getting good grades, and so forth), the students anticipated using quite different strategies to accomplish their ends. Some, for instance, planned to strive hard in order to succeed in college (diligently completing all course assignments, cramming until the end for every exam), while others pursued the goal of success partly by defending themselves against failure (imagining how they would cope with the "worst-case" scenario, for example). Thus, another reason why Mischel may have failed to find much behavioral consistency could have been that he had too narrow a notion of the concept of "traits". When researchers include in the idea of "traits" people's strategies for accomplishing life goals, a good deal of behavioral consistency does seem to emerge.

A third reason why Mischel may have had trouble finding evidence of behavioral consistency could have been that some of the studies he used failed to observe subjects in enough situations. How fair is it, critics ask, for a researcher to give a subject the chance to contribute spare change to a worthy cause and to donate blood to a blood bank and then, if the two responses are dissimilar, conclude that there is little evidence for a stable trait of generosity? Yet this is essentially what some psychologists have done: they have based their conclusions on a very small sample of behaviors. When other researchers have observed behavior across many situations, much greater consistency has been found.

The need to assess behavior a variety of situations has been taken into account in what is called the act frequency approach to personality. The act frequency approach measures the relative frequency of acts that people agree are characteristic of some broad dispositional category. The category "submissiveness", for example, is characterized by such acts as walking out of a store when you have been shortchanged, continuing to apologize for some minor mistakes, and letting your partner choose the movie that the two of you will see. By tallying up the frequency of these and many similar acts, you get a measure of how consistent a person's submissive behaviors really are. Research is now underway to discover the relationship between act-trend data derived from the act frequency approach and data derived form other methods of assessing behavioral tendencies.

Patterns and Conclusions

The evidence indicates that behavior is probably not as consistent as psychologists once believed, but neither is it totally inconsistent. Many times our behavior is quite predictable from one context to another, suggesting that inner traits, as well as situations, influence how we act. The interplay of traits and situations, moreover, is often highly complex. Traits not only influence behavior directly by encouraging certain responses, but they also influence it indirectly by affecting the kinds of situations in which we choose to place ourselves[5]. A man with the trait of low self-confidence, for instance, may fail to strive for career advancement partly because he sees himself as low in ability. But at he same time his low self-confidence may prompt him to seek out jobs that are safe and unchallenging—jobs, in short, that place few demands on him.

The view that traits and situations interact is widely accepted today. A major task for contemporary psychologists is to unravel just how this interaction takes place in particular cases. Consider, for example, some recent investigations into the causes of child abuse. It has been found that a sizable minority of battered children have traits that adults find annoying—hyperactivity, constant fussing, a particularly grating cry, and so forth. Obviously, this is insufficient reason for a normal adult to beat a child. But when these traits are presented to a parent who is emotionally unstable to begin with and under a great deal of stress, the result may be uncontrolled aggression. This theory is supported by the fact that many battered children have brothers or sisters who are not similarly abused, and some go on to be further abused by foster parents who have no past record of severely mistreating their children. The battered child, in turn, may intensify the original abrasive behavior in response to this abuse. So the parent responds with more abuse, and on its goes in a tragic interplay of traits and situation. It is hard to say which of these factors is most important. Without either, the abuse might never occur. Many psychologists believe that much future research in personality is likely to focus on just such complex interactions between situations and traits.

from: *Psychology* (third edition), Camile B. Wortman & Elizabeth F. Loftus

Words and Expressions

consistent	adj.	[kənˈsistənt]	连贯一致的
adolescence	n.	[ˌædəulsəns]	青春期
stable	adj.	[ˈsteibl]	稳定的
adaptability	n.	[ədæptəˈbiliti]	适应性
stability	n.	[stəˈbiliti]	稳定性
extraversion	n.	[ˌekstrəˈvəːʃən]	外向性；外倾性
context	n.	[ˈkɔntekst]	环境；背景
correlation	n.	[ˌkɔriˈleiʃən]	相互关系；相关(性)
underlying	adj.	[ˈʌndəˈlaiiŋ]	潜在的
beholder	n.	[biˈhəuldə]	目睹者
psyche	n.	[ˈsaiki(ː)]	灵魂；精神
bias	n.	[ˈbaiəs]	偏见；偏爱
generosity	n.	[ˌdʒenəˈrɔsiti]	慷慨；宽大
enduring	adj.	[inˈdjuəriŋ]	持久的；不朽的
reticent	adj.	[ˈretisənt]	沉默寡言的

demeanor	n.	[diˈmiːnə]	行为；风度
disposition	n.	[dispəˈziʃən]	性情；脾气
intuition	n.	[ˌintju(ː)ˈiʃən]	直觉
subject	n.	[ˈsʌbdʒikt]	受实验者
submissiveness	n.	[səbˈmisivnis]	柔顺；服从
interplay	n.	[ˈintə(ː)ˈplei]	相互影响
hyperactivity	n.	[ˌhaipə(ː)ˈræktiviti]	活动过度；极度活跃
battered	n.	[ˈbætəd]	打扁了的
abrasive	adj.	[əˈbreisiv]	生硬粗暴的
interaction	n.	[ˌintərˈækʃən]	交互作用

personality characteristics	个性特点
activity level	活动水平
attention span	注意广度
intuitive perception	直觉感知
perceptual bias	知觉偏见
primary effect	最初印象
act frequency approach	行为频率方法
inner dispositions	内在性情
behavioral consistency	行为一致性

Difficult Sentences

① For instance, when James Conley measured the traits of several hundred adults at three different times in their lives, he discovered that extraversion, neuroticism, and impulse control in particular remained remarkable stable even over a forty-five-year period.
康利测量了几百位成年人一生中三个不同时期的个性，他发现即便是长达四十五年的时间，外向性、神经质以及冲动控制尤其能保持显著的稳定性。

② Thus people who score high on a scale measuring generosity are often only slightly more willing than other people to give money to charity, to donate blood, or to perform other acts typically considered signs of a generous nature.

因此在衡量慷慨程度时获得过高分的人,经常不比其他人更愿意为慈善捐钱,献血或做其他被认为是慷慨的行为。

③ The answer, Mischel and others say, is that the traits a particular person possesses lie as much in the eye of the beholder as in the psyche of the beheld.

米切尔和其他人说,答案是一个人拥有的个性在于观看者的眼中也同样在于被观看者精神中。

④ So persuasive were their arguments at the time they were proposed that many psychologists came to accept the view that situations generally exert a more powerful influence on human behavior than do inner dispositions.

他们提出的论点在当时是如此的有说服力以至于许多心理学家接受情景通常比内在性情对人类行为的影响更大这一观点。

⑤ Traits not only influence behavior directly by encouraging certain responses, but they also influence it indirectly by affecting the kinds of situations in which we choose to place ourselves.

个性不仅通过促进某些反应直接影响行为,而且还通过影响我们选择所处的情景来间接影响行为。

Phrases and Patterns

1. incline ... to 使……有……倾向

   But in general, people's central traits, according to trait theorists, incline them to behave similarly in many different contexts.

   但是一般而言,据个性理论家所说,人们的主要个性使他们在很多不同的环境下做出相似的行为。

2. conform to 符合;遵照

   This view of relative consistency in human behavior conforms to our intuitive perceptions, and a large number of psychologists accepted it for many years.

人类行为的相对一致性与我们的直觉感知相符合,许多年来很多心理学家接受该观点。

Remarkably, the intuitive judgments of these experts did not conform to statistical principles with which they were thoroughly familiar.

显然,这些专家的直觉判断与他们所熟知的统计学原则不符。

3. be bound to 一定要

As a result, when researchers study a large group of randomly selected people regarding an arbitrarily chosen trait, the behavior on average is bound to appear only slightly consistent.

因此,当研究人员随机挑选一组人并研究任意选择的一项个性,平均来看它们的行为一定有些微的一致。

Other morphemes can exist only if they are bound to other morphemes.

只有它们一定要成为词素时,其他的词素才存在。

7.3 Contextualized Personality: Traditional and New Assessment Procedures

背景人格:传统的和新的评估程序

In this section we identify four deserving areas for future research including: (a) construct and predictive validity studies; (b) the examination of combinations of hypothetical (traditional) and subtle (novel) assessment procedures; (c) the investigation of antecedents and outcomes of intra-individual variability in personality; and (d) the examination of assimilation or contrast effects within a context.

Construct and Predictive Validity

The most important immediate need for future research relates to the examination of the convergent and discriminant validity of these traditional and novel assessment strategies. That is, there is a need to validate all procedures vis-à-vis: (a) each other; (b) knowledgeable informant reports (e. g. supervisors, romantic partners, and friends); and (c) external criteria (e. g. job performance). For example, in one such study described briefly earlier, Heller and Watson examined the convergence between explicit measures of work and home identity with spouse ratings. Our findings indicated that neuroticism, agreeableness, and conscientiousness ratings of spouses were more closely related to partner's self ratings of their home identity than they were to partner's self ratings of their work identity. This approach can be easily expanded to include more comprehensive investigations of multiple contexts, and multiple informants within these contexts, as well as to include multiple methods for assessing contextual personality[①].

Moreover, it is important to investigate the unique and joint predictive validity of both hypothetical and subtle contextual personality measures against external criteria, most notably against objective criteria (e. g. job performance and turnover, marital dissolution). This is important as some of the aforementioned previous research employing self-reports of attitudes and other self-conceptions as criteria may have been susceptible to common-method bias concerns, as well as problems of overlap in content between predictors and criteria (i. e., the "criterion contamination" problem).

Investigation of Combinations of Subtle and Traditional Approaches

Another intriguing area of future research is the examination of the implications of different combinations of explicit and subtle measures of contextual personality. For example, consider a person who rates herself as highly conscientious at work, whereas the aggregation of her state assessments of conscientiousness at work actually indicates she is low on this contextual trait. We suspect that this incongruence may cause her to experience substantial role confusion, job dissatisfaction, and may also negatively influence her job performance levels[2]. Thus, it may be useful to avoid simply viewing the two types of assessments as competitors (e. g. by examining their unique effects in a multiple regression framework), and instead to examine the statistical interaction between them, wherein the focus shifts to the investigation of meaningful combinations of the two types of measures.

Investigation of Antecedents and Outcomes of Variability in Contextual Personality

Using both explicit and subtle types of assessment procedures, future research should examine both old and new questions in the study of intra-individual variability in personality. For example, what is the magnitude of role- or culture-based within-individual variability in personality? How does it compare to the magnitude of between-individual variability in personality? Recent statistical advances in multi-level modeling may be especially conducive for answering such questions.

Another important issue relates to the antecedents of this contextual variability. Are they dispositional factors such as self-monitoring, self-concept clarity, self-construal, or (low) self-esteem? Are they related to contextual or situational differences such as differences in goals, audiences, and expectations in different contexts? Or is it the case, perhaps, that both dispositional and situational factors are causing these fluctuations in personality?

Finally, what are the implications of contextual personality variability for both hedonic and eudaimonic well-being? For instance, consider the "social chameleon" who is very different at her work as a CEO and at home as a mother, or a Chinese-Canadian who is very different with her Canadian friends than her Chinese parents. Is she happier than a person who is more consistent across roles or cultures? Does she function more effectively than someone who is more consistent across roles or cultures?

Conceptually, a differentiated self could be indicative of high levels of adaptation and specialization in response to environmental demands or, conversely, of fragmentation of the self and a lack of a sense of coherence or unity[3]. Role-based variability in personality findings reported by Sheldon et al. and Donahue et al. lend support for the fragmentation view by indicating that a more differentiated self is associated with lower levels of well-being. However, these initial findings are based on explicit measures of personality within roles and on a limited conceptualization of the well-being construct. Thus, future research should examine the link between role-based personality variability and well-being using multiple assessments of personality variability, as well as examine the implications of this variability on individuals' life satisfaction, depression levels, as well as sense of purpose, self-acceptance, and vitality. In addition, it would be interesting to examine whether these effects on well-being are moderated by self-monitoring; that is, are those high on self-monitoring less bothered by their inconsistency in personality across cultures or social roles compared to their low self-monitoring peers[4]?

The well-being implications of culture-based variability in personality represent a novel and intriguing question. A large divergence in personality could be associated with a sense of incoherence, confusion, and conflicting tendencies (i. e., low levels of well-being). Alternatively, if these different culture-based personalities are stored in separate knowledge structures that are rarely activated simultaneously, then this divergence may indicate a high level of adaptability to a new culture and <u>serve as</u> a buffer against stress (i. e., high levels of well-being).

Alternatively, individual differences in Bicultural Identity Integration (BII; that is, how bicultural experience their dual culture identities) may moderate the relation between culture-based variability in personality and well-being. That is, whereas high BIIs (i. e. , those that see the two cultures as compatible and integrated) may benefit from greater culture-based variability in personality, their low BII peers (i. e. , those that see the two cultures as oppositional and difficult to integrate) may have a more negative experience of confusion and conflict when trying to manage their different culture-based personalities (i. e. , a negative association between personality variability and well-being). All of these possibilities are speculative at this point and empirical data are very much needed to examine the well-being implications of culture-based variability in personality.

Examination of Assimilation or Contrast Effects within a Context

Our discussion of the three subtle approaches to assessing contextual personality may have created an erroneous perception that contextual cues are always associated with an assimilation effect; that is, that individuals always conform or adapt the appropriate thoughts, feelings, and behaviors associated with a context. This is not always the case; indeed, people may show contrast effects such that specific contextual cues may lead to or activate patterns of thoughts, feelings, or behaviors that are inconsistent with the context[⑤]. Consider, for example, a Chinese-Canadian living in Canada for many years returning to China for a visit after several years. We suspect that such a person may feel a bit out of place in his home country and, consequently, may actually feel more Canadian during his visit than when in Canada. Future research should examine the prevalence of assimilation and contrast effects both within- and between-individuals, as well as the situational (e. g. extremity of contextual cues) and dispositional (e. g. BII, self-monitoring) antecedents of these conflicting effects.

To summarize, the four diverse assessment approaches discussed in this manuscript enable an in-depth assessment of contextualized variability in personality, ensuring both the internal validity and external validity of findings, as well as minimizing concerns regarding potential demand characteristics. These approaches can help researchers uncover the magnitude, antecedents (e. g. social roles, culture, goals, self-monitoring), and well-being consequences of intra – individual variability in personality. Moreover, they further point to the need to supplement traditional global assessments of personality with more contextual ones that <u>take into account</u> situational influences. <u>As such</u>, these studies represent a first step in a larger program of research that examines processes of consistency and change in personality/self, their antecedents, and their implications.

from: *http://www. psych. uiuc. edu, written by Daniel Heller, David Watson, Jennifer Komar, Ji-A Min and Wei Qi Elaine Perunovic*

Words and Expressions

contextualized	adj.	[kɔnˈtekstjuəlaizd]	使……融入背景的
validity	n.	[vəˈliditi]	有效性
assessment	n.	[əˈsesmənt]	评估;估价
variability	n.	[veəriəˈbiləti]	可变性
assimilation	n.	[əˌsimiˈleiʃən]	同化
vis-à-vis	prep.	[viːzɑːˈviː]	同……相比;关于
rating	n.	[ˈreitiŋ]	评价;地位
implicit	adj.	[imˈplisit]	暗示的;含蓄的
explicit	adj.	[iksˈplisit]	清楚的;直率的
incongruence	n.	[inˈkɔŋgruəns]	不一致
regression	n.	[riˈgreʃən]	衰退

construal	n.	[kən'stru:əl]	解释;说明
hedonic	adj.	[hi:'dɔnik]	享乐主义的
eudaimonic	adj.	[ju:'daimnək]	幸福说的;快乐说的
fluctuation	n.	[ˌflʌktju'eiʃən]	波动;起伏
chameleon	n.	[kə'mi:ljən]	多变的人
conceptualization	n.	[kənˌseptju'lai'zeiʃən]	概念化
divergence	n.	[dai'və:dʒəns]	分歧
buffer	n.	['bʌfə]	缓冲器
dual	adj.	['dju(:)əl]	双重的
extremity	n.	[iks'tremiti]	末端;极端

"criterion contamination" problem	"标准污点"问题
role-based personality variability	基于角色的人格可变性
multiple assessments of personality variability	人格可变性的多重评估
within-individual variability	个体内部可变性
between-individual variability	个体之间的可变性

Difficult Sentences

① This approach can be easily expanded to include more comprehensive investigations of multiple contexts, and multiple informants within these contexts, as well as to include multiple methods for assessing contextual personality.
这种方法可以很容易地延伸到包括多种背景和置于该背景下的多种信息更加全面的研究上,而且还包括评估背景人格的多种方法。

② We suspect that this incongruence may cause her to experience substantial role confusion, job dissatisfaction, and may also negatively influence her job performance levels.
我们怀疑这种不一致性可能会使她体验到强烈的角色混乱和工作不满,也可能对她的工作表现水平有负面的影响。

③ Conceptually, a differentiated self could be indicative of high levels of adaptation and specialization in response to environmental demands or, conversely, of fragmentation of the self and a lack of a sense of coherence or unity.

从概念上来讲,不同的自我对环境需求会表示出高度的适应性和特殊性,或相反地表示出高度的自我分裂和缺乏一致感和统一感。

④ In addition, it would be interesting to examine whether these effects on well-being are moderated by self-monitoring; that is, are those high on self-monitoring less bothered by their inconsistency in personality across cultures or social roles compared to their low self-monitoring peers?

另外,研究这些对幸福影响是否因自我监控而减弱将是很有趣的,换句话说,与自我监控程度较低的人相比,那些自我监控程度较高的人较少地受到跨文化或社会角色人格矛盾的烦扰。

⑤ This is not always the case; indeed, people may show contrast effects such that specific contextual cues may lead to or activate patterns of thoughts, feelings, or behaviors that are inconsistent with the context.

事实并非如此,实际上人们会表现出相反的效果,具体的背景线索可导致或激活与背景不一致的思想、感情或行为模式。

Phrases and Patterns

1. serve as 用于;当作

    Alternatively, if these different culture-based personalities are stored in separate knowledge structures that are rarely activated simultaneously, then this divergence may indicate a high level of adaptability to a new culture and serve as a buffer against stress.

    如果这些不同的基于文化的人格被储存在很难同时被激活的分别的知识结构中,那么这种分歧会显示出对新文化的高度适应性,并成为缓解压力的缓冲器。

Such external stimuli that serve as anticipated rewards for certain behaviors are called incentives.

当作对某种行为的预期奖赏的这种外部刺激被称为动机。

2. take into account 考虑；顾及

Moreover, they further point to the need to supplement traditional global assessments of personality with more contextual ones that take into account situational influences.

此外，他们进一步指出有必要用更多地考虑到情境影响的情景评估来补充传统的综合人格评估。

The person's happiness, relation to social norms, and ability to cope—as well as society's ability to cope with the person—are all taken into account.

个人与社会规范相关的幸福和个人处理社会问题的能力以及社会与个人相处的能力都被考虑进去了。

3. as such 同样地

As such, these studies represent a first step in a larger program of research that examines processes of consistency and change in personality/self, their antecedents, and their implications.

同样地，这些研究代表了对一致性与人格/自我变化过程、它们的前提和它们的含义的研究的一项大计划的第一步。

Questions

1. If, as the humanistic perspective suggests, reality is subjective, how can individuals ever hope to agree on anything?
2. What are the best new ideas that you learned from the theories of personality? What are the least helpful ideas to you?
3. Which of the four diverse assessment approaches are you interested in? Why?

8

Psychological Disorders
心理混乱症

【本章导读】 本章主要阐述心理混乱症的几种行为。第 1 篇文章概述心理反常行为,给出了心理反常行为的多种定义,从而使读者从多角度了解它。第 2 篇文章主要介绍焦虑症,列举了几种常见的焦虑症,并且做出了简明扼要的阐释。第 3 篇文章讲述了社会恐惧症的影响及特征。

8.1 Understanding Abnormality
解读心理反常行为

Most kinds of abnormal behavior are far less dramatic than the symptoms of the wall-pounding schizophrenic; in fact, most people with psychological disorders seem "normal" most of the time[①]. Attempts to define abnormality make it clear that the standards that separate normal and abnormal behavior are not as clear-cut as we might assume.

To establish the line between normal and abnormal behavior, we must first divide thought patterns and behavior that the community considers acceptable from those that are considered unacceptable. These standards may change from one society to another and from time to time within the same society.

The simplest way to define abnormal behavior is <u>in terms of</u> norm violation. Each society has a set of social norms—rules that prescribe "right" and "wrong" behavior—by which its members live. Social norms cover every aspect of life, from the person one may marry to the food one may eat. Since these rules are absorbed in childhood during the process of socialization, we <u>take</u> them so much <u>for granted</u> that we notice them only when they are broken.

Norms can change, as they have in American society during the past few decades. Not many years ago, for example, a divorced parent who engaged in sexual activity might lose custody of his or her children, but today this behavior has become acceptable. <u>By contrast</u>, behavior that once would have been considered normal—beating an unruly child so severely as to cause injury—is now seen as child abuse. This shifting nature of norms as a standard tends to enforce conformity and to mark the nonconformist as "abnormal"[2]. In spite of these problems, norms remain the dominant standard of our culture because they have been so deeply engrained.

Another way to define abnormal behavior is in terms of its statistical rarity. Using statistical abnormality as the standard, we consider people abnormal when their behavior differs greatly from that of the majority (the "average"). This is a simple way of making a diagnosis, and this approach is used in some areas of psychological functioning—for instance, people who score below a certain level on intelligence tests are considered retarded[3]. The use of statistical definition of abnormality, however, does present problems. One problem is that we have no way to distinguish between the two extremes above and below the "average": according to this definition, both geniuses and retardates are considered "abnormal". An even greater problem is the fact that, from a statistical standpoint, some abnormality must exist. Even if we could improve general intelligence so that no one scored below what is now considered "normal", some people would score lower than others. These people, whose level of functioning would once have been normal, would then be classified as abnormal.

Less restrictive than norm violation or statistical rarity is the standard of personal discomfort, which is based on an individual's self-assessment. According to this definition, only those who are distressed by their own thoughts or behavior are abnormal. This standard is also faulty, primarily because the same behavior patterns can make one person miserable but bother another only a little④. In fact, some people (schizophrenics, rapists, and murderers, for example) may be violent or dangerous and not feel any distress at all. Limiting the definition to personal discomfort, then, gives us no yardstick for evaluating any specific behavior.

A fourth definition is the standard of maladaptive behavior. If a physically healthy person cannot hold a job, deal with family and friends, or get out of bed in the morning, most of us would agree that he or she is psychologically disturbed. In many cases, severe personal distress accompanies such behavior patterns. The advantage of maladaptive behavior as a standard is that it focuses on a person's behavior <u>in relation to</u> the behavior of others. The major disadvantage is that "adaptive behavior", like normality, is subjectively defined and difficult to apply as a consistent standard. Germans who cooperated in the genocidal programs of the Nazi regime had adapted to the demands of their society: their behavior would be considered "adaptive", despite being morally objectionable.

Finally, we can define abnormality in terms of its deviation from an ideal. The trouble with this definition is that it immediately labels most of us as abnormal, because ideal adjustment is beyond the grasp of most people. The pursuit of such an ideal can make people feel disturbed or seriously inadequate when in fact they are only imperfect human beings. In addition, the definition of the ideal personality can change as quickly and as often as social norms do.

These ways of defining abnormal behavior do not exhaust the possibilities. We might define any behavior that makes observers uncomfortable as "abnormal", or any behavior that is unpredictable, incomprehensible, or simply unconventional⑤. None of the definitions is perfect. In practice, the judgment of abnormality, whether made by diagnosticians or by family and friends, is usually based on a combination of standards. The person's happiness, relation to social norms, and ability to cope—as well as society's ability to cope with the person—are all taken into account.

In summary, Abnormality can be defined as norm violation, as deviation from a statistical average, as personal discomfort, as maladaptive behavior, or as deviation from as ideal personality. Explanations of abnormality are primarily either biogenic-based on physical causes—or psychogenic-based on maladaptive behavior causes. Major perspectives of mental disorders are neuroscientific, psychoanalytic, behavioral, social cognitive, and humanistic-existential. Classifying abnormal behavior allows researchers and clinicians to exchange information about disordered behavior and to describe a person's problems in a way that increases the chances of selecting proper treatment and predicting the course of behavior. Classification can be a disadvantage if it labels people as "sick", makes us think we have explained the behavior, or stigmatizes people and inappropriately influences treatment.

from: *Psychology Today*: *An Introduction*, *Richard R. Bootzin*, *Gordon H. Bower*, *Jennifer Crocker*, *Elizabeth Hall*, *Von Hoffmann Press*, 1991

Words and Expressions

schizophrenic	adj.	[ˌskidzəuˈfrenik]	精神分裂症的
norm	n.	[nɔːm]	标准；规范
violation	n.	[ˌvaiəˈleiʃən]	违反；违背；妨碍；侵害
custody	n.	[ˈkʌstədi]	保管
enforce	vt.	[inˈfɔːs]	强迫；执行；坚持；加强
conformity	n.	[kənˈfɔːmiti]	一致；符合
engrain	vt.	[inˈgrein]	染成木纹色；使根深蒂固；[喻]使遍体渗透
rarity	n.	[ˈrɛəriti]	稀有
retarded	adj.	[riˈtɑːdid]	智力迟钝的；发展迟缓的
retardate	n.	[riˈtɑːdeit]	白痴；低能者
discomfort	n.	[disˈkʌmfət]	不便之处；不适
maladaptive	adj.	[ˌmæləˈdæptiv]	不适应的；适应不良的；不利于适应的；显示不适应的
deviation	n.	[ˌdiːviˈeiʃən]	背离
diagnostician	n.	[ˌdaiəgnɔsˈtiʃən]	诊断医生；诊断专家
biogenic	adj.	[ˌbaiəuˈdʒenik]	源于生物的；生物所造成的
psychoanalytic	adj.	[ˈsaikəuˌænəˈlitik]	心理分析的
stigmatize	vt.	[ˈstigmətaiz]	打烙印；诬蔑

abnormal behavior	反常行为
psychological disorders	心理混乱
norm violation	违背常规
psychological functioning	心理功能
intelligence test	智力测验
behavior pattern	行为方式
ideal personality	理想人格
social norms	社会规范

Difficult Sentences

① Most kinds of abnormal behavior are far less dramatic than the symptoms of the wall-pounding schizophrenic; in fact, most people with psychological disorders seem "normal" most of the time.
大多数反常行为都远远没有严重的精神分裂症具有戏剧性；事实上，许多有心理混乱的人在大多数时间看起来都是正常的。

② This shifting nature of norms as a standard tends to enforce conformity and to mark the nonconformist as "abnormal".
行为标准的性质变化，意在加强其整合适应性，同时使那些不适应变化的人成为"异类"。

③ This is a simple way of making a diagnosis, and this approach is used in some areas of psychological functioning—for instance, people who score below a certain level on intelligence tests are considered retarded.
这是一种简单的诊断反常行为的方法，而且这种方法被用在心理功能鉴定的一些方面，比如，智力测验分数低于某个水平的人就被视为智力迟钝。

④ This standard is also faulty, primarily because the same behavior patterns can make one person miserable but bother another only a little.
这种标准也是错误的，主要原因是同样的行为方式可能使一个人很痛苦，而另一个人却不怎么被妨碍。

⑤ We might define any behavior that makes observers uncomfortable as "abnormal", or any behavior that is unpredictable, incomprehensible, or simply unconventional.
我们也许把任何使观察者不舒服的行为定义为反常行为，或者把任何不可预测的行为、不易理解的行为，或简单地讲，不符合传统的行为定义为反常行为。

Phrases and Patterns

1. in terms of 根据;按照;用……的话;在……方面

   The simplest way to define abnormal behavior is in terms of norm violation.

   按照违背规范与否来定义反常行为是最简单的方法。

   An implication of the first general principle is that the Harvard Law ought to be understandable in terms of properties of the nervous system, and of the second is that knowing something of how the nervous system works should help to make sense of the Law.

   第一个一般原则的意义在于哈佛法可以帮助理解神经系统的特性方面;第二个原则的意义在于一旦我们对神经系统的作用规律有一些了解的话,我们就能更好地理解哈佛法。

2. take ... for granted 认为……理所当然

   Since these rules are absorbed in childhood during the process of socialization, we take them so much for granted that we notice them only when they are broken.

   因为在我们孩童时代接受社会化过程的时候已经吸收了这些社会规则,所以我们认为这些社会规则理所当然是这样的,只有当我们违背它们时,我们才注意到它们。

   We take it so much for granted that you may not have been aware that it was happening until you read this paragraph.

   直到读了这段文字,你才意识到它的出现,我们认为这是理所当然的。

3. by contrast 对照;对比

   By contrast, behavior that once would have been considered normal—beating an unruly child so severely as to cause injury—is now seen as child abuse.

   例如,把不听话的孩子打伤的行为在过去被认为是正常的,与此相比,在现在被视为是虐待儿童。

4. in relation to 关于;涉及;与……相比

The advantage of maladaptive behavior as a standard is that it focuses on a person's behavior in relation to the behavior of others.

把不利于适应的行为作为标准的优点是它关注了一个人的行为和其他人的行为的对比。

8.2 Anxiety States
焦虑状态

In anxiety states, the emotional response is diffused and not <u>related to</u> any one particular situation or stimulus. In these disorders, the anxiety is said to be "free-floating". We can distinguish four types of anxiety states, and they will be considered in the following sections.

Panic Disorder

A panic disorder involves brief periods of exceptionally intense spontaneous anxiety. These periods come and go suddenly, usually lasting only a few minutes, and their occurrence is unpredictable. They seem to come "<u>out of the blue</u>" and can even start during sleep (nocturnal panic attacks). In addition to intense psychological feelings of apprehension, fear, and terror, the individual experiences physical symptoms that can include shortness of breath, heart palpitations, chest pains, choking or smothering sensations, dizziness, feelings of unreality, tingling of the extremities, hot and cold flashes, sweating, faintness, and trembling or shaking[①]. Because of the physical symptoms, an individual who is having a panic attack may think that he or she is having a heart attack. One patient who <u>suffered from</u> panic attacks said, "Most people only face dying once; I do it a couple of times a week! It's scary."

Panic attacks are very frightening. Individuals who experience panic attacks become concerned about losing control and often think that they are "going crazy", and therefore they sometimes begin avoiding public places in favor of staying home, where they feel safe[2]. If the avoidance becomes extreme, the individual may be diagnosed as suffering from a panic disorder with agoraphobia rather than simply from a panic disorder. Between attacks, the individual is often anxious about possible impending attacks, therefore causing an elevated general level of anxiety. Because of that, sometimes individuals suffering from a panic disorder are erroneously diagnosed as suffering from a generalized anxiety disorder.

It is important not to confuse panic attacks with the intense periods of arousal that are associated with physical exertion or the stress of real life-threatening situations. Furthermore, it should be noted that for many years panic attacks were misdiagnosed as cardiac or respiratory problems and treated accordingly, of course with no benefit to the patient. Fortunately, now that panic attacks are recognized as a psychological disorder, they receiving widespread attention in the medical and public press, and the likelihood of misdiagnosis has been greatly reduced.

The panic disorder is thought to be rather common; in one study of undergraduate students it was found that 2.4% met the criteria for having a panic disorder.

Generalized Anxiety Disorder

The generalized anxiety disorder involves general, persistent anxiety that lasts for at least a month and is not associated with any particular object or situation. The anxiety is present constantly, and there is no escape from it. The prolonged nature of the anxiety separates it from the panic disorder, and it is usually less intense than what is seen in the panic disorder.

The generalized, omnipresent nature of the anxiety results in some additional problems that are not seen in the other anxiety disorders.

Because the anxiety is general and not associated with a particular object, the individual does not know from where the threat and doom will come and must therefore be exceptionally vigilant and must continually scan the surroundings for the threat[3]. This may result in debilitating effects such as distractibility and fatigue. To imagine what a generalized anxiety disorder is like, think about how you feel just before taking an exceptionally important examination, and then imagine those feelings lasting for months without your knowing why you are upset.

Posttraumatic Stress Disorder

The posttraumatic stress disorder has undoubtedly existed through history, but it has only gained widespread attention since it was observed in veterans of the Vietnam conflict. The major symptom of this disorder is the reexperiencing of a traumatic event. The traumatic events that precipitate this disorder are extreme; they include natural disasters (floods, earthquakes), accidental disasters (plane crashes, fires), and deliberate disasters (wars, torture, death camps, rape, assaults).

The reexperiencing may take the form of recurrent painful memories of the event, recurrent dreams of nightmares about the event, or "flashbacks" in which for some period of time (usually minutes or hours but sometimes longer) the individual relives the event and behaves as though experiencing the event at that moment[4]. This reexperiencing phenomenon can persist for many years after the event.

In addition to the reexperiencing, there is often a general numbing of responsiveness or reduced involvement with the external world. This psychic numbing is apparent in diminished interest in usual activities, feelings of detachment from others, and blunted emotional responses when the individual is not reexperiencing the traumatic experience. In short, the individual has a limited and emotionally flattened life that is punctuated with intense emotional experiences involving the earlier trauma.

Finally, a number of other symptoms that are sometimes associated with a posttraumatic stress disorder reflect the individual's continuing general arousal. These symptoms include hyper alertness, problems with sleep, guilt about surviving when others did not, trouble concentrating, avoidance of activities that arouse memories of the traumatic event, and heightened arousal upon exposure to events that symbolize or resemble the traumatic event.

Obsessive-Compulsive Disorder

The obsessive-compulsive disorder involves recurrent obsessions or compulsions or both. An obsession is a persistent idea, thought, image, or impulse that an individual cannot get out of his or her mind. Because they are not under voluntary control and are often repugnant to the individual, obsessions are said to be ego-dystonic[5]. We all occasionally go through periods when we cannot get a thought or a tune out of our heads, although usually the content is not distasteful, the episodes do not last too long, and they would not be classified as obsessions or abnormal.

Obsessions and worries both involve perseverative thinking, but there are important differences between them and they should not be confused. In general, worries are usually related to everyday experiences (e. g. work, money, family), occur in the form of a thought, are not usually repugnant, are seen as controllable, and are not usually resisted by the individual. In contrast, obsessions generally revolve around a unique topic (e. g. dirt or contamination, death, aggression), often involve impulses as well as thoughts, are often repugnant, are seen as uncontrollable, and are resisted by the individual.

A compulsion is a behavior that is performed over and over in a stereotyped fashion. The behavior appears to be designed to achieve some goal (handwashing to avoid germs), but it is actually senseless and ineffective (the hands were not dirty to begin with). The individual realizes the irrationality of the behavior and does not get any particular pleasure from it but becomes tense and anxious if the behavior is not performed. Clinically common compulsions include handwashing, counting, checking, and touching. As with obsessions, compulsions can seriously disrupt normal functioning. Apart form interfering with normal activities, compulsions can have other serious effects. For example, an individual with a handwashing compulsion may wash his or her hands until the skin has literally been scrubbed away.

Behaviors such as eating, drinking, and gambling when done excessively are sometimes referred to as "compulsive". However, that is an incorrect use of the term because pleasure is derived from those activities, even if they lead to negative outcomes. True compulsions are not pleasurable, except for the fact that they may briefly forestall anxiety.

Acute Stress Disorder

The acute stress disorder is a new disorder that made its first appearance in DSM-IV and involves a period of intense anxiety that lasts for one month or less. This anxiety could stem from some transient situational factor such as a natural disaster or personal experience (attack, rape). This disorder is of interest because it may provide the basis for a subsequent posttraumatic stress disorder.

Now that you have an understanding of the major anxiety disorders, we can consider the questions that are asked and steps that are taken in diagnosing them.

from: Abnormal Psychology, David S. Holmes, New York: Harper Collins College Publishers, 1994

Words and Expressions

diffuse	v.	[di'fju:z]	散播;传播;扩散;(使)慢慢混合
panic	n.	['pænik]	惊慌;恐慌;没有理由的
nocturnal	adj.	[nɔk'tə:nl]	夜的;夜曲的
palpitation	n.	[pælpi'teiʃ(ə)n]	心悸
choking	adj.	['tʃəukiŋ]	窒息的;憋闷的;透不过气来的
smother	v.	['smʌðə]	窒息
agoraphobia	n.	[ægərə'fəubiə]	[心]广场恐怖;旷野恐怖;陌生环境恐怖
impending	n.	[im'pendiŋ]	迫近
elevate	vt.	['eliveit]	举起;提拔;振奋;提升职位
erroneous	adj.	[i'rəunjəs]	错误的;不正确的
omnipresent	adj.	[ɔmni'prezənt]	无所不在的
vigilant	adj.	['vidʒilənt]	警惕着的;警醒的
debilitate	vt.	[di'biliteit]	使衰弱;使虚弱
fatigue	n.	[fə'ti:g]	疲乏;疲劳;累活;[军]杂役
posttraumatic	adj.	[ˌpəusttrɔ:'mætik]	[医]外伤后的
precipitate	vt.	[pri'sipiteit]	猛抛;使陷入;促成;使沉淀
relive	vt.	['ri:'liv]	重新过活;再体验
numbing	adj.	['nʌmiŋ]	使麻木的;使失去感觉的
obsessive	adj.	[əb'sesiv]	强迫性的;分神的
compulsive	adj.	[kəm'pʌlsiv]	强制的;强迫的;由强迫产生的;禁不住的
impulse	n.	['impʌls]	推动;刺激;冲动;推动力
repugnant	adj.	[ri'pʌgnənt]	不一致的
ego	n.	['i:gəu]	自我;利己主义;自负

anxiety states	焦虑状态
panic disorder	恐慌型混乱
generalized anxiety disorder	综合焦虑型混乱
posttraumatic stress disorder	伤后压力型混乱
obsessive-compulsive disorder	强制强迫型混乱
acute stress disorder	急性压力型混乱

Difficult Sentences

① In addition to intense psychological feelings of apprehension, fear, and terror, the individual experiences physical symptoms that can include shortness of breath, heart palpitations, chest pains, choking or smothering sensations, dizziness, feelings of unreality, tingling of the extremities, hot and cold flashes, sweating, faintness, and trembling or shaking.
除忧惧、害怕、恐惧等强烈的心理感觉之外,个体还会经历一些身体上的症状,例如,呼吸短促、心悸、胸痛、窒息不透气感、头昏眼花、不现实感、绝境体验、冷热交替、流汗、晕眩、颤抖或者摇摇欲坠。

② Individuals who experience panic attacks become concerned about losing control and often think that they are "going crazy", and therefore they sometimes begin avoiding public places in favor of staying home, where they feel safe.
经历过恐慌袭击的人变得非常注意自己是否失控,从而经常担心自己变得疯狂,因此有时他们开始避免出入公众场所而宁愿呆在安全的家里。

③ Because the anxiety is general and not associated with a particular object, the individual does not know from where the threat and doom will come and must therefore be exceptionally vigilant and must continually scan the surroundings for the threat.
因为这种焦虑是综合性的而不与任何一个具体的物体相联系,

个人不知道威胁和厄运从哪里来,所以个人必须特别警惕而且必须不断地审视周围的威胁。

④ The reexperiencing may take the form of recurrent painful memories of the event, recurrent dreams of nightmares about the event, or "flashbacks" in which for some period of time (usually minutes or hours but sometimes longer) the individual relives the event and behaves as though experiencing the event at that moment.

这种再体现有很多形式,比如,对过去事件的痛苦回忆,对过去事件的噩梦梦魇,或者闪回到过去某个时间(通常是几分钟或几小时,有时也会更长一些),一个人似乎在重新经历过去的事情。

⑤ Because they are not under voluntary control and are often repugnant to the individual, obsessions are said to be ego-dystonic.

因为这些困扰不受主动控制而且经常与个人意志不一致,所以困扰据说是自我失调。

Phrases and Patterns

1. relate to 涉及;与……有关

   In anxiety states, the emotional response is diffused and not related to any one particular situation or stimulus.

   在焦虑状态中,情感反应是扩散的,不涉及任何一个具体的情景或刺激物。

   A person's actual performance of behaviors related to the trait.

   一个人的实际行为表现与个性有关。

2. out of the blue 突然地

   They seem to come "out of the blue" and can even start during sleep (nocturnal panic attacks).

   它们来得突然,甚至能在睡眠中发生(夜间恐慌袭击)。

3. suffer from 忍受;遭受

   One patient who suffered from panic attacks said, "Most people only face dying once; I do it a couple of times a week! It's scary."

一个遭受恐慌袭击的病人说:"大多数人只面对一次死亡;而我一周就得面对几次。简直太可怕了。"

But if you're suffering from social anxiety disorder, these emotional and physical symptoms are severe and disruptive to your life.

但是如果你忍受社会焦虑混乱症,这些情感和身体上的症状是严重的和分裂性的。

4. in favor of 赞同;有利于

They sometimes begin avoiding public places in favor of staying home, where they feel safe.

有时候他们开始避免出入公共场所,而更愿意呆在安全的家里。

5. rather than 胜于

If the avoidance becomes extreme, the individual may be diagnosed as suffering from a panic disorder with agoraphobia rather than simply from a panic disorder.

如果极端地避免出入公共场所,这个人就会被诊断为陌生环境恐惧症而不只是简单的恐慌性混乱。

In contrast, most psychologists study behavior only in their own society, and they take specific behaviors or mental processes as the topic for analysis, rather than the society itself.

相反,大多数心理学家只在自己的社会里研究行为,他们分析的话题是具体的行为或思维活动而不是社会本身。

8.3 Social Phobia
社会恐惧症

What Is Social Anxiety Disorder (Social Phobia)?

Social anxiety disorder, also called social phobia, is defined as an overwhelming and disabling fear of scrutiny, embarrassment, or humiliation in everyday social situations which leads to avoidance of potentially pleasurable and meaningful activities[①]. Most people experience some shyness or nervousness in certain social or work situations, but for someone with social anxiety disorder, the anxiety is so extreme that it can become debilitating.

Social anxiety disorder is common, affecting from 7 to 13 percent of American adults in any given year, making it the third most common psychiatric disorder in the United States after depression and alcohol abuse[②]. Unlike other anxiety disorders, which affect women more than men, social anxiety disorder is an equal problem for both men and women. Adolescents and young adults, who often are unsure of themselves around others and concerned with image and conformity, are especially susceptible to social anxiety. However, social anxiety disorder is sometimes seen in children under twelve.

You may have social anxiety disorder if your feelings keep you from your work or isolate you from activities with others. Warning signs of social phobia include:

· Intense worry for days or even weeks before an upcoming social situation.

· Extreme fear of being judged by others, especially people you don't know.

· Excessive self-consciousness and anxiety in everyday social situations.

· Fear that you'll act in ways that that will embarrass or humiliate yourself.

· Avoidance of social situations to a degree that limits your activities and causes disruptions to your daily life.

Is Social Anxiety Disorder the Same as Shyness?

The short answer is "No, it's much worse." Social anxiety disorder is a kind of extreme shyness: extreme to the point of avoiding social situations and causing disruption to social and professional relationships③.

For example, if you get the jitters before making a speech or presentation, that's considered pretty normal. If you call in sick to avoid making the presentation, that's a clue that your anxiety exceeds normal levels. The shy guy might be too nervous to ask someone to dance at a party, but the person with social anxiety disorder, sure that everyone will decide his clothes are uncool and that he'll spill a drink on himself, will skip the party altogether.

A person with social phobia might <u>fail to</u> attend the first meeting of a class or conference because she knows she'll be asked to introduce herself. Another might worry all week about a weekly team meeting at work, deathly afraid that he'll be required to describe what he's working on or even answer a question. Some people with social anxiety disorder find it difficult to pick up a phone and call the cable company (what if the person on the other end thinks her request is stupid?), stand in line at the supermarket (he knows people aren't really staring at him, but he feels as if they are), or simply walk down the street (what if she has to talk to someone?).

According to the Social Phobia/Social Anxiety Association (SP/SAA), people with social phobia usually find their anxiety triggered by situations such as:

- Being introduced to other people.
- Being teased or criticized.
- Being the center of attention.
- Being watched or observed while doing something.
- Having to speak in public.
- Meeting people in authority.
- Attending parties or other social gatherings.

- Becoming embarrassed.
- Meeting other people's eyes.
- Eating, talking, or making phone calls in public.

People with social anxiety disorder usually recognize that their fears are irrational, but they <u>can't help feeling</u> fearful and allowing their fears to affect the way they conduct their lives. Social anxiety sufferers often experience negative thought patterns that <u>contribute to</u> and prolong their anxiety. If you have social phobia, you may find yourself overwhelmed by thoughts like:

- "I'll act uncomfortable or awkward."
- "I'll look stupid or incompetent."
- "I'll seem weird or strange."
- "I'll feel embarrassed."
- "I'll be boring."

How Are Children Affected by Social Phobia?

In children, the extreme shyness, timidity, and fear of embarrassing themselves that are hallmarks of social anxiety disorder are especially distressing because children are less able to understand that their fears aren't based on reality. Again, there's nothing abnormal about a child being shy, but children with social phobia often avoid everyday activities and situations such as playing with other kids, reading in class, speaking to adults, or ordering food in restaurants[④].

The Cincinnati Children's Hospital Medical Center reports that social anxiety disorder in children is triggered by situations such as speaking in front of the class, talking with unfamiliar children, writing on the board, performing in front of others, taking tests, and interacting with strangers. Typical thoughts among such children are:

- "I hope the teacher doesn't <u>call on</u> me."
- "I'm going to make a mistake."

- "Everybody's staring at me."
- "Nobody likes me."

Children showing symptoms of social anxiety disorder may avoid eye contact, speak inaudibly, or fidget and tremble. They may be sweaty or clammy and complain of dizziness, headaches, or stomach aches. Often, children with social phobia don't want to go to school.

Children with social anxiety are often lonely, have fewer friends than other children their age, and report symptoms of depression⑤. The center also warns that children who develop social anxiety before the age of twelve are not likely to outgrow the disorder. Left untreated, many children with social anxiety disorder grow up to be socially anxious adults and continue to have problems in interpersonal situations.

What Are the Symptoms of Social Anxiety Disorder?

Almost everyone experiences symptoms of social anxiety from time to time. But if you're suffering from social anxiety disorder, these emotional and physical symptoms are severe and disruptive to your life. If your lifestyle is consistently limited by your fear of negative evaluation and your distress over the anxiety you suffer when socializing, it is likely that you have social anxiety disorder.

Emotional Symptoms
- Disabling fear of one or more social situations.
- Fear of being watched or judged by others.
- Fear that others will notice your physical symptoms of anxiety.
- Fear of embarrassing yourself in public.

Physical Symptoms
- Racing heart or palpitations.
- Blushing.
- Excessive sweating.

- Dry throat and mouth.
- Trembling.
- Muscle tension.
- Trouble talking.
- Nausea.
- Stomach upset.
- Diarrhea.

The Anxiety Disorders Association of America has a brief social phobia self-test that you can complete, print out, and share with a mental health professional if you are experiencing symptoms of social anxiety disorder.

from : http://www. helpguide. org

Words and Expressions

phobia	n.	[ˈfəubjə]	恐惧症
scrutiny	n.	[ˈskru:tini]	详细审查
debilitate	v.	[diˈbiliteit]	使衰弱;使虚弱
adolescent	n.	[ˌædəuˈlesnt]	青少年
conformity	n.	[kənˈfɔ:miti]	一致;符合
humiliate	v.	[ˈhju(:)ˈmilieit]	羞辱;使丢脸;耻辱
disruption	n.	[disˈrʌpʃən]	中断;分裂;瓦解;破坏
jitters	n.	[ˈdʒitəz]	神经过敏
spill	vt.	[spil]	使溢出;使散落;洒;使流出;使摔下;倒出
trigger	v.	[ˈtrigə]	引发;引起;触发
tease	adj.	[ti:z]	取笑;奚落;欺负;嘲弄
prolong	v.	[prəˈlɔŋ]	延长;拖延
overwhelm	vt.	[ˈəuvəˈwelm]	淹没;覆没;受打击;制服;压倒
awkward	adj.	[ˈɔ:kwəd]	难使用的;笨拙的

hallmark	n.	['hɔːlmɑːk]	特点
distressing	adj.	[dis'tresiŋ]	悲伤的;使痛苦的;使烦恼的
interact	v.	[ˌintər'ækt]	互相作用;互相影响
fidget	v.	['fidʒit]	坐立不安;烦躁;慌张;(不安地或心不在焉地)弄;玩弄
clammy	adj.	['klæmi]	湿粘的;湿冷的
dizziness	n.	['dizinis]	头昏眼花
outgrow	v.	[aut'grəu]	过大而不适于;出生;长出;年久丧失(某种习惯、兴趣等)
disruptive	adj.	[dis'rʌptiv]	使破裂的;分裂性的
evaluation	n.	[iˌvælju'eiʃən]	估价;评价;赋值
racing	adj.	['reisiŋ]	比赛的
palpitation	n.	[pælpi'teiʃ(ə)n]	心悸
blush	v.	[blʌʃ]	脸红;羞愧;呈现红色;使成红色
nausea	n.	['nɔːsjə]	反胃;晕船;恶心;作呕
diarrhea	n.	[ˌdaiə'riə]	痢疾;腹泻

social anxiety disorder	社会焦虑混乱症
social phobia	社会恐惧症
psychiatric disorder	精神病型的混乱症
self-consciousness	自我意识
Anxiety Disorder Association	焦虑混乱症协会
cincinnati Children's Hospital Medical Center	辛辛那提儿童医疗中心
social phobia self-test	社会恐惧症自我测试
mental health professional	心理健康专家

Difficult Sentences

① Social anxiety disorder, also called social phobia, is defined as an overwhelming and disabling fear of scrutiny, embarrassment, or humiliation in everyday social situations which leads to avoidance of potentially pleasurable and meaningful activities.

社会焦虑混乱症,也叫作社会恐惧症,其定义是一种无法抵抗的、无能为力的对日常社会情境的恐惧,如被详细审查、处境尴尬、表现羞耻等,这种恐惧导致人们逃避潜在的娱乐和有意义的活动。

② Social anxiety disorder is common, affecting from 7 to 13 percent of American adults in any given year, making it the third most common psychiatric disorder in the United States after depression and alcohol abuse.

社会焦虑混乱症是普遍的,每年影响7%至13%的美国成人,成为美国继忧郁和酗酒之后排名第三的最普遍的精神错乱症之一。

③ Social anxiety disorder is a kind of extreme shyness: extreme to the point of avoiding social situations and causing disruption to social and professional relationships.

社会焦虑混乱症是一种极端的害羞,极端到逃避社会环境,甚至导致社会关系和人际关系的瓦解。

④ Again, there's nothing abnormal about a child being shy, but children with social phobia often avoid everyday activities and situations such as playing with other kids, reading in class, speaking to adults, or ordering food in restaurants.

再者说,小孩害羞没什么异常的,但是有社会恐惧症的孩子经常逃避日常社会活动和环境,比如,跟别的小孩一块儿玩耍,在课堂上朗读,跟大人讲话,或者在饭店点餐。

⑤ Children with social anxiety are often lonely, have fewer friends than other children their age, and report symptoms of depression.

有社会恐惧症的孩子通常是孤独的,朋友比同龄人少,以及表现出忧郁症状。

Phrases and Patterns

1. fail to 未能

    A person with social phobia might fail to attend the first meeting of a class or conference because she knows she'll be asked to introduce herself.

    有社会恐惧症的人可能不会去参加第一次班会或其他会议,因为她知道在第一次会议上她肯定会被要求自我介绍。

    The psychological approach fail to explain why only certain goods are bought impulsively.

    心理学的方法未能解释为何只有某些货物会被冲动地购买。

2. can't help doing 忍不住做

    People with social anxiety disorder usually recognize that their fears are irrational, but they can't help feeling fearful and allowing their fears to affect the way they conduct their lives.

    有社会焦虑混乱症的人们通常认为他们的恐惧是没有理性的,但是他们忍不住感到恐惧并任由这种恐惧影响他们的生活方式。

3. contribute to 有助于

    Social anxiety sufferers often experience negative thought patterns that contribute to and prolong their anxiety.

    忍受社会焦虑症的人经常采取消极思考方式,反之,消极思考又增长和延长社会焦虑。

    Together, their efforts have contributed to our understanding of formal reasoning processes as well as the mental shortcuts we routinely use—shortcuts that may sometimes lead our reasoning capabilities astray.

    总的来说,他们的努力有助于对我们理解正式的推理过程以及我们常用的心理捷径,但这些捷径会把我们的推理能力引入歧途。

4. call on 号召;呼吁;邀请;访问;指派;要(学生)回答问题

    I hope the teacher doesn't call on me.

    我希望老师不点我回答问题。

Questions

1. How to define abnormality?
2. How many anxiety states are explained? Give a brief description of each one.
3. Can you compare and contrast panic disorder, generalized anxiety disorder, posttraumatic stress disorder, obsessive-compulsive disorder, and acute stress disorder?

9

Social Psychology
社会心理学

【本章导读】 本章第1篇文章总述社会心理学的本质特征。第2篇文章讲解社会原形和图式理论,以及社会原形和图式在现实生活中的应用。第3篇文章运用社会心理学解释了一个相对具体的例子,即男人和女人在冲动时的购买行为的差异,他们购买的物品对象、购买决策和购买时的自我形象都存在很大的差异。

9.1　The Nature of Social Psychology
社会心理学的本质

Social psychology according to one classic definition, represents "an attempt to understand and explain how the thought, feeling, and behavior of individuals are influenced by the actual, imagined, or implied presence of others". The core of this definition is that social psychology studies how people influence people. The topics of conformity, obedience, persuasion and attitude change, and group processes all address interpersonal influence. Many of the questions we posed about people's behavior after the American earthquake focused on different varieties of social influence.

Social psychologists study not only social influences on behavior, but nonsocial influences on social behavior as well. For example, emergencies and anxiety-provoking events like the American earthquake can lead people to seek out others. The physical environment can affect friendships or aggression. Note that these findings lie in the realm of social psychology because they study influences on social behavior, even though these influences do not come from other people.

There is yet another way to define social psychology—through the kinds of explanations it offers for social behaviors. Examine Figure 9.1, which visually presents the factors that a social scientist might use to explain human behavior, including broad explanations (such as evolutionary and cultural factors), individual-level explanations (such as individual rearing and family history), and internal factors (such as personality traits and attitudes). Social psychologists tend to emphasize some of these explanations more than others. To illustrate, let's consider a particular kind of social behavior—aggression. What leads people to be aggressive? Even more specifically, what led to violence between Armenians and the peoples of Azerbaijan? Let's begin providing possible answers to these questions by looking first at the top level of Figure 9.1— "group-level" explanations.

To understand human aggression, it may be useful to examine the biological groups to which humans belong—mammals, primates, and our species, Homo sapiens. Clearly, Siamese fighting fish and laboratory rats show different patterns of aggression than do human beings; some of these differences are biologically based. Could the ethnic unrest in the Soviet Union be due in part to evolutionary factors? For example, is it possible that people have evolved with a tendency to be more aggressive to "outsiders" than to "our own kind"?

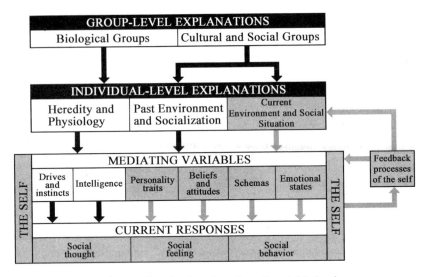

Figure 9.1　Levels of explanation of social behavior

Human aggression is also influenced by cultural and social groups. Some societies, like that of the Arapesh of New Guinea, are reported to be quite peaceful and cooperative, whereas others, like that of the Mundugumor (also of New Guinea), are reported to be dominating and aggressive. Although most societies show some degree of violence and aggression, absolute levels can vary dramatically across different cultures. In the mid-1980s the United States reported 8.5 homicides per 100 000 people, Canada reported 2.3, and Great Britain reported only 0.7. Why these differences? It seems likely that cultural and sociological factors, not biology, are responsible. To return to our example of aggression in Armenia and Azerbaijan, we might study cultural attitudes toward aggression in each of these Soviet republics.

Each individual's unique heredity and physiology (Figure 9.1) may influence aggression. For example, there is some evidence that males, perhaps in part because of the effects of male hormones, are on

<u>average</u> more aggressive than females. Although the news reports from Armenia and Azerbaijan contain no reference to the gender of the warring "gangs", it seems likely that they were largely composed of males.

An individual's past environment can <u>exert a potent effect on</u> social behavior. For example, child-rearing practices and learning early in life may influence a person's aggressiveness later in life. One explanation for the observed tendency for women to be less aggressive than men is that girls and women are consistently taught to be less aggressive by family members, their peers, and the mass media①. In Armenia and Azerbaijan, residents may have learned during their childhoods ethnic prejudices that later fostered aggressive behaviors.

A person's current situation can also exert a potent influence on behavior. Indeed, this type of explanation is particularly emphasized in social psychology. For example, one famous theory holds that frustration inevitably leads to aggression. In a classic study Hovland & Sears found a significant correlation between the health of the economy and the lynching of blacks in the old South. Presumably, as whites were frustrated by economic bad times, they vented their resulting hostility on "safe" targets, namely blacks. According to the frustration-aggression hypothesis, factors in the current situation—specifically, anything that thwarts achievement of a desired goal—lead to aggression②. Armenians living in Azerbaijan presumably felt frustrated and harassed by the non-Armenian majority, and perhaps these feelings contributed to ethnic violence.

Consider another possible situational influence on aggression—media violence. Do violent TV shows and movies lead to aggressive behavior in some individuals? For now we'll simply note that this question focuses on how the past environment and the current environment may affect a person's level of aggressiveness. It is interesting to note that ethnic unrest in the Soviet Union was preceded by a period of "glasnost"—that is, of increased openness in the Soviet media—which allowed people striving for greater ethnic recognition to become more aware of other ethnic struggles in the Soviet Union[③].

Many topics central to social psychology deal with the influence of current situational pressures on individuals' behavior: Research on conformity investigates how pressures from groups of people induce individuals to shift their stated attitudes and beliefs, research on attitude change examines how persuasive messages can change people's opinions, and research on group processes probes how being in a group affects individuals' performance and decision making[④]. Because social psychology often focuses on social influence, it makes sense that the social setting should be seen as an important explanatory variable in social psychology.

When we consider the third level of boxes in Figure 9.1, mediating variables, we seem to slip inside the skin of the individual. Such explanatory variables cannot be directly observed, but rather must be inferred from behavior. For example, we may infer that our friend has the trait of aggressiveness because he always gets into fights. We might further explain that his high level of aggression is due to his aggressive "drives" or his strong aggressive "instincts". Perhaps we might observe also that his "attitude" that it is good for men to be strong and aggressive leads him to be aggressive in many settings. In Soviet Armenia and Azerbaijan, prejudiced attitudes undoubtedly contributed to the reported aggression.

Social psychologists tend to study some of these mediating variables more than others. Beliefs and attitudes have traditionally been among those most studied by social psychologists. Beliefs comprise the cognitive information people hold about various people and things. Attitudes are evaluative responses (that is, reactions of liking or disliking) to people and things. Beliefs and attitudes have always intrigued social psychologists because of these concepts presumed close relation to a host of important social behaviors, including aggression, discrimination, altruism, and attraction[5].

In recent years, social psychologists have studied intensively a number of cognitive mediators of social behavior. For example, the concept of cognitive schemas has recently been at the forefront of social psychological theory and research. A schema—a kind of mental model or theory that people hold—contains the information we have about social groups and social settings, and even about ourselves.

from: *Introduction to Social Psychology*, Richard A. Lippa, Wadsworth Publishing Company, 1990

Words and Expressions

address	vt.	[əˈdres]	向……致辞;演说;写姓名地址;从事;忙于
Armenia	n.	[ɑːˈmiːnjə]	亚美尼亚(亚美尼亚共和国)
Azerbaijan	n.	[ˌɑːzəbaiˈdʒɑːn]	阿塞拜疆
mammal	n.	[ˈmæməl]	哺乳动物
primate	n.	[ˈpraimit]	首领;大主教;灵长类的动物
Siamese	n.	[saiəˈmiːz]	暹罗人[语];暹罗猫
New Guinea	n.	[njuːˈgini]	新几内亚岛(位于太平洋)
homicide	n.	[ˈhɔmisaid]	杀人;杀人者
heredity	n.	[hiˈrediti]	遗传;形质遗传
physiology	n.	[ˌfiziˈɔlədʒi]	生理学
hormone	n.	[ˈhɔːməun]	荷尔蒙;激素
lynching	n.	[ˈlintʃiŋ]	处私刑
vent	v.	[vent]	放出;排出;发泄
hostility	n.	[hɔsˈtiliti]	敌意;恶意;不友善;敌对;对抗;反对
harassed	adj.	[ˈhærəst]	疲倦的;厌烦的

glasnost	n.	[ˈglɑːsnɔːst]		公开性;公开化
induce	vt.	[inˈdjuːs]		劝诱;促使;导致;引起;感应
probe	vt.	[prəub]		(以探针等)探查;查明
variable	n.	[ˈvɛəriəbl]		变数;可变物;变量
intrigue	vt.	[inˈtriːg]		激起……的兴趣;用诡计取得
altruism	n.	[ˈæltruizəm]		利他主义;利他
mediator	n.	[ˈmiːdieitə]		调停者;仲裁人;[宗]中保(指耶稣,《圣经·新约》中称他是上帝和人之间的中保)

social psychology	社会心理学
social behavior	社会行为
personality traits	个性特征
cognitive schema	认知模式
mental model	智力模型

Difficult Sentences

① One explanation for the observed tendency for women to be less aggressive than men is that girls and women are consistently taught to be less aggressive by family members, their peers, and the mass media.

据观察女人的攻击性比男人小,一种解释就是女孩和女人接受来自家庭、同龄人以及媒体的教育都是要求她们攻击性小些。

② According to the frustration-aggression hypothesis, factors in the current situation—specifically, anything that thwarts achievement of a desired goal—lead to aggression.

根据挫折攻击假设,当前情形的因素,尤其是阻碍既定目标实现的因素,会导致攻击行为。

③ It is interesting to note that ethnic unrest in the Soviet Union was preceded by a period of "glasnost"—that is, of increased openness in the Soviet media—which allowed people striving for greater ethnic recognition to become more aware of other ethnic struggles in the Soviet Union.

媒体开放才使得人们追求更大的种族认同,同时更加关心前苏联其他的种族斗争,但是前苏联的种族动荡却先于媒体公开化时代,即前苏联媒体日益开放的时代,是非常有趣的事情。

④ Many topics central to social psychology deal with the influence of current situational pressures on individuals' behavior: Research on conformity investigates how pressures from groups of people induce individuals to shift their stated attitudes and beliefs, research on attitude change examines how persuasive messages can change people's opinions, and research on group processes probes how being in a group affects individuals' performance and decision making.

许多以社会心理学为中心的话题都研究当前的情形压力对个人行为的影响。例如,一致性调查研究来自人群的压力是怎样导致个人固有的态度和信念改变的;态度改变调查研究劝导话语如何改变人们的观点;小组作用调查研究身处集体中是怎样影响个人的行为和决定的。

⑤ Beliefs and attitudes have always intrigued social psychologists because of these concepts presumed close relation to a host of important social behaviors, including aggression, discrimination, altruism, and attraction.

信念和态度总是刺激社会心理学家的研究兴趣,因为他们认为这两个概念与许多社会行为紧密相关,包括攻击行为、歧视行为、利他主义和吸引力。

Phrases and Patterns

1. due to 由于；应归于

   We might further explain that his high level of aggression is due to his aggressive "drives" or his strong aggressive "instincts".

   我们会进一步解释他的高强度的攻击性是由于他的侵略的"动力"或是他强烈的侵略"本能"。

2. on average 平均起来

   There is some evidence that males, perhaps in part because of the effects of male hormones, are on average more aggressive than females.

   有些证据证明，平均而言男性比女性的攻击性更大，可能部分来自于男性荷尔蒙的影响。

   As a result, when researchers study a large group of randomly selected people regarding an arbitrarily chosen trait, the behavior on average is bound to appear only slightly consistent.

   因此，当研究人员随机挑选一组人并研究任意选择的一项个性，平均来看它们的行为一定有些微的一致。

3. exert an effect/influence on 对……施加影响

   An individual's past environment can exert a potent effect on social behavior.

   一个人过去的环境能够对他的社会行为产生潜在的影响。

   So persuasive were their arguments at the time they were proposed that many psychologists came to accept the view that situations generally exert a more powerful influence on human behavior than do inner dispositions.

   他们提出的论点在当时是如此的有说服力以至于许多心理学家接受情景通常比内在性情对人类行为的影响更大这一观点。

4. strive for 奋斗；争取

   Some, for instance, planned to strive hard for success in college.

例如，一些人打算努力奋斗为了在大学中获得成功。
5. make sense 有意义

Because social psychology often focuses on social influence, it makes sense that the social setting should be seen as an important explanatory variable in social psychology.
因为社会心理学经常关注社会影响，社会环境应当被视为一个重要的解释性变量，所以考虑媒体暴力因素是有意义的。

Another way to make sense of the variety of emotion terms is to identify which emotions are basic, in the sense that they share some kind of underlying biological foundation or are universal, and which are subordinate, or variations on the basic emotions.
另一种理解各种情感术语的方法是确定哪些情感是基本的，他们享有根本的生物基础或者是普遍的；哪些是基本情感的下级情感或变形情感。

9.2 Schemas and Stereotypes
图式与定型

Each person we meet is a unique individual, a fact that makes our social world extremely varied and complex. However, if we were actually to treat each person as unique, our cognitive abilities to attend to and think about others would quickly be overwhelmed[①]. Consequently, we simplify matters by forming mental representations of types of people on the basis of important or noticeable similarities and differences between them. In other words, we categorize people, just as we categorize objects and events. There are many ways to categorize others—for example, by their dominant personality traits (extroverts, approval seekers), by their occupations or roles (mothers, lawyers), or by their membership in large social categories defined by physical attribute (race, gender, age).

Although these categorizations are initially based on perceptible differences among types of people, such as skin color or number of wrinkles on the face, we quickly make additional generalizations about what members of a category are like. Women, we might decide, are more emotional, whereas men are more reliable in a crisis. Eventually, we develop complex mental representations of different types of people, containing all the information that we know or believe to be generally true of them. These mental representations are called stereotypes. A stereotype may be either an accurate or an inaccurate generalization about what members of a category are like.

Stereotypes are useful in social situations because knowing a person's category membership suggests what we should <u>look for</u> (or <u>look out for</u>) in them, enables us to predict what they will be like and how they will behave, and helps us to remember their characteristics. Stereotypes also affect our interpretations of others' behavior. In one study, white schoolchildren were shown stick-figure drawings of children while the experimenter read stories about the characters in the drawings. The stories were ambiguous, or open to interpretation. For example, one story read, "Mark was sitting at his desk, working on his social studies assignment, when David started poking him in the back with the eraser end of his pencil. Mark just kept on working. David kept poking him for awhile, then he stopped." Some subjects were told that David was black, others that he was white. Subjects tends to rate David's behavior as mean and threatening when he was described as black and as playful and friendly when he was described as white[②]. Thus, subjects' stereotypes about blacks and whites led them to interpret exactly the same behavior differently.

Stereotypes also affect our causal attributions of other people's behavior. We tend to attribute behavior that fits our stereotypes to stable characteristics or personality traits and to attribute behavior that violates our stereotypes to temporary influences on behavior[3]. For example, in one study, subjects learned that a person had been successful at a stereotypically masculine task. When the person was described as male, subjects tended to attribute his success to ability, whereas when the target was described as female, they attributed her success to luck or effort.

Moreover, simply believing is that a group of people are in the same category leads us to perceive a set of people as similar to one another and different from members of other categories.

Finally, we tend to organize and remember information about people according to their category membership. In one study, subjects listened to a tape recording of a discussion among six male teachers, three black and three white. As each of the teachers spoke, subjects saw a slide of the speaker. Subjects were then given a list of all the statements made during the discussion and a set of photographs of the speakers, and were asked to match each speaker with the statements he had made. Subjects were more likely to make within-race errors (that is, to attribute a statement made by a black to the wrong black) than across-race errors (that is, to attribute a statement made by a black to a white, or vice versa), indicating that they had organized information in memory according to the race of the speaker. Similar within-group errors have been found when the speakers were male and female rather than black and white.

>   *Father, Mother, and Me,*
>   *Sister and Auntie say,*
>   *All the people like us are We,*
>   *and everyone else is They.*
>   *And They live over the sea,*
>   *While we live over the way,*
>   *But—would you believe it—They look upon We*

As only a sort of They!

Rudyard Kipling

This poem describes the pervasive human tendency to categorize people into ingroups (us) and outgroups (them)—in other words, into the broadest possible stereotypes or schemas. Note that those two stereotypes are set up in opposition to each other, with positive emotions linked to the ingroup and negative emotions to the outgroup.

Even when group boundaries are determined by some arbitrary criterion—such as people who draw the letter "A" out of a hat versus people who draw the letter "B"—people will accept those group boundaries and favor the ingroup over the outgroup. This ingroup bias is expressed in prejudice (negative evaluations of the outgroup) and in discrimination (the allocation of more rewards or resources to ingroup members than to outgroup members). Ingroup bias persists even when randomly selected members do not know the other members of their ingroup, and even when they personally have nothing to gain by favoring the ingroup④.

The mere fact of categorization into "us" and "them" is sufficient to produce discrimination against outgroups. In one study, eight adolescents in the Netherlands were randomly divided into two teams of four. After both groups completed a few simple tasks, the researcher announced that members of one group would get transistor radios. The lucky group would be determined by the flip of a coin. Once the radios had been distributed, the adolescents rated the members of each group. Hostility was already apparent. The adolescents in each group saw the other group—the outgroup—as less open, less responsible, and less desirable as friends.

This ingroup/outgroup division has a number of cognitive effects, which can reinforce negative stereotypes and make discrimination and prejudice more likely. First, members of the ingroup tend to assume that outgroup members are similar to one another and different from the ingroup. When researchers divided people into two groups on the basis of artistic preferences, the members of each group assumed that fellow members held opinions and beliefs similar to their own, even on matters that had nothing to do with art. Thus, differences between groups are exaggerated and differences within groups are minimized. Second, and paradoxically, people see their ingroup as more diverse than the outgroup members. Third, appraisals of outgroup members are polarized: for example, competent outgroup members may be evaluated very positively, but incompetent outgroup members will be strongly rejected.

Given these tendencies, it is not surprising that information about ingroup and outgroup members seems to be processed differently. Negative acts of outgroup members tend to be remembered, but negative acts of fellow ingroup members are easily forgotten. Attributions of causes for ingroup and outgroup behavior are also made very differently. In a variation of the fundamental attribution error, we attribute ingroup members' successes to their personal qualities and ascribe their failures to situational factors beyond their control[5]. We do the opposite for outgroup members, attributing their successes to the situation and their failures to their personal weaknesses. Thus, ingroup and outgroup divisions lead to a number of cognitive biases that can create further divisions between the groups and practically guarantee that such rifts will persist.

from: *Psychology Today*: *An Introduction*, *Richard R. Bootzin*, *Gordon H. Bower*, *Jennifer Crocker*, *Elizabeth Hall*, *Von Hoffmann Press*, 1991

Words and Expressions

stereotype	n.	['stiəriəutaip]	定型;典型;[印]铅版;陈腔滥调;老套
attribute	n.	[ə'tribju(:)t]	属性;品质;特征;加于;归结于
attribution	n.	[,ætri'bju:ʃən]	归因
categorize	v.	['kætigəraiz]	加以类别;分类
generalization	n.	[,dʒenərəlai'zeiʃən]	一般化;普遍化;概括;广义性
perceptible	adj.	[pə'septəbl]	可察觉的;显而易见的
masculine	adj.	['mɑ:skjulin]	男性的;男子气概的;阳性的
perceive	v.	[pə'si:v]	感知;感到;认识到
pervasive	adj.	[pə:'veisiv]	普遍深入的
arbitrary	adj.	['ɑ:bitrəri]	任意的;武断的;独裁的;专断的
criterion	n.	[krai'tiəriən]	(批评判断的)标准;准据;规范
prejudice	n.	['predʒudis]	偏见;成见;损害;侵害
discrimination	n.	[dis,krimi'neiʃən]	辨别;歧视
allocation	n.	[,æləu'keiʃən]	分配;安置
adolescent	n.	[,ædəu'lesnt]	青少年
Netherlands	n.	['neðələndz]	荷兰(地区名)
transistor	n.	[træn'zistə]	[电子]晶体管
paradoxical	adj.	[,pærə'dɔksikəl]	荒谬的
polarize	v.	['pəuləraiz]	(使)偏振;(使)极化;(使)两极分化
ascribe	vt.	[əs'kraib]	归因于;归咎于
rift	n.	[rift]	裂缝;裂口;断裂;长狭谷;不和

mental representation	精神方面的代表
social category	社会范畴
category membership	某类别的成员资格
transistor radio	晶体管收音机
situational factor	外在因素

Difficult Sentences

① However, if we were actually to treat each person as unique, our cognitive abilities to attend to and think about others would quickly be overwhelmed.

然而,如果我们真的认为每个人都是独一无二的,那么我们对他人的认知能力和想法将很快变得泛滥起来。

② Subjects tends to rate David's behavior as mean and threatening when he was described as black and as playful and friendly when he was described as white.

如果大卫是黑人,人们就会认为他的行为是卑鄙的、危险的;如果大卫是白人,人们就会认为他的行为是顽皮的、友好的。

③ We tend to attribute behavior that fits our stereotypes to stable characteristics or personality traits and to attribute behavior that violates our stereotypes to temporary influences on behavior.

我们趋向于把符合我们传统范式的行为归结为固定的性格特点或人格特点,而把违背传统模式的行为归结为行为受到临时影响。

④ Ingroup bias persists even when randomly selected members do not know the other members of their ingroup, and even when they personally have nothing to gain by favoring the ingroup.

持组内偏见观点的人坚持认为随机选择的成员不知道其他的组员情况,他们个人即便帮助组内成员也别无所求。

⑤ In a variation of the fundamental attribution error, we attribute ingroup members' successes to their personal qualities and ascribe their failures to situational factors beyond their control.

在众多基本的归因错误中,我们把组内成员的成功归因于他们的个人能力,而把他们的失败归因于不可控的外在因素。

Phrases and Patterns

1. look (out) for 寻找;期待;留心;期待;物色

   Stereotypes are useful in social situations because knowing a person's category membership suggests what we should look for (or look out for) in them, enables us to predict what they will be like and how they will behave, and helps us to remember their characteristics.

   传统模式在社会环境中非常有用,因为了解一个人在所属类别的成员资格需要我们自己探寻,能帮助我们预测他们的样子以及他们的行为,还能帮助我们记住他们的特点。

2. attribute to 归因于

   When the person was described as male, subjects tended to attribute his success to ability, whereas when the target was described as female, they attributed her success to luck or effort.

   当他是男人时,我们说他的成功是他的能力强,但如果是女人成功了,我们就说这个女人很幸运或者很努力。

   We tend to attribute behavior that fits our stereotypes to stable characteristics or personality traits and to attribute behavior that violates our stereotypes to temporary influences on behavior.

   我们趋向于把符合我们传统模式的行为归结为固定的性格特点或人格特点,而把违背传统范式的行为归结为行为受到临时影响。

3. have nothing to do with... 与……无关

   When researchers divided people into two groups on the basis of artistic preferences, the members of each group assumed that fellow members held opinions and beliefs similar to their own, even on matters that had nothing to do with art.

当研究者把人们按艺术特长分为两组,每组的成员都假设他们组内的成员持有与他本人相似的观点,甚至对待与艺术无关的事情他们也这么想。

4. ascribe to 归因于

He ascribes his well-being to a sound constitution.

他把他的幸福生活归因于一个健康的体质。

9.3 Objects, Decision Considerations and Self-Image in Men's and Women's Impulse Purchases

男人和女人冲动购买的对象、决定和自我形象

Consumer Goods and Self-Image

In developed techno-industrial countries, the consumption of material goods has changed radically in nature, particularly during the last century. A focus on buying provisions to satisfy the physical needs of self and one's immediate network of people has increasingly shifted towards using goods as modern—or postmodern—means of acquiring and expressing a sense of self-identity. Material goods are consumed not only for their functional benefits, but also as symbolic signifiers of taste, lifestyle and identity. Thus, the central assumption of this paper is that consumers buy, and relate to, sets of products in a way that fits their preferred self-image. We see material consumption as involving a lot more than the rational cost-benefit concerns of "economic man" as assumed by orthodox economics or the detailed information-processing about single goods and brands by the "purchase decision-maker" in mainstream marketing and consumer research.

Shopping as a major leisure and lifestyle activity suggests the increasing importance and frequency of unplanned, non-necessity purchases. Indeed, there is emerging evidence that impulse buying constitutes a substantial "non-rational" segment of purchasing behavior, which is present in "normal" consumer behavior, but which can assume such excessive proportions that individuals find themselves in considerable financial debt and psychological distress. Empirical studies on "shopping addiction" or "compulsive buying" have been carried out recently in the United States, Canada, Germany and the United Kingdom. All suggest that extreme impulse (compulsive) buying is on the increase, affecting an estimated 5% to 10% of the adult population, and that at least occasional bouts of impulse buying are much more common than that. Scherhorn et al. describe 25% of German adults as showing some mild compulsive shopping tendencies.

Fairly recent developments in consumer psychology and cultural studies in particular, but also in social psychology, emphasize the importance of "symbolic consumption" for understanding the ways in which consumers construct, maintain and express their self-identity. In contrast to mainstream consumer research, the "symbolic consumption" perspective proposes that consumers do not just consume actual products, but also—or even instead—consume the symbolic meanings of those products. Purchasing consumer goods is thus a significant element in the construction and maintenance of consumers' self-identities, in the attainment of social status, and in attempts to make oneself "feel better".

Social psychological studies demonstrate empirically that, in addition to the functional and use-related benefits they offer, material possessions are used to express and communicate personal and social aspects of identity. In addition, Wicklund and Gollwitzer demonstrate that people acquire and display material symbols—amongst other strategies—to compensate for perceived inadequacies in certain dimensions of their self-concept: a process they term symbolic self-completion.

This literature shows that consumer goods and material possessions have become important symbols of identity: both in the way we see ourselves, and in the way we perceive the identity of others. If we accept that extended self-definition is linked to the meaning of consumer goods, we might expect from this that gender, as a major social category, would exert a strong influence on either the items bought, or the reasons for buying them, or both[1].

Gender and Consumption

Consistent evidence has emerged in previous British and American studies that women and men relate differently to their material possessions. Dittmar classified lists of subjects' favorite possessions into different categories of material objects, and found some gender differences in choices: women listed more objects of sentimental value, while men chose more items relating to leisure and finances. However, gender differences were pronounced in orientations towards sets of material goods: <u>by comparison</u>, women saw their possessions as important because of the emotional comfort they provide and the relationships with others they symbolize, while, men referred more to use-related, activity-related and self-expressive features of possessions. These differences can be interpreted as reflecting male and female gender identity, because they echo the distinction between male self-oriented, activity-centered identity construction and female other-oriented, relationship-centered identity construction described in both the sociological and social psychological literature.

More recent is still needed to investigate whether different types of objects and different types of considerations are important to women and men at the point of purchase, but a recent study with compulsive shoppers suggests that clothes, jewellery, and cosmetics were bought more by women, and high-tech, electronic and sports equipment more by men[2]. Our previous study on gender identity and impulse buying showed in a "normal" consumer sample that men tend to impulsively buy instrumental and leisure items projecting independence and activity, while women tend to buy symbolic and self-expressive goods concerned with appearance and emotional aspects of self.

Explanatory Models of Impulse Buying

Impulse buying has been of theoretical and practical significance to economics, consumer behavior, and psychology. Yet, many aspects of impulse buying remain largely unexplored, specifically which kinds of products tend to be purchased impulsively, and why. We propose that a social psychological model is needed to address these questions, which remain unanswered by previous explanatory models.

The term "impulse buying" has had different meanings to different theoretical perspectives. It is important to disentangle these before attempting to examine behaviors which may have quite different underlying motivations. For example, presumably there is a considerable difference between "reminder impulse buying" (in which a shopper remembers the need for an essential item on seeing it in the shop), and "pure impulse buying" (a novelty or escape purchase which breaks the normal buying pattern)[3]. Consumer behaviorists have tended to regard any unplanned purchases as impulse buying, while economists and psychologists have generally studied the (possibly "irrational") aspects of pure impulse buying. At the outset we note that none of these traditions has investigated why some items (e.g. fashionable clothes) are more susceptible to impulse buying that others (e.g. basic kitchen equipment), or the underlying reasons for impulse buying.

Informed by the still predominant rational choice perspective on economic agents, the standard economic explanation of impulse buying has been the discounting model, which assumes that impulse buyers discount the future at too rapid a rate. Thus, the benefits of the desired object at the point of imminent purchase outweigh the (future) problem of paying the bill. However, these preferences switch later, when the buyer comes to pay the bill and regrets the purchase[4]. A similar model is Winston's stochastic preference model, in which people are assumed to randomly switch between two sets of different preferences: a myopic set which pushes the shopper towards the purchase, and a far-sighted set which remembers that the bill must be paid. In both models, no explanation is given of why myopic preferences exist, or of why certain objects are more susceptible to impulse buying than others. The mainstream consumer behavior and marketing approach has produced atheoretical lists of those goods that <u>are likely to</u> be bought impulsively. This information may be useful for choosing goods for sales promotions, and is also unusual in recognizing that certain goods have a greater potential to be bought on impulse than others. However, it does not explain why, nor predict beyond the particular goods studied. Moreover, these studies tend to use purely behavioral definitions of impulse buying, such as regarding a purchase as impulsive if it was not on the buyer's original shopping list.

Psychological approaches have fallen into two types: cognitive and clinical[5]. The cognitive approach places impulsive shopping within the framework of impulse control in general. This work has shown show that impulse control improves with developmental stage, and can be used as individual difference parameter to predict performance on certain cognitive tasks. Like the economic and consumer behavior approaches, the cognitive literature assumes a rational decision maker. In contrast, the clinical psychological literature has been concerned with the excessive buying of compulsive shoppers. This approach treats compulsive shopping as similar to other types of impulsive, addictive or obsessive-compulsive disorders, and therefore cannot explain "normal" impulsive buying, which some have argued lies on a continuum with compulsive buying. Again, all psychological approach fail to explain why only certain goods are bought impulsively.

from: *Dr. Helga Dittmar, Sociology and Social Psychology Group, School of Social Sciences, Arts E. University of Sussex, Brighton, Falmer, BN1 9QN, East Sussex, England*

Words and Expressions

provision	n.	[prə'viʒən]	供应;(一批)供应品;预备;防备
signify	v.	['signifai]	表示;意味
rational	adj.	['ræʃənl]	理性的;合理的;推理的
orthodox	adj.	['ɔːθədɔks]	正统的;传统的;保守的;东正教的
excessive	adj.	[ik'sesiv]	过多的;过分的;额外的

proportion	n.	[prə'pɔːʃən]	比例;均衡;面积;部分
bout	n.	[baut]	一回;一场;回合;较量
perspective	n.	[pə'spektiv]	透视画法;透视图;远景;前途;观点
perceive	v.	[pə'siːv]	察觉
orientation	n.	[ˌɔ(ː)rien'teiʃən]	方向;方位;定位;倾向性;向东方
sociological	adj.	[ˌsəuʃiə'lɔdʒikəl]	社会学的;社会学上的
disentangle	v.	['disin'tæŋgl]	解开;松开
outset	n.	['autset]	开端;开始
susceptible	adj.	[sə'septəbl]	易受影响的;易感动的;容许……的
discount	n.	['diskaunt]	折扣
stochastic	adj.	[stəu'kæstik]	随机的
myopic	adj.	[mai'ɔpik]	近视的
atheoretical	adj.	[eiˌθiə'retikəl]	非理论的;与理论无关的
parameter	n.	[pə'ræmitə]	参数;参量;起限定作用的因素
continuum	n.	[kən'tinjuəm]	连续统一体;连续统;闭联集

consumer goods	消费者商品
self-image	自我形象
material goods	物质商品
self-identity	自我身份
impulse buying	冲动购买
compulsive buying	强迫购买
consumer psychology	消费者心理
symbolic consumption	象征性消费

social status 社会地位
gender differences 性别差异
sales promotion 商品促销

Difficult Sentences

① If we accept that extended self-definition is linked to the meaning of consumer goods, we might expect from this that gender, as a major social category, would exert a strong influence on either the items bought, or the reasons for buying them, or both.

如果我们认为延展的自我定义与消费者商品相关,我们由此可能得出这样的结论:作为一个主要的社会类别,性别对商品购买或者对购买原因或者两者都起到很强的作用。

② More recent is still needed to investigate whether different types of objects and different types of considerations are important to women and men at the point of purchase, but a recent study with compulsive shoppers suggests that clothes, jewellery, and cosmetics were bought more by women, and high-tech, electronic and sports equipment more by men.

不同的物品和不同的考虑是否对男人和女人购买行为很重要仍需要进一步研究,但是最近一项对强迫购买者的研究表明女人更愿意买衣服、珠宝和化妆品,男人更愿意买高科技产品、电子产品和运动设备。

③ For example, presumably there is a considerable difference between "reminder impulse buying" (in which a shopper remembers the need for an essential item on seeing it in the shop), and "pure impulse buying" (a novelty or escape purchase which breaks the normal buying pattern).

例如,暗示冲动消费和纯粹冲动消费之间大概有一个很大的区别,即暗示冲动消费指购物者在商店看到某件商品时突然记起需要购买这件必需品;而纯粹冲动消费指打破常规购买模式的新奇购买或逃避购买。

④ Thus, the benefits of the desired object at the point of imminent purchase outweigh the (future) problem of paying the bill. However, these preferences switch later, when the buyer comes to pay the bill and regrets the purchase.

因此,即将购买时需求商品的好处大于即将买单的问题。然而,这种倾向后来在购买者买单时就改变了,购买者开始后悔买东西了。

⑤ Psychological approaches have fallen into two types: cognitive and clinical.

心理学上的研究方法分成两类:认知的方法和临床的方法。

Phrases and Patterns

1. carry out 完成;实现;贯彻;执行

   Empirical studies on "shopping addiction" or "compulsive buying" have been carried out recently in the United States, Canada, Germany and the United Kingdom.

   最近在美国、加拿大、德国和英国进行了关于购买瘾和强迫购买的经验研究。

   This study was carried out during a 20 year period form 1945 to 1965 and was quite revealing.

   从1945年到1965年的二十年,该研究一直在进行,而且还很有启示作用。

2. by comparison 比较起来

   However, gender differences were pronounced in orientations towards sets of material goods: by comparison, women saw their possessions as important because of the emotional comfort they provide and the relationships with others they symbolize, while, men referred more to use-related, activity-related and self-expressive features of possessions.

然而,性别差异体现在物质购买的倾向上。比较起来,女人把自己的拥有物看得很重要,因为物质商品能给她们感情安慰以及它们象征着人与别的东西的联系;而男人注重物质商品的实用性、活动相关性和自身的表现特征。

The computer—by comparison—is backward.

比较而言,计算机是落后的。

3. tend to 注意;趋向

Yet, many aspects of impulse buying remain largely unexplored, specifically which kinds of products tend to be purchased impulsively, and why.

冲动购买的许多方面都有待研究,尤其是容易被冲动购买的商品品种和原因。

We tend to attribute behavior that fits our stereotypes to stable characteristics or personality traits and to attribute behavior that violates our stereotypes to temporary influences on behavior.

我们趋向于把符合我们传统范式的行为归结为固定的性格特点或人格特点,而把违背传统范式的行为归结为受临时影响的行为。

4. be likely to 可能

The mainstream consumer behavior and marketing approach has produced atheoretical lists of those goods that are likely to be bought impulsively.

主流消费行为和市场通道产生了非理论的容易冲动购买的商品名单。

Furthermore, we assume that the same sort of event is more likely to occur in the future.

而且,我们推断同样的事件很有可能在将来发生。

Questions

1. What does social psychology study?
2. How does social psychology explain social behavior?
3. What is stereotype?
4. How do stereotypes affect human's social behaviors? And how are stereotypes embodied between ingroups and outgroups?

10

Feature: New Development of Applied Psychology
专题：应用心理学研究新进展

【本章导读】 本章介绍应用心理学研究新进展。第 1 篇文章主要介绍了健康心理学、压力、紧张性刺激、压力反应的生理机能、压力与免疫系统以及压力与心血管疾病。第 2 篇文章主要讲述人的性格和压力之间的关系。乐观对待压力的人性格勇敢；悲观对待压力的人性格懦弱。孤独症就是一种性格缺陷。孤独症的定义、表现和形成原因在文中都一一被阐述。第 3 篇文章是一篇论文，论述了通过强调动机和意志对行为的影响的区别及关注开始并维持健康行为，包括五个问题：影响行为关键的动机因素、影响行为的关键的意志因素、对于意图－行为调解因素的最近的研究是如何使我们更进一步了解意志对健康行为的影响的、混淆连续和阶段模式所产生的问题、划分开始和维持健康行为的界限的意义。第 4 篇是一篇短文，改变行为能改善健康。第 5 篇至第 8 篇是论文摘要，都是近年来应用心理学研究的新进展。

10.1 Health and Stress
健康与压力

For thousands of years, people in many cultures around the world have believed that people's mental state, their behavior, and their health are linked. Today, <u>scientific evidence for</u> this belief <u>has been documented</u>. We know, for example, that through their impact on psychological and physical processes, the stresses of life can influence physical health. Researchers have also associated anger, hostility, pessimism, depression, and hopelessness with the appearance of physical illnesses. Similarly, poor hearth has been linked to such behaviors as lack of exercise, inadequate diet, smoking, and alcohol and drug abuse.

Prior to the 20th century, the principal threats to health were contagious diseases caused by infectious agents—diseases such as smallpox, typhoid fever, diphtheria, yellow fever, malaria, cholera, tuberculosis, and polio. Today, none of these diseases is among the leading killers in the developed countries. They are tamed by improvements in nutrition, public hygiene, sanitation, and medical treatment. Unfortunately, the void left by contagious diseases has been filled all too quickly by chronic diseases that develop gradually, such as heart disease, cancer, and stroke. Psychosocial factors, such as stress and lifestyle, play a large role in the development of these chronic diseases. The growing recognition that psychological factors influence physical health has led to the emergence of a new specialty in psychology. Health psychology is concerned with how psychosocial factors relate to the promotion and maintenance of health and with the causation, prevention, and treatment of illness. Hearth Psychology is a field within which psychology devotes to understanding psychological influences on how people stay healthy, why they become ill, and how they respond when they do get ill. Health psychology is related to a broader interdisciplinary field called behavioral medicine, whose goals are essentially the same as those of health psychology: using knowledge from the behavioral sciences to promote scientific understanding of health and illness[①]. Researchers and practitioners come to behavioral medicine from many sciences—including psychology, medicine, medical sociology, medical anthropology, and health education about behavioral factors associated with health and illness, and to promote preventive and treatment efforts to reduce the prevalence of illness and minimize its effects.

Stress

Stress is basic to life—no matter how wealthy, powerful, attractive, or happy you might be. It comes in many forms—a difficult exam, an automobile accident, waiting in a long line, a day on which everything goes wrong. Mild stress can be stimulating, motivating, and sometimes desirable. But as it becomes more severe, stress can bring on physical, psychological, and behavioral problems. Stress is the process that occurs as individuals adjust to or deal with environmental circumstances that disrupt, or threaten to disrupt, their physical or psychological functioning[②]. Thus stress involves a transaction between people and their environments. The environmental circumstances (such as exams or accidents) that cause people to make adjustments are called stressors. Stress reactions are the physical, psychological, and behavioral responses (such as nausea, nervousness, and fatigue) that people display in the face of stressors. Interestingly, some people are more strongly affected by stressors than other people, or may be more affected on one occasion or another. Why? The answer appears to <u>lie in</u> mediating factors that influence the transaction between people and their environments.

Mediating factors include variables such as the extent to which people can predict and control their stressors, how they interpret the threat involved, the social support they get, and their stress-coping skills. These mediating factors dampen or amplify a stressor's impact. Thus, stress is not a specific event but a process in which the nature and intensity of stress responses depend to a large degree on how stressors are mediated by factors such as the way people think about them and the skills they have to cope with them. Aversive stimuli can harm people's health. Many of these harmful effects are produced not by the stimuli themselves but by our reactions to them. The word stress was borrowed from engineering, in which it refers to the action of physical forces of mechanical structures. The word can be a noun or a verb; and the noun can refer to situations or the individual's response to them. Because of this potential confusion, psychologists refer to "stressful" stimuli and situations as stressors and to the individual's reaction as a stress response. The word stress will refer to the general process. The physiological responses that accompany the negative emotions prepare us to threaten rivals or fight them, or to run away from dangerous situation. The term stress has been used in different ways by different theorists. We'll define stress as any circumstances that threaten or are perceived to threaten one's well-being and that thereby tax one's coping abilities. The threat may be to immediate physical safety, long-range security, self-esteem, reputation, peace of mind, or many other things that one values.

Stressors

For humans most stressors have both physical and psychological components. Athletes, for example, are challenged by the demands of physical exertion, as well as by the pressure of competition. Here, we focus on psychological stressors. Even very pleasant promotion may be desirable, but the upgrade usually brings new pressures as well.

Similarly, people often feel exhausted after a vacation. Still, the events and situations most likely to be associated with stress are unpleasant ones—those involving daily hassles and frustrations, negative life changes and stains, and catastrophes[3]. Daily hassles are minor irritations, pressures, and annoyances that, if experienced only occasionally, would not be significant stressors. But when experienced more regularly, hassles can have cumulative effects. Life changes and strains can be major stressors, particularly if the changes are negative and if they force a person to make adjustments. Divorce, illness in the family, unemployment, difficulties at work, and moving to a new city are just a few examples of changes and strains that create demands to which people must adjust. Being unable to earn a decent living because of adverse economic conditions or job discrimination constitutes another long-term strain that acts as a stressor. Catastrophic events are shocking, potentially life-threatening experiences. Examples include traumas such as physical or sexual assault, military combat, fire, tornadoes, torture, or accidents involving loved ones. Catastrophic events can lead to serious psychological disorders.

Physiology of the Stress Response

The autonomic and endocrine responses are the ones that can have adverse effects on health. Because threatening situations generally call for vigorous activity, the autonomic and endocrine responses that accompany them are catabolic; that is, they help to mobilize the body's energy resources. The sympathetic branch of the autonomic nervous system is active, and the adrenal glands secrete epinephrine, norepinephrine and steroid stress hormones. Epinephrine affects glucose metabolism, causing the nutrients stored in muscles to become available to provide energy for strenuous exercise. Along with norepinephrine, the hormone also increases blood flow to the muscles by increasing the output of the heart.

In doing so, it also increases blood pressure, which, over the long term, contributes to cardiovascular disease.

The Immune System and Stress

The body's first line of defense against invading substances and microorganisms is the immune system. Components of the immune system kill of inactivate foreign or harmful substances in the body such as viruses, bacteria, and cancer cells. If the immune system is impaired—by stressors, for example—a person is left more vulnerable to colds, mononucleosis, and many other infectious diseases. Disabling of the immune system is the process by which the human immunodeficiency virus (HIV) leads to AIDS and leaves the HIV-infected person defenseless against infections or cancers. The activity of immune system cells can be either strengthened or inhibited by a number of systems, including the endocrine system and the central and autonomic nervous systems. It is through these connections that stress-related psychological and emotional factors can affect the functioning of the immune system. The precise mechanisms by which the nervous system affects the immune system are not yet fully understood. But there is evidence that the brain can influence the immune system indirectly by altering the secretion of hormones that modify circulating T-cells and B-cells and directly by making connections with the immune organs, such as the thymus, where T-cells and B-cells are stored[4]. Researchers have shown convincingly that people under stress are more likely than their less stressed counterparts to develop infectious diseases and to experience reactivation of latent viruses responsible for oral herpes (cold sores) or genital herpes[5]. The relationship between stress and the immune system is especially important in persons who are HIV-positive but do not yet have AIDS. Their immune systems are already seriously compromised, so further stress-related decrements could be life threatening. Recent research indicates that psychological stressors are associated with the progression of HIV-related illnesses.

Stress and Cardiovascular Disease

One of the most important causes of death is cardiovascular diseases—diseases of the heart and the blood vessels. Cardiovascular diseases can cause heart attacks and strokes; heart attacks occur when the blood vessels that serve the heart become blocked, while strokes involve the blood vessels in the brain. The two most important risk factors in cardiovascular disease are high blood pressure and a high level of cholesterol in the blood. The degree to which people react to potential stressors may affect the likelihood that they will suffer from cardiovascular disease. For example, Wood examined the blood pressure of people who had been subjected to a cold pressor test in 1934, when they were children. The cold pressor test reveals how people's blood pressure reacts to the stress caused by their hand being placed in a container of ice water for 1 minute. Wood and his colleagues found that 70 percent of the subjects who hyperreacted to cold pressor test when they were children had high blood pressure, compared with 19 percent of whose who showed little reaction to the rest. A study with monkeys showed that individual differences in emotional reactivity are a risk factor for cardiovascular disease. Manuck fed a high-cholesterol diet to a group of monkeys, which increase the likelihood of their developing coronary artery disease. They measured the animals' emotional reactivity by threatening to capture the animals. (Monkeys avoid contact with humans, and they perceive being captured as a stressful situation.) The animals who showed the strongest negative reactions eventually developed the highest rates of coronary artery disease. Presumably, these animals reacted more strongly to all types of stressors, and their reactions had detrimental effects on their health. Apparently, at least some of the differences in emotional reactivity displayed by individual animals are caused by genetic differences in brain chemistry and function.

In fact, a wide variety of stress—producing events in a person's life can increase the susceptibility to illness.

Words and Expressions

hostility	n.	[hɔs'tiliti]	敌意;恶意;不友善
pessimism	n.	['pesimizm]	悲观;悲观主义
contagious	adj.	[kən'teidʒəs]	传染性的
smallpox	n.	['smɔːlpɔks]	天花
typhoid	n.	['taifɔid]	伤寒症
diphtheria	n.	[dif'θiəriə]	白喉
malaria	n.	[m'ɔləriə]	疟疾
cholera	n.	['kɔlərə]	霍乱
tuberculosis	n.	[tjuˌbəːkju'ləusis]	肺结核
polio	n.	['pəuliəu]	脊髓灰质炎;小儿麻痹症
sanitation	n.	[sæni'teiʃən]	卫生;卫生设施
void	n.	[vɔid]	空间;空旷
practitioner	n.	[præk'tiʃnəə]	从业者;开业者
anthropology	n.	[ˌænθrə'pɔlədʒi]	人类学
formidable	adj.	['fɔːmidəbl]	强大的;令人敬畏的
nausea	n.	['nɔːsjə]	反胃;晕船;恶心
nervousness	n.	['nəːvəsnis]	神经过敏
catastrophe	n.	[kə'tæstrəfi]	大灾难;大祸
hassle	n./v.	['hæsl]	激战
tornado	n.	[tɔː'neidəu]	旋风;龙卷风,
torture	n.	['tɔːtʃə]	折磨;痛苦
catabolic	adj.	[ˌkætə'bɔlik]	分解代谢的;异化的
epinephrine	n.	[ˌepi'nefrin]	肾上腺素
glucose	n.	['fluːkəus]	葡萄糖

norepinephrine	n.	['nɔˌrepi'nefrin]	去甲肾上腺素
cardiovascular	adj.	[ˌkɑːdiəu'væskjulə]	心脏血管的
microorganism	n.	[maikrəu'ɔːgəniz(ə)m]	微生物
mononucleosis	n.	[ˌmɔnəuˌnjuːkli'əusis]	单核细胞增多症
thymus	n.	['θaiməs]	胸腺
herpes	n.	['həːpiːz]	疱疹
decrement	n.	['dekrimənt]	消耗
pressor	n.	['presə]	增压物质
cholesterol	n.	[kɔ'lestərəul]	胆固醇
coronary	adj.	[səˌseptə'biliti]	冠的;花冠的;冠状的

contagious disease	接触传染病
chronic disease	慢性病
health psychology	健康心理学
adrenal gland	肾上腺
blood pressure	血压
immune system	免疫系统
human immunodeficiency virus (HIV)	人体免疫缺陷病毒;艾滋病病毒
AIDS (Acquired immune deficiency system)	艾滋病;获得性免疫缺陷综合症
cardiovascular disease	心血管病
coronary artery disease	冠心病

Difficult Sentences

① Health psychology is related to a broader interdisciplinary field called behavioral medicine, whose goals are essentially the same as those of health psychology: using knowledge from the behavioral sciences to promote scientific understanding of health and illness.
健康心理学涉及一门更广阔的跨学科领域即行为医学,其目标

根本上与健康心理学相同:利用行为科学的知识提高对健康与疾病的理解。

② Stress is the process that occurs as individuals adjust to or deal with environmental circumstances that disrupt, or threaten to disrupt, their physical or psychological functioning.

压力指个体适应或应付能够干扰或即将干扰身体或心理机能周围的环境的过程。

③ Still, the events and situations most likely to be associated with stress are unpleasant ones—those involving daily hassles and frustrations, negative life changes and stains, and catastrophes.

尽管如此,有可能与压力有关的事件和情况是令人不愉快的——包括日常争论、挫折、负面的人生变化与污点以及大灾难。

④ But there is evidence that the brain can influence the immune system indirectly by altering the secretion of hormones that modify circulating T-cells and B-cells and directly by making connections with the immune organs, such as the thymus, where T-cells and B-cells are stored.

有证据显示大脑能通过改变荷尔蒙的分泌间接影响免疫系统,荷尔蒙的分泌能更改 T 细胞和 B 细胞,还通过接通免疫器官如:储备 T 细胞和 B 细胞的胸腺来直接影响免疫系统。

⑤ Researchers have shown convincingly that people under stress are more likely than their less stressed counterparts to develop infectious diseases and to experience reactivation of latent viruses responsible for oral herpes (cold sores) or genital herpes.

研究者令人信服地表明处在压力下的人比压力小的人更易得传染病并更易再次感染口疮或生殖器疱疹的潜伏性病毒。

Phrases and Patterns

1. ... scientific evidence for ... has been documented ……的科学依据已有文献记载

Today, scientific evidence for this belief has been documented.
现今,该理念的科学依据已有文献记载。

2. lie in 在于

The answer appears to lie in mediating factors that influence the transaction between people and their environments.
答案就在于影响人与环境之间各项事务的中介因素。

Note that these findings lie in the realm of social psychology because they study influences on social behavior, even though these influences do not come from other people.
要注意的是这些发现存在于社会心理学领域,因为他们研究对社会行为的影响,尽管这些影响不是来自其他人。

3. be vulnerable to 易受……的攻击

If the immune system is impaired—by stressors, for example—a person is left more vulnerable to colds, mononucleosis, and many other infectious diseases.
例如,如果一个人的免疫系统受到紧张性刺激的侵害,那么他就易患感冒、单核细胞增多症和许多其他传染病。

10.2 Stress and Personality
压力与人格

Some of the stress-mediating factors reflect enduring cognitive habits, individual differences in how people think about stressors and the world in general. Cognitive habits often seen as part of hardy personalities appear to help insulate people from the ill effects of stress, while others, often seen in disease-prone personalities, may leave people especially vulnerable to those effects[①]. One component of hardy personality seems to be dispositional optimism, belief or expectancy that things will work out positively. Optimistic students, for example, experience fewer physical symptoms at the end of the academic term, and optimistic coronary bypass surgery patients have been shown to heal faster than pessimists and to perceive their quality of life following coronary surgery to be higher than those with less optimistic outlooks. Optimism might provide a stress-buffering effect. Among HIV-positive gay men, for example, dispositional optimism has been associated with lower psychological distress, fewer worries, and lower perceived risk of acquiring full-blown AIDS. These effects appear due in part to optimists' tendency to use challenge-oriented, problem-focused coping strategies that attack stressors directly, whereas pessimists use emotion-focused coping such as denial and avoidance[2]. Another study of HIV-positive gay men showed that active coping strategies <u>are associated with</u> improved functioning of the immune system. Do more optimistic people live longer overall? The results would suggest just that, but a seventy-year longitudinal study found that children who were optimistic in childhood actually tended to die younger than their more pessimistic age-mates. The measures optimism used in that study were different from those used today, so this result should be interpreted with caution. Still, it suggests that factors in addition to optimism are probably important in surviving the effects of life's stressors.

 People who tend to think of stressors as temporary and who do not always blame themselves for the onset of stressors appear to be harmed less by them. This cognitive stance can be quite adaptive, especially when combined with a challenge orientation. Its benefits can also be seen, however, among many devout people whose religious beliefs prompt them to think of poverty, disease, and other objective stressors, not as challenges to be overcome, but as temporary conditions to be endured until their suffering is rewarded. There is also a flip side to these relationships between cognitive patterns and vulnerability to stress. That is, stress-related health problems tend to be more common among people who persist at mentally evading stressors; who perceive them as long-term, catastrophic threats that they brought on themselves; and who are pessimistic about their ability to overcome the stressors[③]. In short, individual differences in how stressors are perceived and interpreted can combine with emotional and other factors to increase or decrease vulnerability to mental and physical problems. Our review of personality and other factors that can alter the impact of stressors should make it obvious that what is stressful for a given individual is not determined simply by predispositions, coping styles, or situations. What seems most important are interactions between the person and the situation, the mixture of each individual's resources and the specific characteristics of the situations encountered. The potentially fatal impact of stressors lies primarily in their ability to alter physiological arousal. A moderate level of arousal may improve a person's ability to perform a task, but overarousal or underarousal can interfere with the efficient processing of information and with performance. Overarousal is also dangerous because, as arousal increases above a moderate level, it is the performance of complex and difficult task—such as dealing with aircraft emergencies—that is most likely to be disrupted. Why? One reason is that increased arousal strengthens the tendency to perform behaviors that are most dominant, the ones a person knows best. This reaction may aid performance of an easy, familiar task like riding a bike; but on more difficult or unfamiliar tasks, the well-learned behaviors elicited by overarousal may not be the right ones. For example, when overaroused by frustration or time pressure, American tourists in countries where cars are driven on the left side of the road, such as Britain or Japan, tend to revert to their old habit of entering the right-hand lane as they make right turns. This tendency causes numerous head-on collisions each year. Overarousal created by stressors also impairs performance on difficult tasks by interfering with people's ability to think clearly about complex material. For one thing, it tends to narrow the range of attention. The consequent inability to scan a wide range of creative solutions may add to the time needed to solve problems or reason efficiently. Stress-narrowed attention may intensify difficulties with problem solving on thought and language. For example, stress can accentuate the tendency to cling to mental sets, which are well established, though possibly inefficient, approaches to problem. More specifically, stress can intensify functional fixedness, which is the tendency to use objects for only one purpose. Decision making may also suffer when people face stressors. People who normally consider carefully all aspects of a situation before making a decision may, under stress, act impulsively and sometimes foolishly. Couples whose dating relationships have been full of conflict may suddenly decide to break up and then, just as suddenly, get married. High-pressure salespeople try to take advantage of people's tendency to act impulsively when under the influence of stressors by creating artificially time-limited offers or by telling customers that others are waiting to buy the item they are considering. Research on the links among stress, thinking, and performance has helped to highlight the importance of reducing the stress under which people perform complex tasks. For years, commercial pilots have been limited in the number of hours they may fly per day, and air-traffic controllers are encouraged to take breaks every two hours. But sometimes, as when an engine is on fire or a nuclear reactor malfunctions, extreme stress is inevitable.

Autism

When a child is born, the parents normally expect to love and cherish it and to be loved and cherished in return. Unfortunately, approximately 4 in every 10 000 infants are born with a disorder that impairs their ability to return their parents' affection. The symptoms of autistic disorder include a failure to develop normal social relations with other people, impaired development of communicative ability, and lack of imaginative ability. The syndrome was named and characterized by Kanner, who chose the term (auto, "self", -ism, "condition") to refer to the child's apparent self-absorption[④]. The disorder afflicts boys three times more often than girls. Infants with autistic disorder do not seem to care if they are held, or they may arch their backs when picked up, as if they do not want to be held. They do not look or smile at their caregivers. If they are ill, hurt, or tired, they will not look to someone else for comfort. As they get older, they do not enter into social relationships with other children and avoid eye contact with them. Their language development is abnormal or even nonexistent. They often echo what is said to them, and they may refer to themselves as others do—in the second or third person. For example, they may say, "You want some milk?" to mean "I want some milk". They may learn words and phrases by rote, but they fail to use them productively and creatively. Those who do acquire reasonably good language skills talk about their own preoccupations, without regard for other people's interests. They usually interpret other people's speech literally. For example, when an autistic person is asked, "Can you pass the salt?" he may simply say "Yes" and not because he is trying to be funny or sarcastic. Autistic people generally show abnormal interests and behaviors. For example, they may show stereotyped movements, such as flapping their hand back and forth or rocking back and forth. They may become obsessed with investigating objects, sniffing them, feeling their texture, or moving them back and forth. They may become attached to a particular object and insist on carrying it around with them. They may become preoccupied in lining up objects or in forming patterns with them, oblivious to everything else that is going on about them. They often insist on following precise routines and may become violently upset when they are hindered from doing so. They show no make-believe play and are uninterested in stories that involve fantasy. Although most autistic people are mentally retarded, not all are; and unlike most retarded people, they may be physically adept and graceful[5]. Some have isolated skills, such as the ability to multiply two four-digit numbers very quickly, without apparent effort. As you can see, autistic disorder includes affective, cognitive, and behavioral abnormalities. Frith, Morion, and Leslie suggest that the impaired socialization, communicative ability, and imagination that characterize autism stem from abnormalities in the brain that prevent the person from forming a "theory of mind". That is, the person is unable "to predict and explain the behavior of other humans in terms of their mental states". He or she just cannot see things from another person's point of view. As one autistic man complained, "Other people seem to have a special sense by which they can read other people's thoughts".

Possible Causes

When Kanner first described autism, he suggested that it was of biological origin; but not long afterward, influential clinicians argued that autism was learned. More precisely, it was taught—by cold, insensitive, distant, demanding, introverted parents. Bettelheim believed that autism was similar to the apathetic, withdrawn, and hopeless behavior. Some professionals saw the existence of autism as evidence for child abuse and advocated that autistic children be removed from their families and placed with faster parents. Nowadays, researchers and mental health professionals almost universally believe that autism is caused by biological factors and that parents should be given help and sympathy, not blame. Careful studies have shown that the parents of autistic children are just as warm, sociable, and responsive as other parents. In addition, parents with one autistic child often raise one or more normal children. If the parents were at fault, we should expect all of their offspring to be autistic.

Heritability

Some forms of autism appear to be heritable. As we shall see, there appear to be several hereditary causes, as well as some nonhereditary ones. Between 2 and 3 percent of the siblings of people with autism are themselves autistic. That figure may seem low, but it between 50 and 100 times the expected frequency of autism in the general population (4 cases per 10 000 people). As Jones and Szatmari noted, many parents stopped having children after an autistic child is born for fear of having another one with the same disorder; if they did not, the percentage of autistic siblings would be even larger. The best evidence for genetic factors in autism comes from twin studies. These studies indicate that the concordance rate for monozygotic twins is as high as 96 percent, while the rate for dizygotic twins appears to be no higher than that for normal siblings. This difference is extremely large and indicates that autism is highly heritable. It also implies that autism is caused by a combination of several genes. Folstein and Piven also report that in the relatively few cases of monozygotic twins who are discordant for autism, the affected member was likely to have had a history of obstetric complications. This finding suggests that like schizophrenia and obsessive-compulsive disorder, autism can be caused by both hereditary and nonhereditary factors. Investigators have suggested that autism is associated with some specific genetic disorders, such as phenylketonuria, Tourette's syndrome, and fragile X syndrome. Phenylketonuria (PKU) is caused by an inherited lack of an enzyme that converts phenylalanine (an amino acid) into tyrosine (another amino acid). Excessive amounts of phenylalanine in the blood interfere with the myelinization of neurons in the central nervous system, much of which takes place after birth. When PKU is diagnosed soon after birth, it can be treated by putting the infant on a low-phenylalanine diet. The diet keeps the blood level of phenylalanine low, and myelinization of the central nervous system takes place normally. However, if PKU is not diagnosed and an infant born with this disorder receives foods containing phenylalanine, the amino acid accumulates and the brain fails to develop normally. The result is a severe mental retardation—and, in some cases, autism. Obsessive-compulsive disorder and Tourette's syndrome appear to be linked genetically. The same may be true for autism.

Words and Expressions

stressor	n.	['stresə]	[心]紧张性刺激
insulate	v.	['insjuleit]	使绝缘;隔离
prone	adj.	[prəun]	倾向于
vulnerable	adj.	['vʌlnərəb(ə)l]	易受攻击的;易受……的攻击
outlook	n.	['autluk]	景色;风光;观点;见解;展望;前景
buffer	n.	['bʌfə]	缓冲器
distress	n.	[dis'tres]	悲痛;穷困;不幸;危难;忧伤
longitudinal	adj.	[lɔndʒi'tju:dinl]	经度的;纵向的
onset	n.	['ɔnset]	攻击;进攻;有力的开始;肇端;[医]发作
stance	n.	[stæns]	姿态
devout	adj.	[di'vaut]	虔敬的;诚恳的
flip	adj.	[flip]	无礼的;冒失的;轻率的
predisposition	n.	[pri:dispə'ziʃən]	易患病的体质
elicit	v.	[i'lisit]	得出;引出;抽出;引起
revert	v.	[ri'və:t]	回复
impair	v.	[im'pɛə]	削弱
accentuate	v.	[æk'sentjueit]	重读;强调;着重强调

reactor	n.	[ri(ː)ˈæktə]	反应堆
autism	n.	[ˈɔːtizəm]	[心]自我中心主义;孤独症
arch	v.	[ɑːtʃ]	(使)弯成弓形
rote	n.	[rəut]	死记硬背;机械的做法;生搬硬套
preoccupation	n.	[pri(ː)ˌɔkjuˈpeiʃən]	当务之急
obsess	v.	[əbˈses]	迷住;使困扰
retard	v.	[riˈtɑːd]	延迟;使减速;阻止;妨碍;阻碍
adept	adj.	[əˈdept]	熟练的;拿手的
clinician	n.	[kliˈniʃən]	[医]临床医生;临床教师
apathetic	adj.	[ˌæpəˈθetik]	缺乏兴趣的;缺乏感情的;无动于衷的
heritability	n.	[ˌheritəˈbiləti]	遗传可能性
sibling	n.	[ˈsibliŋ]	兄弟;姐妹;同胞;同属
concordance	n.	[kənˈkɔːdəns]	和谐
monozygotic	adj.	[ˌmɔnəzaiˈgɔtik]	[动]单卵的;单精合子的
dizygotic	adj.	[ˌdaizaiˈgɔtik]	[生]两合子的;两受精卵的
discordant	adj.	[disˈkɔːdənt]	不调和的;不和的;[乐]不悦耳的;不和谐的
obstetric	adj.	[ɔbsˈtetrik]	产科的
schizophrenia	n.	[ˌskizəuˈfriːniə]	[心]精神分裂症
phenylketonuria	n.	[ˌfenəlˌkiːtəˈnjuəriə]	[医]苯丙酮尿;苯丙酮酸尿症(一种先天性代谢异常)
enzyme	n.	[ˈenzim]	[生化]酶
phenylalanine	n.	[ˌfenəlˈæləniːn]	苯基丙氨酸
amino	adj.	[ˈæminəu]	[化]氨基的
tyrosine	n.	[ˈtirəsiːn]	[生化]酪氨酸
myelinization	n.	[ˌmaiəlinaiˈzeiʃən]	髓鞘化;髓鞘形成

| diagnose | v. | [ˈdaiəgnəuz] | 诊断 |
| retardation | n. | [ˌriːtɑːˈdeiʃən] | 延迟 |

Difficult Sentences

① Cognitive habits often seen as part of hardy personalities appear to help insulate people from the ill effects of stress, while others, often seen in disease-prone personalities, may leave people especially vulnerable to those effects.

常见于勇敢性格的认知习惯似乎可以帮助人们免受压力的负面影响;而常见于有疾病倾向性格的其他习惯也许使人们特别易受疾病影响。

② These effects appear due in part to optimists' tendency to use challenge-oriented, problem-focused coping strategies that attack stressors directly, whereas pessimists use emotion-focused coping such as denial and avoidance.

出现这些影响,部分是由于乐观主义者倾向于用挑战的、问题焦点的处理技巧去直接面对紧张性刺激;然而悲观主义者却用否定和逃避等情感中心的方法去处理它。

③ That is, stress-related health problems tend to be more common among people who persist at mentally evading stressors; who perceive them as long-term, catastrophic threats that they brought on themselves; and who are pessimistic about their ability to overcome the stressors.

也就是说压力引起的健康问题更容易出现在以下三种人群中,一种人总是从内心逃避紧张性刺激;一种人认为紧张性刺激是他们自己带给自己的长期的、灾难性的威胁;还有一种人对自己克服紧张性刺激的能力总是抱以悲观的态度。

④ The symptoms of autistic disorder include a failure to develop normal social relations with other people, impaired development of communicative ability, and lack of imaginative ability. The syndrome was named and characterized by Kanner, who chose the term (auto, "self", -ism, "condition") to refer to the child's apparent self-absorption.

孤独症的症状包括不能与其他人发展正常的社会关系,交际能力薄弱以及缺乏想象力。这种症状是由 Kanner 命名和描述的,他选用表示自我的"auto"和表示情况的"ism"合成"autism"来指儿童明显的自闭症。

⑤ Although most autistic people are mentally retarded, not all are; and unlike most retarded people, they may be physically adept and graceful.

尽管大多数孤独症患者是智力迟钝的,但不是所有孤独症患者都是这样;相反与之形成鲜明对比的是,有些孤独症患者在身体某些方面是超常熟练和突出。

Phrases and Patterns

1. be associated with... 与……发生联系
   Another study of HIV-positive gay men showed that active coping strategies are associated with improved functioning of the immune system.
   另一个对 HIV 阳性并快乐的人的研究表明,积极处理问题的策略与免疫系统的改良机能有关。
   Investigators have suggested that autism is associated with some specific genetic disorders, such as phenylketonuria, Tourette's syndrome, and fragile X syndrome.
   调查者认为孤独症与苯丙酮酸尿症、Tourette 症状和脆弱的 X 症状等特殊的基因无序有关。
2. interfere with... 干涉;干扰
   A moderate level of arousal may improve a person's ability to perform a task, but overarousal or underarousal can interfere with the efficient processing of information and with performance.

适当水平的激励也许能提高一个人完成任务的能力,但是过度激励和低度激励却干扰有效的信息处理和任务完成过程。
Excessive amounts of phenylalanine in the blood interfere with the myelinization of neurons in the central nervous system, much of which takes place after birth.
血液中过量的苯基丙氨酸可以干扰中央神经系统神经元的髓鞘形成,这种干扰大多发生在出生后。

3. back and forth 来来往往地;来回地
For example, they may show stereotyped movements, such as flapping their hand back and forth or rocking back and forth.
例如,他们也许表现出如来回拍打手掌或者来回摇摆身子等孤独症患者典型的行为。
They may become obsessed with investigating objects, sniffing them, feeling their texture, or moving them back and forth.
他们也许会沉迷于反复研究某些物体,用鼻子闻它们,触摸它们的质地,或者来回舞动它们。

10.3 Initiation and Maintenance of Health Behaviors
启动及维持健康行为

The Health Action Process Approach (HAPA) has made important contributions to understanding health behavior change through emphasizing the distinction between motivational and volitional influences on behavior and focusing attention on maintenance as well as initiation of health behaviors[①]. The present commentary draws out a number of issues in relation to the contribution of the HAPA to our understanding of health behaviors. Five issues are highlighted: What are the key motivational influences on behavior? What are the key volitional influences on behavior? How does recent research on intention-behavior moderators provide further insights into volitional influences on health behaviors? What are the problems of blurring a distinction between continuum and stage models as is done in the HAPA? What is the value of a distinction between initiation and maintenance of a health behavior?

Introduction

Schwarzer's review of modeling health behavior change raises a number of important issues in relation to how we predict and change the initiation and maintenance of health behaviors. The review particularly focuses on the Health Action Process Approach (HAPA) and its contribution to understanding in this area. Prominently this work emphasizes a distinction between motivational and volitional influences on behavior. In the motivational "phase", the HAPA emphasizes self-efficacy, outcome expectancies, risk perceptions, and intentions. This is consistent with various overviews of the key determinants of various health behaviors, although other accounts tend to consider risk perceptions as more distal determinants of behavior. In the volitional "phase" the HAPA emphasizes the importance of self-efficacy, action planning, and coping planning. This is perhaps where the contribution of the HAPA is most novel as few other comprehensive models of the volitional influences on behavior have achieved prominence. The presented evidence appears to provide good support for a focus on these particular volitional variables, although as Schwarzer notes there are a number of other volitional variables that might be considered here. The visual presentation of the model emphasizes important differences between initiation, maintenance, and relapse recovery, although this aspect of the model is not a focus of the present article. These are important and useful contributions to our understanding of the initiation and maintenance of health behaviors. The present commentary draws out a number of issues in relation to the contribution of the HAPA to our understanding of health behaviors. Five such issues are highlighted: What are the key motivational influences on behavior? What are the key volitional influences on behavior? How does research on intention-behavior moderators help identify key volitional influences? What are the problems of blurring a distinction between continuum and stage models? and What is the distinction between initiation and maintenance?

Key Motivational Influences on Behavior

Considerable research effort has been devoted to identifying the key determinants of health behaviors. Much of this research has focused on motivational factors and a number of the prominent models in this area show considerable overlap in terms of the key determinants included. Most consistent evidence supports important roles for self-efficacy, outcome expectancies, and goal intentions as determinants of health behaviors.

The motivational phase of Schwarzer's HAPA shows most close resemblance to Bandura's Social Cognitive Theory (SCT), although there is also a degree of overlap with models such as the Theory of Planned Behavior (TPB). Neither of these models places as much emphasis on risk perceptions which have generally been found to be more distal determinants of intentions and behavior and/or been treated as outcome expectancies. The operationalisation of the HAPA indicates that different types of outcome expectancies are worth distinguishing (positive and negative), although there tends to be a focus on positive outcome expectancies. Research with the TPB has shown social outcome expectancies (normative beliefs) to be important predictors of at least some health behaviors, while other research suggests the value of assessing both positive and negative outcome expectancies and distinguishing between instrumental and affective outcomes[2]. A novel aspect of the HAPA is the distinguishing among different types of self-efficacy. However, there are, as yet, only a few studies that have made this distinction, with the vast majority of research focusing on "action" self-efficacy. It remains for further research to confirm the value of distinguishing types of self-efficacy in the way data from the HAPA would suggest rather than adopting the more parsimonious approach of considering a single type of self-efficacy. One can imagine that similar types of intentions, outcome expectancies, and risk perceptions could be distinguished and provide some additional predictive power, although the resulting model might be open to criticism in terms of lack of parsimony.

Thus while the HAPA clearly identifies some of the key determinants of health behavior in the motivational phase, other variables may also be important while the emphasis on risk perceptions is less strongly supported in the literature.

Key Volitional Influences on Behavior

One of the important contributions of the HAPA has been to focus attention on the importance of volitional variables. Such variables come into play once the decision (intention) to act has been made. The HAPA focuses attention on self-efficacy and planning, and Schwarzer's paper presents a number of studies to support the role of these variables. Planning can take a number of forms and different forms may have different levels of effectiveness for individuals and behaviors. Even very specific plans like implementation intentions (the forming of if-then plans) have not shown universal effectiveness. Unfortunately the science of volition is not yet as advanced as that of motivation. Volitional models identify a wide range of variables that might be important in translating intentions into action and it is not yet clear that self-efficacy and planning are necessarily the key variables, although they do appear to be likely candidates. Volitional processes that enable an individual to maintain a strong intention to act (i. e. intention stability) may represent another good candidate.

Moderators of the Intention-Behavior Relationship

A significant body of work in recent years has examined the role of moderators of the intention-behavior relationship (i. e. variables that influence the magnitude of relationships between intention and behavior). The value of this work for applied researchers lies in identifying when there is or is not an "intention-behavior gap". From a theoretical perspective, such moderators may help elucidate the volitional variables important in translating intentions into action.

A range of moderator variables have been examined. These include anticipated regret, moral norms, past behavior, accessibility, direct experience, involvement, certainty, ambivalence, affective-cognitive consistency, temporal stability, and conscientiousness. For example, anticipated regret has been posited as a moderator of intention-behavior relationships on the basis that high levels of regret may bind people to their intentions and so strengthen their intentions because failing to act would be associated with aversive affect③. Several studies have demonstrated this effect in relation to exercising and smoking initiation. Abraham and Sheeran also reported a similar moderating effect of anticipated regret on exercise intention-behavior relationships. Impressively, a second study by these authors manipulated regret and demonstrated similar moderation effects. Temporal stability appears to be a particularly important moderator of intentions' relationship with behavior. In the Cooke and Sheeran review it emerged as the strongest moderator. As Ajzen has argued, "to obtain accurate prediction of behavior, intentions... must remain reasonably stable over time until the behavior is performed". Intentions measured prior to performance of a behavior may change as a result of new information or unforeseen obstacles resulting in a reduced predictive power. The moderating role of temporal stability of intentions has been addressed in several recent studies of health behaviors. Conner, Sheeran, Norman, and Armitage found intention stability moderation effects for both attending health screening and eating a low fat diet. In both cases, intentions were stronger predictors of behavior when intentions were stable. Conner et al. showed intentions stability to show moderation effects for smoking initiation. In addition, Conner, Norman, and Bell demonstrated similar effects for intention stability for healthy eating over a period of six years. Sheeran and Abraham showed intention stability to both moderate the intention-behavior relationship for exercising and importantly to mediate the impacts of various other moderators of the intention-behavior relationship (e.g. anticipated regret, certainty, etc.). This suggests that a number of these other moderators may have their effect on intention-behavior relationships through changing the temporal stability of intentions. It seems likely that intentions to act must remain stable in any "volitional phase" of action and so identification of the volitional factors promoting intention stability is important. Nevertheless, the stability of intentions is an emergent property of an individual's intention and subsequent research may well show it to be dependent on other more directly modifiable aspects of intentions (e.g. prioritising one particular intention/goal over other competing intentions/goals).

A final moderator of intention-behavior relationships that might help elucidate key volitional variables is the personality dimension of conscientiousness. Three studies have examined this relationship. Conner et al. reported conscientiousness to moderate the impact of intentions to exercise on exercise behavior, but only for exercise completed in non-usual weeks. Similarly, Rhodes et al. reported conscientiousness to significantly moderate the intention-exercise behavior relationship, with higher levels of conscientiousness associated with stronger intention-behavior relationships. Based on these findings, future research might usefully examine the strategies conscientious individuals use to enact their health behavior intentions. For example, do conscientious individuals simply try harder, are they less distracted, and/or do they formulate clearer plans? Clearer planning would be consistent with the focus Schwarzer's work suggested. Rhodes et al. similarly suggest the value of goal-setting and time management interventions with those low in conscientiousness. Rhodes et al.'s finding that it was the industriousness-ambition facet of conscientiousness that moderated the intention-behavior relationship rather than the orderliness or reliability facets is also relevant④. The industriousness-ambition facet is most closely linked to planning.

Distinguishing Between Continuum and Stage Models

As Schwarzer notes, the key distinction between continuum and stage models is that in continuum models there is a linear relationship between predictor variables and action; while in stage models there is no such necessary linear relationship, different variables may predict progression at different stages. Schwarzer appears to suggest that the HAPA, in specifying phases of action, can take on characteristics of both a continuum and stage model. In relation to a continuum model, it has been noted that the HAPA possesses a number of similarities to the TPB and that it might be useful to formally test the predictive power of the two. In relation to a stage model, it has been suggested that the HAPA implies that it is useful to specify at least *three* stages: (a) a pre-intentional stage, in which the person has not formed an intention with respect to the target behavior; (b) a post-intentional, pre-actional (or planning) stage, in which the person has formed an intention to perform the target behavior; and (c) an actional stage, in which the person has initiated the behavior, although Sutton goes on to criticise the HAPA for not specifying the factors that determine stage transition. Given these important differences between continuum and stage models the value of introducing a half-way category of "phase models" that possess the characteristics of continuum and stage models depending on how they are tested is questionable[5].

Distinctions Between Initiation and Maintenance of Health Behaviors

The HAPA and other stage models have played an important role in emphasizing the differences between initiation and maintenance of a health behavior. Much research in this area has focused on initiation. This is quite appropriate for behaviors where the health benefits are associated with one off performance (e. g. immunisation). However, for some health behaviors (e. g. healthy eating, exercise) there is little or no health benefit unless the behavior is maintained over a prolonged period of time and initiation may be necessary but not sufficient for these health benefits to accrue. For such maintenance behaviors we need to try to understand and predict the factors which determine maintenance over prolonged periods of time. Similar to the development of theories in relation to volitional influences on behavior, there is as yet rather limited development of theories in relation to maintenance of health behaviors. However, it is worth noting that the need to distinguish initiation and maintenance is a key component of various stage models.

A limited number of theories suggest that different factors may be important in the decision to initiate a behavior compared to the decision to maintain a behavior. These theories specify that either different factors or the same factors acting via different processes may be important in determining the decision to initiate or maintain a behavior. For example, satisfaction with the outcome of the behavior (e. g. quit smoking) may be important in the decision to maintain, but not initiate, a behavior. In contrast, self-efficacy may be an important determinant of both initiation and maintenance behaviors but may act in different ways or be of different types. Also, the extent to which the motivation to perform the behavior is internalised is suggested to be key to maintenance in Self-Determination Theory. Finally, the importance of how lapses are dealt with is a key component of the Relapse Prevention Model and is a further aspect emphasized in the HAPA.

The HAPA has made a useful contribution here in emphasizing some of the factors important in relation to initiation, maintenance, and recovery from relapse. However, further research is required, particularly in relation to maintenance and relapse recovery. Although several key factors have been highlighted (e. g. self-efficacy), others may remain. In addition, we need clearer theoretical accounts of how these variables interact to produce maintenance of a health behavior including the processes important in recovery from a relapse in a behavior.

Words and Expressions

initiation	n.	[iˌniʃiˈeiʃən]	开始
maintenance	n.	[ˈmeintinəns]	维护;保持
motivational	adj.	[ˌməutiˈveiʃənəl]	动机的;有关动机的
volitional	adj.	[vəuˈliʃənəl]	意志的
commentary	n.	[ˈkɔməntəri]	评论;评述
moderator	n.	[ˈmɔdəreitə]	调解者
blur	v.	[blə:]	把(界线)弄得模糊不清
prominently	adv.	[ˈprɔminəntli]	显著地
expectancy	n.	[ikˈspektənsi]	期待;期望
determinant	n.	[diˈtə:minənt]	决定性因素
distal	adj.	[ˈdistəl]	末梢的
relapse	n.	[riˈlæps]	回复原状

normative	adj.	[ˈnɔːmətiv]	标准化的
affective	adj.	[əˈfektiv]	情感的
parsimonious	adj.	[ˌpɑːsiˈməunjəs]	吝啬的；节俭的
implementation	n.	[ˌimplimenˈteiʃən]	执行
elucidate	v.	[iˈljuːsideit]	阐明；说明
ambivalence	n.	[æmˈbivələns]	正反感情并存
temporal	n.	[ˈtempərəl]	当时的；暂时的
conscientiousness	n.	[ˌkɔnʃiˈenʃəsnis]	尽责
posit	v.	[ˈpɔzit]	安置
bind	v.	[baind]	约束
aversive	adj.	[əˈvəːsiv]	令人嫌恶的
impressively	adv.	[imˈpresivli]	令人难忘地
mediate	v.	[ˈmiːdieit]	仲裁；调停
prioritise	v.	[praiˈɔritaiz]	把……区分优先次序
enact	v.	[iˈnækt]	扮演
facet	n.	[ˈfæsit]	方面
linear	adj.	[ˈliniə]	线的；直线的；线性的
immunization	n.	[ˈimjuːnaizeiʃən]	免疫性
internalise	v.	[inˈtəːnlaiz]	使成为主观

Difficult Sentences

① The Health Action Process Approach (HAPA) has made important contributions to understanding health behavior change through emphasizing the distinction between motivational and volitional influences on behavior and focusing attention on maintenance as well as initiation of health behaviors.
通过强调动机和意志对行为的影响的区别及关注开始并维持健康行为，健康行动过程法(HAPA)对于我们了解健康行为变化做出了重要贡献。

② Research with the TPB has shown social outcome expectancies (normative beliefs) to be important predictors of at least some health behaviors, while other research suggests the value of assessing both positive and negative outcome expectancies and distinguishing between instrumental and affective outcomes.

针对TPB做的研究显示:社会结果期待(标准化的信念)是预测至少某些健康行为的重要因素,而其他研究显示:评价正的和反的结果期待及区分功用的和情感的结果是很有价值的。

③ For example, anticipated regret has been posited as a moderator of intention-behavior relationships on the basis that high levels of regret may bind people to their intentions and so strengthen their intentions because failing to act would be associated with aversive affect.

例如,因为无作为往往与令人厌恶的情感联系在一起,高度的懊悔可能使人们更依附于他们的意图因而巩固他们的意图,因此意料中的懊悔一直被用来调解意图和行为的关系。

④ Rhodes et al.'s finding that it was the industriousness-ambition facet of conscientiousness that moderated the intention-behavior relationship rather than the orderliness or reliability facets is also relevant.

Rhodes等人发现:缓和了意图-行为关系的是尽职尽责的人所表现出的勤奋努力、充满抱负的一面,而不是他们做事有条理或可靠的一面。

⑤ Given these important differences between continuum and stage models the value of introducing a half-way category of "phase models" that possess the characteristics of continuum and stage models depending on how they are tested is questionable.

考虑到连续模式和阶段模式的重大差异,是否有必要引入一种介入中间的根据测试方式拥有连续模式和阶段模式两者的特征的"阶段性模式"还值得怀疑。

Phrases and Patterns

1. draw out 探讨

   The present commentary draws out a number of issues in relation to the contribution of the HAPA to our understanding of health behaviors.

   本篇评论探讨的几个问题与 HAPA 对我们了解健康行为做出的贡献有关。

   This paper draws out some teaching approaches in College English Teaching.

   这篇论文探讨几种大学英语教学方法。

2. provide further insights into... 使我们进一步了解了……

   How does recent research on intention-behavior moderators provide further insights into volitional influences on health behaviors?

   对于意图 - 行为调解因素的最近的研究是如何使我们更进一步了解意志对健康行为的影响的?

   Her autobiography provides further insight into the way government actually works.

   她的自传使我领悟到政府的实际运作方式。

3. It remains for further research to... 有待进一步研究……

   It remains for further research to confirm the value of distinguishing types of self-efficacy in the way data from the HAPA would suggest rather than adopting the more parsimonious approach of considering a single type of self-efficacy.

   根据 HAPA 所显示的数据来区分几种自我效验是否强于采纳只考虑单一一种自我效验的更省事的方法,还有待进一步研究。

   It remains for further research to confirm the extent to which human brain has been developed.

   人的大脑在多大程度上已被开发还有待进一步研究。

4. on the basis that/of 根据

Is it safe to predict the result on the basis of one opinion poll?
根据一次民意测验来预测结果可靠吗？

10.4 Changing Behavior Can Improve Your Health
改变行为能改善健康

The Chief Medical Officer for Northern Ireland has said this is the decade to encourage people to change their eating habits and lifestyles.

In his first report as Chief Medical Officer for Northern Ireland, Dr Michael McBride said: "While the health of the population is improving, not everyone is benefiting from these improvements."

Dr McBride said: "While health professionals and Government can help in bringing about improvements—all of us as individuals need to take control of our own behaviours and lifestyles, in order to make a real difference."

Commenting on the alarming rise in obesity Dr McBride said: "Over 20% of Primary One children are overweight or obese. Junk food and a lack of exercise are contributing to the problem. The importance of a healthy diet and taking more exercise is well recognized by all of us. We must act now to avoid a future where many of our children could face significant health problems such diabetes, heart disease and cancer."

Dr McBride welcomed the ban on smoking in public places saying: "It will save lives and protect the health of many workers. But we cannot be complacent as 350 000 people here are still smoking. Too many young people still smoke, Northern Ireland has the second highest percentage in Europe of 14 year olds who smoke. We must re-double our efforts to encourage people to kick the habit and avoid serious illness such as cancer and heart disease①."

In his Report, the Chief Medical Officer also highlighted a number of other significant health challenges including binge drinking, poor dental health, the rise in sexually transmitted infections, suicide and mental health saying: "These are issues which continue to challenge us in the medical professional and as a society."

Many of these issues and the resulting ill health and premature death have a disproportionate effect on people who live in the more deprived areas②. Dr McBride said: "Sadly where we live can have a major effect on our health and can determine how long we will live. Those in our community who live in the most deprived areas have the poorest health."

Words and Expressions

obesity	n.	[əuˈbisiti]	肥胖；肥大
diabetes	n.	[ˌdaiəˈbiːtiːz]	糖尿病；多尿症
highlight	v.	[ˈhailait]	使显著
premature	adj.	[ˌpreməˈtjuə]	太早的；未成熟的
disproportionate	adj.	[ˌdisprəˈpɔːʃənit]	不成比例

Difficult Sentences

① We must re-double our efforts to encourage people to kick the habit and avoid serious illness such as cancer and heart disease.
我们必须加倍努力鼓励人们戒除不良习惯，避免患癌症和心脏病那样的疾病。

② Many of these issues and the resulting ill health and premature death have a disproportionate effect on people who live in the more deprived areas.
许多这些问题以及由此导致的身体疾病和夭折对生活在缺乏食

物地区的人们有着极大的影响。

10.5　Psychology: Is It Applied Enough
心理学:它的应用是否足够

Pieter J. D. Drenth

Abstract

The question "Is psychology applied enough?" can be regarded in two ways. In the first place, it could refer to the distinction "pure versus applied science", and the reproach that modern scientific experimental psychology has little to offer to the practitioner. It is argued that this distinction has lost much of its topicality in modern science, and certainly with respect to psychology. In this sense "applied psychology" is an outmoded notion. Secondly, it could refer to the question whether psychology is utilised enough in dealing with the great many pressing problems in modern society. And it is shown that this question cannot be answered in the affirmative. Too often psychological aspects of problems escape notice and too often potential psychological contributions are neglected in governmental and organisational decision-making, also in cases where such a contribution would prove valuable indeed. A number of reasons for such a neglect are discussed and some ways of improvement are suggested.

Words and Expressions

reproach　　　　n.　　　[ri'prəutʃ]　　　　责备

practitioner	n.	[præk'tiʃənə]	从业者
topicality	n.	[tɔpi'kæliti]	时事性
outmoded	adj.	[aut'məudid]	过时的
notion	n.	['nəuʃən]	观念;想法
utilise	v.	['juːtilaiz]	利用
pressing	adj.	['presiŋ]	紧迫的
affirmative	adj.	[ə'fəːmətiv]	肯定的
escape	v.	[is'keip]	逃过(注意)

10.6 Theory-Based Health Behavior Change: Developing, Testing, and Applying Theories for Evidence-Based Interventions
基于理论的健康行为的改变:开发、测试和以证据为基础的干预应用理论

Sonia Lippke, Jochen P. Ziegelmann

Abstract

Theories are needed to explain and predict health behavior, as well as for the design and evaluation of interventions. Although there has been a history of developing, testing, applying, and refining health behavior theories, debates and limitations in evidence exist: The component of theories which, for example, predicts change should be better elaborated so that we can more easily understand what actually drives behavior change. Theories need to be empirically testable in two ways. Theories need to specify a set of changeable predictors to describe, explain, and predict behavior change, and they should enable us to design an effective intervention that produces exactly those changes in behavior that are predicted by the relevant theory. To make this possible, theories need to be specified in such a way that they can be rigorously tested and falsified. Moreover, for the design of theory-based interventions it must be possible to derive change techniques from the theory and to use them to generate changes in behavior. Based on eight state-of-the-science articles that make conceptual and empirical contributions to the current debate on health behavior theories, various approaches are discussed to gain further insights into explaining and changing health behaviors and the iterative process of theory development.

Words and Expressions

intervention	n.	[ˌɪntə(ː)ˈvenʃən]	干涉
refine	v.	[rɪˈfaɪn]	精练
component	n.	[kəmˈpəunənt]	成分
elaborate	v.	[ɪˈlæbərət]	详细阐述
empirically	adv.	[emˈpɪrikəli]	以经验为主地
testable	adj.	[testəbl]	可测试的
specify	v.	[ˈspesifai]	详细说明
rigorously	adv.	[ˈrigərəsli]	严格地
falsify	v.	[ˈfɔːlsiˌfai]	伪造
derive	v.	[dɪˈraiv]	得自
generate	v.	[ˈdʒenəˌreit]	产生
conceptual	adj.	[kənˈseptʃuəl]	概念上的
empirical	adj.	[emˈpɪrikəl]	完全根据经验的
iterative	adj.	[ˈitərətiv]	重复的;反复的

10.7　Positive Health
积极健康

Martin E. P. Seligman

Abstract

I propose a new field: positive health. Positive health describes a state beyond the mere absence of disease and is definable and measurable. Positive health can be operationalised by a combination of excellent status on biological, subjective, and functional measures[①]. By mining existing longitudinal studies, we can test the hypothesis that positive health predicts increased longevity (correcting for quality of life), decreased health costs, better mental health in aging, and better prognosis when illness strikes[②]. Those aspects of positive health which specifically predict these outcomes then become targets for new interventions and refinements of protocol[③]. I propose that the field of positive health has direct parallels to the field of positive psychology, parallels that suggest that a focus on health rather than illness will be cost saving and life saving. Finally, I suggest a different mode of science, the Copenhagen-Medici model, used to found positive psychology, as an appropriate way of beginning the flagship explorations for positive health.

Words and Expressions

| definable | adj. | [dɪˈfaɪnəbl] | 可定义的 |
| operationalise | v. | [ˌɒpəˈreɪʃənlaɪz] | 使用于操作；使开始运转； |

			实施
status	n.	['steitəs]	身份;地位;情形;状况
mine	v.	[main]	挖掘;开采;布雷;破坏
longevity	n.	[lɔn'dʒeviti]	长命;寿命;供职期限;资历
prognosis	n.	[prɔg'nəusis]	预后
refinement	n.	[ri'fainmənt]	精致;(言谈，举止等的)文雅;精巧
protocol	n.	['prəutəkɔl]	草案;协议
flagship	n.	['flægʃip]	旗舰

positive health　　　　　　　　积极的健康
the Copenhagen-Medici model　　哥本哈根-梅第奇模型

Difficult Sentences

① Positive health can be operationalised by a combination of excellent status on biological, subjective, and functional measures.
积极健康可以通过结合生物的、主观的、功能的方法在优良的状况下测量。

② By mining existing longitudinal studies, we can test the hypothesis that positive health predicts increased longevity (correcting for quality of life), decreased health costs, better mental health in aging, and better prognosis when illness strikes.
通过挖掘现有的纵向研究,我们能检验一个假设,该假设认为积极健康可以延长寿命(校正生活质量),降低健康成本,人老时心理会更健康,得病时态度会更乐观。

③ Those aspects of positive health which specifically predict these outcomes then become targets for new interventions and refinements of protocol.

于是,具体预测这些结果的积极健康的那些方面就成为干预和改进新草案的目标。

10.8 Positive Psychology and the Illness Ideology: Toward a Positive Clinical Psychology
积极心理学和疾病意识:对于积极临床心理学

James E. Maddux

Abstract

This article challenges traditional views of the proper subject matter of clinical psychology, the nature of psychological adjustment and maladjustment, and the roles and functions of clinical psychologists. Toward this end, the article discusses clinical psychologists' *conceptions* of psychological adjustment and maladjustment and of the *difference* between psychological adjustment and maladjustment. It describes and challenges the *illness ideology* that has prevailed in clinical psychology for the past century—an ideology that has been socially constructed rather than scientifically constructed[①]. This ideology consists of not only a set of assumptions about the nature of psychological adjustment and the "territory" of clinical psychology but also a language that influences the way clinical psychologists and others think about the field[②]. It then offers a statement of a new mission for and vision of clinical psychology based on the values of positive psychology[③].

Words and Expressions

ideology	n.	[ˌaidlˈɔlədʒi]	意识形态
clinical	adj.	[ˈklinikəl]	临床的;病房用的

prevail	v.	[pri'veil]	流行;盛行;获胜;成功

positive psychology　　　　　积极心理学
illness ideology　　　　　　　疾病意识
clinical psychology　　　　　临床心理学
psychological adjustment　　心理调节
psychological maladjustment　心理失调

Difficult Sentences

① It describes and challenges the *illness ideology* that has prevailed in clinical psychology for the past century—an ideology that has been socially constructed rather than scientifically constructed.

本文描述并挑战过去一个世纪里临床心理学对疾病的意识形态的理解,本文认为对疾病的意识形态是社会建构的,而不是科学建构的。

② This ideology consists of not only a set of assumptions about the nature of psychological adjustment and the "territory" of clinical psychology but also a language that influences the way clinical psychologists and others think about the field.

对疾病的意识形态不仅包括一套关于心理调节的性质和临床心理学领域的假设,还包括影响临床心理学家和其他人看待该领域的方法的语言。

③ It then offers a statement of a new mission for and vision of clinical psychology based on the values of positive psychology.

然后,本文提出了一种以积极心理学价值为基础的临床心理学的新任务和新视野的论述。

Questions

1. Do you think there are some links between human health and mental state? Why? Give examples.
2. What role do the mediating factors play in stress?

3. In what ways does the stress affect the cardiovascular system?
4. How does the brain influence the immune system indirectly?
5. Please briefly state the relationship of personality and stress by examples.
6. What is autism? What are the stereotyped behaviors of an autistic person? Are there any exceptional?
7. What are the possible causes of autism? Can you explain it by heritable aspects?
8. What are the key motivational influences on behavior?
9. What are the key volitional influences on behavior?

PART TWO
ACADEMIC INFORMATION

第二部分 专业学术信息

国外著名期刊

1. Mind

网址：http://mind.oxfordjournals.org

Mind 是由牛津大学出版社代表心理学会发行的期刊。它是心理学领域中首要的期刊,季度发行,有 100 多年的历史,它涉及认识论、纯粹哲学、语言哲学、逻辑哲学、心理哲学。在心理学领域享有盛名。

2. The American Journal of Psychology

网址：http://www.press.uillinois.edu/journals/ajp.html

The American Journal of Psychology 是由伊利诺斯大学出版社发行,1887 年创刊,是心理学领域中首个以英语为语言的期刊。其中涉及最著名和最有影响力的心理学家的最具创新性和建设性的文章。其领域涉及基本的心理科学、心理学领域核心的理论和实验,它从哲学和历史的角度关注心理学的重要话题：意识和无意识过程的作用、记忆的重现和形式、问题解决和推理、语言和思维的联系等很多方面。

3. Psychological Review

网址：http://www.apa.org/journals/rev/

Psychological Review 是由美国心理学会发行的季刊。主要发表在科学心理学的任何领域有重要理论贡献的文章。它偏好前沿理论的文章,也涉及对既定领域的替代性理论的系统性评价。

4. The Monist

网址：http://monist.buffalo.edu/

The Monist 是由海格勒研究所发行,主要发表关于特殊哲学话题的文章,是世界上最古老的哲学期刊之一,由爱德华·海格勒于 1888 年创刊,季度发行。

5. Psychological Bulletin

网址：http://www.apa.org/journals/bul/

Psychological Bulletin 是由美国心理学会发行的双月刊。发表科学心理学领域中评价性和综合性的研究观点以及问题的诠释。重要的研究报告仅以说明为目的。综合评论和研究结论主要是经验研究,寻求从多种角度和假设条件下的综合性结论。

国外心理学协会

1. APA(the American Psychological Association)

网址:http://www.apa.org/

会员设置和组织规模:美国心理学协会位于美国华盛顿,是一个代表美国心理学领域的科学和专业的组织。拥有会员148 000人,是全世界最大的心理学家协会。至1996年,共有普通心理学会、心理学教学学会、实验心理学会、生理与比较心理学会、发展心理学会等53个专业分会,7个地区分会:东部心理学会(1930),中西部心理学会(1938),新英格兰心理学会(1963),东南部心理学会(1955),西部心理学会(1938),西南部心理学会(1954),洛杉矶心理学会(1930)。另有53个地方分会。

工作语言、主要活动和出版物:工作语言为英语。每年八九月间举行一次学术年会,进行学术交流和学会主席换届选举。为表彰对心理学做出贡献的心理学家,设立各种心理科学奖,每年评选一次。出版刊物《心理学文摘》《心理学评论》《美国心理学家》《实验心理学报》《心理学通报》《人格和社会心理学报》等15种,以及《心理学——21世纪的职业:科学的问题的解决者》等著作。

2. The Association for Contextual Behavioral Science(ACBS)

网址:http://www.contextualpsychology.org

2005年创立,致力于认知和行为科学理论和实践的发展,以期减轻人们的痛苦,提高人类生活质量。

3. International Union of Psychological Science(IUPsyS)

网址:http://www.iupsys.org/

1951年成立于瑞典斯德哥尔摩。它致力于在研究机构之间建立全世界的联系,将促进心理科学和技术发展提高到国际高度。

联系人:Prof. Picrre Ritchie(秘书长)

通讯地址:
School of Psychology
University of Ottawa
145 Jean-Jacques Lussier St., P. O. Box 450
Stn A. Ottawa, ON K1N 6N5, Canada
E-mail: pritchie@uottawa.ca

工作语言、主要活动和出版物:工作语言为英语。每4年举办一次国际心理学大会,规模为6 000人左右,组织学术交流,介绍学科最新发展,促进国际性项目的科学研究等,会后还举办以发展中国家青年学者为主要对象的高级培训研讨班(ARTS-Advanced Research Training Seminar)。在两次大会之间组织以推动某一地区性的心理学发展为目的地区性会议。出版物有《国际心理学杂志》(International Journal of Psychology,1966年创刊)和《国际心理学家名录》以及会议文集等。还有《心理科学国际手册》(International Handbook of Psychology)于2000年出版。

会员设置和组织规模:设国家会员(National Member)和联系会员(Affiliated Organization);截至2001年2月,有国家会员68个及12个联系会员(如:国际应用心理学会 IAAP、国际跨文化心理学会 IACCP 等)。

4. International Association of Applied Psychology (IAAP)
网址:http://www.iaapsy.org/
于1920年在瑞士日内瓦成立,原名称为国际心理技术学会,1955年起改为现名。它是国际心理科学联合会的下属国际心理学团体。

会员设置和组织规模:这个学会下设有7个委员会:工作、财务、学术、会员、出版、职业和心理测验,分别负责有关方面的工作或开展各种学术活动。还设有7个专业委员会,即:教育、教学和学校心理学专业;临床、社区心理学专业;应用老年心理学专业;心理学和国家发展专业;环境心理学专业;组织心理学专业及心理评定专业。

工作语言、主要活动和出版物:近年来,每4年召开一次学术大会。会刊为《国际应用心理学评论》半年刊,用英、法两种语言出版。

5. AFRO-ASIAN Psychological Association（AAPA）

亚非心理学会(AAPA)是1990年于巴基斯坦的拉合尔召开第1届亚非心理学大会时经与会代表建议与酝酿成立的。1992年,由中国心理学会负责筹备与组织的第二届亚非心理学大会在北京召开。

联系人:Prof. Bilal Aslam Sufi

通信地址:University of the Punjab,Lahore, Pakistan

工作语言、主要活动和出版物:工作语言为英语,每2年召开一次亚非心理学大会,由19个亚非国家及地区派代表出席,并选举新一届执行委员会。

会员设置和组织规模:分团体会员(国家心理学会)及个人会员两种。凡属亚非地区的国家一级心理学会均可申请参加。入会后有选举权和被选举权。个人会员以个人身份参加,不代表国家,需填表申请,缴纳会费。

6. 国际测验委员会 International Test Commission,简称ITC

网址:http://www.intestcom.org

联系人:Dave Bartram

通信地址:

SHL Group. The Pavilion

1 Atwell Place, Thames Ditton

Surrey KT7 ONE,UK

E-mail:Dave.Bartram@ Shlgroup.com

工作语言、主要活动和出版物:工作语言为英语。每年召开一次理事会,每4年召开一次国际测验大会并改选,规模100人。出版物有 *ITC Bulletin*,每年3月和9月各一期;*ITC Newsletter* 每年6月和12月各一期。

会员设置和组织规模:国际测验委员会1974年成立于加拿大蒙特利尔。设正式会员及联系会员,正式会员是指一个国家的心理学会或委员会,享有选举权和被选举权,联系会员是对心理测验感兴趣的任何机构,包括出版社、机关、医院、学校等。现有正式会员14个,联系会员 24 个。

国内心理学研究所及协会

1. 中国科学院心理研究所(Institute of Psychology, CAS)

网址:http://www.psych.ac.cn/CN/index.html

中国科学院心理研究所成立于1951年,其前身是中央研究院心理研究所(1929),是我国唯一的国家级心理学研究机构,在国内外具有较高的学术地位。

心理研究所是一个应用研究与基础研究并重、具有较强科研实力、以承担国家重大项目为主的科研机构。心理所现设有心理健康重点研究室、认知与实验心理学研究室、发展与教育心理学研究室、社会与经济行为研究中心、行为遗传学研究中心。心理所是国务院学位委员会批准的基础心理学、发展与教育心理学和应用心理学专业的博士和硕士学位授予单位,2000年批准为心理学(涵盖心理学各分支)博士学位授予权单位,并设有心理学博士后流动站。目前博士生104人,硕士生85人,在站博士后21人。研究所还是中国心理学会的挂靠单位,与中国心理学会合办《心理学报》并主办《心理科学进展》发行国内外。

2. 中国心理学会(Chinese Psychological Society)

网址:http://www.cpsbeijing.org/

地址:中国北京中国科学院心理研究所

邮编:100101

电话:86 - 10 - 64888946

传真:86 - 10 - 64855830

Email:xuehui@psych.ac.cn

中国心理学会是由中国心理学工作者组成的公益性、学术性社会团体,是中国科学技术协会的组成部分。创建于1921年,是我国现有的全国性学会中最早成立的学术组织之一。目前,中国心理学会中包含各主要心理学的分支学科领域,现有全国性会员6 000余人。其中研究生会员1 658余人。全国31个省、自治区、直辖市有地方心理学会。

中国心理学会于1980年7月正式加入国际心理科学联合会(International Union of Psychological Science,IUPsyS),1984年加入国际应用心理学会(International Association of Applied Psychology,IAAP),1990年加入亚非心理学会(AFRO-ASIAN Psychological Association,AAPA),1990年加入国际测验委员会(International Test Commission,ITC)。

3. 中国人民大学心理学研究所

网址:http://www.socialpsy.org/

电话:86-10-51662123

Email:webmaster@socialpsy.org

中国人民大学社会心理学研究所成立于1993年,为中国最早建立的社会心理学研究所之一。研究所以社会心理学、工业心理学、心理测量、心理学研究方法、组织行为学、民族心理学、经济心理学、管理心理学、两性心理学为主要研究方向,在学校开设相关课程,进行相关的课题研究,开展积极的对外合作与交流。

研究所现有教授2人,副教授1人,讲师2人。1个博士学位点,1个硕士学位点,授予社会心理学(应用心理学方向)学位。

中国人民大学社会心理学研究所为国家自学考试委员会指定的"社会心理学"科目的负责单位,负责指定教材的编写和考试大纲的制定以及考试命题。

4. 中国心理科学信息中心 ICPsyS(China InfoCenter for Psychological Science)

网址:http://lib.psych.ac.cn/

中国心理科学信息中心由中国科学院心理研究所主办,中国心理学会协办,是一个心理科学的专业信息研究和信息服务机构,是国家和中国科学院知识创新工程的组成部分。

中国心理科学信息中心于2004年3月成立,在线服务平台www.icpsys.cn已于2005年5月发布。

5. 北京大学心理学系

网址:http://www.psy.pku.edu.cn/

Email: xrsh@pku.edu.cn

Tel: 0086 - 10 - 62751831(行政)

北京大学是中国最早传播心理学的学府,早在1900年即开设心理学课程。1917年创立中国第一个心理学实验室,这是中国现代科学心理学的开端,是由著名教育家、北京大学校长蔡元培先生倡导的。1977年,北京大学率先在国内恢复心理学,成立了当时国内第一个心理学系,并归入理科,1978年招收第一批学生。

北京大学心理学系按综合大学规格进行全面的学科建制,从事多方面的研究,提供高质量的综合性高等教育,涵盖心理学各主要方向。心理学系拥有一级学科博士学位授予权,可授予心理学各专业理学或教育学学士、硕士、博士学位,同时设有心理学成人自学考试点,开设大专和专升本教育,还受理在职人员申请硕士、博士学位。

心理学系的科研领域涉及较广泛的方面,包括实验心理学,认知心理学,认知神经科学,生理心理学,心理统计与测量,发展心理学,人格与社会心理学,情绪心理学,比较心理学,临床心理学,医学心理学,工业与管理心理学,消费与广告心理学,人力资源管理、工程心理学等,这一综合特性为培养心理学高等基础与应用心理学人才奠定了重要基础。

6. 中国心理学家网

网址:http://www.cnpsy.net

中国心理学家网是互动式的心理学学习和交流平台,每个登录本站者都是本站的参与者、建设者。本站的参与和建设成员应是各栏目策划者、网页制作者、站标设计者、指导解惑者、资料上传者、浏览网页者、参与活动者、请求咨询者、发表论贴者、指评建议者、发布信息者、网站合作者。安徽医科大学医学心理学系学生为本站的初期建设者。

7. 中国心理网

网址:http://www.psych.gov.cn/

中国心理网是在北京大学心理系、北京师范大学心理学院、中国科学院心理所、清华大学心理咨询中心的心理学专家指导下建立起来,经过国家通信管理局和工商局备案登记的心理学门户网站。

由于本站专家大都是国内乃至国际上知名学者,网站也得到社会各界的支持认可。经过本站的专业培训,可以申请获得首都师范大学的心理学硕士学位和美国 Preston University 的博士学位。

除此之外,中国心理网还致力于优秀心理培训项目的推广和宣传,让更多的社会大众了解、掌握好科学的知识、技能。从网站成立以来,本站和清华大学心理咨询中心一起开展多个工作坊的培训;和中国心理学会临床与咨询专业委员会开展心理病理学、家庭治疗等专项培训以及特聘国内知名心理学家、博士生导师金洪源教授进行学生学习障碍诊断和治疗技术的推广,引起了极大的社会反响和好评。

国内期刊

1.《心理学报》(*Acta Psychologica Sinica*)

期刊名称	心理学报
期刊评价	国内一级
所属学科	心理学
主办单位	中国心理学会,中国科学院心理研究所
出版周期	月刊
创刊时间	1956 年
ISSN	0439－755X
CN	11－1911/B
地址	北京市朝阳区林萃路 16 号院 中国科学院心理研究所《心理学报》编辑部
电话	010－64850861
EMAIL	xuebao@psych.ac.cn
(2016 版)复合影响因子	2.544
(2016 版)综合影响因子	1.371

2.《心理科学进展》(Advances in Psychological Science)

期刊名称	心理科学进展
所属学科	心理学
主办单位	中国科学院心理研究所
出版周期	月刊
创刊时间	1983 年
ISSN	1671 - 3710
CN	11 - 4766/R
地址	北京市朝阳区林萃路 16 号院中国科学院心理研究所《心理科学进展》编辑部
电话	010 - 64850861
EMAIL	jinzhan@ psych. ac. cn
HOMEPAGE	http://journal. psych. ac. cn
期刊栏目	反映心理学各领域的最新研究进展的文章
(2016 版)复合影响因子	2.344
(2016 版)综合影响因子	1.3

3.《心理发展与教育》(Psychological Development and Education)

期刊名称	心理发展与教育
期刊评价	国内二级,国内 B 类
所属学科	心理学
主办单位	北京师范大学发展心理研究所
出版周期	双月刊
创刊时间	1985 年
ISSN	1001 - 4918
CN	11 - 1608/B
地址	北京新街口外大街 19 号(北京师范大学院内)
电话	010 - 58807700
EMAIL	pdae@ bnu. edu. cn
(2016 版)复合影响因子	2.345
(2016 版)综合影响因子	1.363

4.《心理学动态》(*Psychological Science*)

期刊名称	心理科学
所属学科	心理学
主办单位	中国心理协会
出版周期	双月刊
创刊时间	1964 年
ISSN	1671-6981
CN	31-1582B
地址	上海市普陀区中山北路 3663 号华东师范大学内田家炳楼 1202 室
电话	021-62232236
EMAIL	xinlikexue@vip.163.com
(2016 版)复合影响因子	1.155
(2016 版)综合影响因子	0.589

5.《心理学探新》(*Psychological Exploration*)

期刊名称	心理学探新
所属学科	心理学
主办单位	江西师范大学
出版周期	双月刊
创刊时间	1981
ISSN	1003-5184
CN	36-1228/B
地址	江西省南昌市北京西路 437 号 江西师范大学《心理学探新》编辑部
电话	0791-8120281
EMAIL	tanxin@nc.jx.cn
(2016 版)复合影响因子	0.836
(2016 版)综合影响因子	0.434

PART THREE GLOSSARY

第三部分 专业词汇

词汇表

A

abashed	adj.	[əˈbæʃt]	不安的;窘迫的
abnormal	a.	[æbˈnɔːməl]	反常的
abnormality	n.	[ˌæbnɔːˈmæliti]	变态
abrasive	adj.	[əˈbreisiv]	生硬粗暴的
accentuate	v.	[ækˈsentjueit]	重读;强调;着重强调
accessibility	n.	[ˌækəsesiˈbiliti]	易接近;可到达
accommodation	n.	[əˌkɔməˈdeiʃn]	眼调节
accompany	v.	[əˈkʌmpəni]	陪伴;伴奏
acupuncture	n.	[ˈækjupʌŋktʃə(r)]	针刺疗法
adaptability	n.	[ədæptəˈbiliti]	适应性
adept	adj.	[əˈdept]	熟练的;拿手的
address	vt.	[əˈdres]	向……致辞,演说;写姓名地址;从事
adolescence	n.	[ˌædəuˈlesəns]	青春期
adolescent	n.	[ˌædəuˈlesnt]	青少年
aesthetics	n.	[iːsˈθetiks]	美学;美术理论;审美学;美的哲学
affective	adj.	[əˈfektiv]	情感的
affirmative	adj.	[əˈfəːmətiv]	肯定的
agoraphobia	n.	[ˌægərəˈfəubiə]	[心]广场恐惧;旷野恐惧;陌生环境恐惧
akin	adj.	[əˈkin]	同族的;类似的
algorithms	n.	[ˈælgəriðəm]	运算法则
allocation	n.	[ˌæləuˈkeiʃən]	分配;安置
altruism	n.	[ˈæltruizəm]	利他主义;利他
altruistic	adj.	[ˌæltruˈistik]	利他的;无私心的

amateur	adj.	['æmətə(r)]	业余的
ambiguous	adj.	[æm'bigjuəs]	暧昧的;不明确的
ambivalence	n.	[æm'bivələns]	正反感情并存
amino	adj.	['æminəu]	[化]氨基的
anal	adj.	['einəl]	肛门的
analogy	n.	[ə'nælədʒi]	类比
anatomy	n.	[ə'nætəmi]	解剖学
anthropology	n.	[ˌænθrə'pɔlədʒi]	人类学
antithesis	n.	[æn'tiθisis]	对立面
apperception	n.	[ˌæpə'sepʃən]	领悟;知觉
apathetic	adj.	[ˌæpə'θetik]	缺乏兴趣的;缺乏感情的;无动于衷的
appreciation	n.	[əˌpriːʃi'eiʃən]	感谢;感激;正确评价;欣赏;增值
approximation	n.	[əˌprɔksi'meiʃən]	接近;过程或结果
arbitrariness	n.	['ɑːbitrərinis]	任意
arbitrary	adj.	['ɑːbitrəri]	任意的;武断的;独裁的;专断的
arch	v.	[ɑːtʃ]	(使)弯成弓形
Armenia	n.	[ɑː'miːnjə]	亚美尼亚(亚美尼亚共和国)
arousal	n.	[ə'rauzəl]	觉醒;激励
artery	n.	['ɑːtəri]	动脉;要道
arthritis	n.	[ɑː'θraitis]	关节炎
artificiality	n.	[ˌɑːtifiʃ'æliti]	人工
ascribe	vt.	[əs'kraib]	归因于;归咎于
assessment	n.	[ə'sesmənt]	评估;估价
assimilation	n.	[əˌsimi'leiʃən]	同化
associative	adj.	[ə'səuʃjətiv]	联想的
astute	a.	[ə'stjuːt]	敏锐的;精明的

atheoretical	adj.	[ei͵θiə'retikəl]	非理论的;与理论无关的
atropine	n.	['ætrəpi:n]	[药]阿托品(含颠茄碱)
attribute	n.	[ə'tribju(:)t]	属性;品质;特征
attribute	n.	[ə'tribju(:)t]	属性;品质;特征;加于;归结于
attribution	n.	[͵ætri'bju:ʃən]	归因
autism	n.	['ɔ:tizəm]	[心]自我中心主义;孤独症
automatic	a.	[͵ɔ:tə'mætik]	自动的;无意识的;机械的
automatize	v.	[ɔ:'tɔmətaiz]	使自动化
autonomic	a.	[͵ɔ:təu'nɔmik]	自主的
auxiliary	adj.	[ɔ:g'ziljəri]	辅助的
aversive	adj.	[ə'və:siv]	令人嫌恶的
awkward	adj.	['ɔ:kwəd]	难使用的;笨拙的
axon	n.	['æksɔn]	(神经细胞的)轴突
Azerbaijan	n.	[͵ɑ:zəbai'dʒɑ:n]	阿塞拜疆

a rule of thumb	单凭经验的方法
abnormal behavior	反常行为
absolute threshold	绝对阈值
abstract concept	抽象概念
acquired modes of response	习得的反应模式
act frequency approach	行为频率方法
activity level	活动水平
acute stress disorder	急性压力型混乱
adrenal gland	肾上腺
aerial perspective	空间透视
AIDS (Acquired Immune Deficiency System)	艾滋病,获得性免疫缺陷综合症
an inverted U function	反向U功能(曲线)
Anxiety Disorder Association	焦虑混乱症协会

anxiety states			焦虑状态
arousal continuum			激励序列
artificial intelligence			人工智能
atomic reaction			原子反应
attention span			注意广度
auditory cortex			听觉皮层
autonomic nervous system			自主神经系统

B

badger	v.	['bædʒə]	困扰
battered	n.	['bætəd]	打扁了的
beholder	n.	[bi'həuldə]	目睹者
bias	n.	['baiəs]	偏见;偏爱
bind	v.	[baind]	约束
binocular	adj.	[bai'nɔkjulə]	用两眼的
biochemistry	n.	['baiəu'kemistri]	生物化学
biogenic	adj.	[ˌbaiəu'dʒenik]	源于生物的;生物所造成的
biopsychological	adj.	['baiəusaikɔ'lədʒikəl]	生物心理学的;精神生物学的
bloated	adj.	['bləutid]	发胀的
blur	v.	[blə:]	把(界线)弄得模糊不清
blush	v.	[blʌʃ]	脸红;羞愧;呈现红色;使成红色
botanical	adj.	[bə'tænik(ə)l]	植物学的
bout	n.	[baut]	一回;一场;回合;较量
brainstorming	n.	['breinˌstɔ:miŋ]	脑力激荡
bruise	n.	[bru:z]	瘀伤;擦伤
brutal	adj.	['bru:tl]	残忍的;冷酷的
brutish	adj.	['bru:tiʃ]	残酷的
buffer	n.	['bʌfə]	缓冲器

bulge	v.	[bʌldʒ]	凸起
bulk	v.	[bʌlk]	显得大;显得重要

behavior pattern	行为方式
behavioral consistency	行为一致性
behaviorist approach	行为主义研究方法
between-individual variability	个体之间的可变性
binocular cue	双眼线索
biological approach	生物学研究方法
biological needs	生物需求
blood pressure	血压
botanical monograph	植物学专论
brain stem	脑干
brightness constancy	明度常性
building block	积木

C

cap	n.	[kæp]	盖
capability	n.	[ˌkeipəˈbiliti]	能力
cardiovascular	adj.	[ˌkɑːdiəuˈvæskjulə]	心脏血管的
carotid	adj.	[kəˈrɔtid]	颈动脉的
carve	v.	[kɑːv]	刻;雕刻
cast	v.	[kɑːst]	投;抛;投射
catabolic	adj.	[ˌkætəˈbɔlik]	分解代谢的;异化的
categorization	n.	[kæˌtigəraizeiʃən]	类别
categorize	v.	[ˈkætigəraiz]	加以类别;分类
cauliflower	adj.	[ˈkɔːliflauə]	花椰菜
celebrant	n.	[ˈselibrənt]	(主持宗教仪式的)教士
censorship	n.	[ˈsensəʃip]	审查机构;审查制度
cerebellum	n.	[ˌseriˈbeləm]	小脑

cerebral	adj.	['seribrəl]	大脑的
cerebrum	n.	['seribrəm]	大脑
chameleon	n.	[kə'mi:ljən]	多变的人
chaotic	adj.	[kei'ɔtik]	混乱的;无秩序的
characterizable	adj.	['kæeriktəraizəbl]	可描述的
charismatic	adj.	[ˌkæriz'mætik]	有吸引力的
choking	adj.	['tʃəukiŋ]	窒息的;憋闷的;透不过气来的
cholesterol	n.	[kə'lestərəul]	胆固醇
ciliary	adj.	['siliəri]	睫状的
clinician	n.	[kli'niʃən]	[医]临床医生;临床教师
circuitry	n.	['səkitri]	电路系统;电路图
circulation	n.	[ˌsə:kju'leiʃən]	循环
clammy	adj.	['klæmi]	湿冷的
closure	n.	['kləuʒə]	闭合
clumsy	adj.	['klʌmzi]	笨拙的;手脚不灵活的
cognition	n.	[kɔg'niʃən]	认知
cognitive	adj.	['kɔgnitiv]	认知的;认识的,
colliculus	n.	[kɔ'likjuləs]	[解]丘
comatose	adj.	['kəumətəus]	昏睡的;昏睡状态的
commentary	n.	['kɔməntəri]	评论;评述
commonplace	adj.	['kɔmənpleis]	平凡的;普通的
communication	n.	[kəˌmju:ni'keiʃn]	交流;沟通
component	n.	[kəm'pəunənt]	构成要素;
comprise	v.	[kəm'praiz]	包含;由……组成
compulsive	adj.	[kəm'pʌlsiv]	强制的;强迫的;由强迫产生的;禁不住的
compute	v.	[kəm'pju:t]	计算;估计
conceptual	adj.	[kən'septʃuəl]	概念上的
conceptualization	n.	[kənˌseptjuəlai'zeiʃən]	概念化

concordance	n.	[kən'kɔːdəns]	和谐
condensation	n.	[kɔndenˈseiʃən]	浓缩
conduct	v.	[ˈkɔndʌkt]	管理
conduct	n.	[ˈkɔndʌkt]	行为
conductance	n.	[kənˈdʌktəns]	[电工]电导;导率;电导系数
conform	v.	[kənˈfɔːm]	符合
conformity	n.	[kənˈfəːmiti]	一致;符合
congenital	adj.	[kɔnˈdʒenitl]	天生的;先天的
conscientiousness	n.	[ˌkɔnʃiˈenʃəsnis]	尽责
consistency	n.	[kənˈsistənsi]	一致性;连贯性
consistent	adj.	[kənˈsistənt]	连贯一致的
constituent	n.	[kənˈstitjuənt]	委托人;要素
construal	n.	[kənˈstruːəl]	解释;说明
construct	v.	[kənˈstrʌkt]	建造;构造
contemplate	v.	[ˈkɔntempleit]	沉思
context	n.	[ˈkɔntekst]	环境;背景
contextualized	adj.	[kɔnˈtekstjuəlaizd]	使……融入背景的
continuity	n.	[ˌkɔntiˈnjuː(ː)iti]	连续性;连贯性
continuum	n.	[kənˈtinjuəm]	连续统一体;连续统;闭联集
contradictory	adj.	[ˌkɔntrəˈdiktəri]	反驳的;反对的;矛盾的
convergence	n.	[kənˈvəːdʒəns]	会聚;会合点
coordinate	v.	[kəuˈɔːdineit]	协调;调节
corollary	n.	[kəˈrɔləri]	必然的结果;系;推论
coronary	adj.	[ˈkɔrənəri]	冠的;花冠的;冠状的
correlation	n.	[ˌkɔriˈleiʃən]	相互关系;相关(性)
correspond	v.	[kɔrisˈpɔnd]	符合;相当;相应
cortex	n.	[ˈkɔːteks]	(植物的)皮层;树皮;(脑或肾的)皮层;皮质
cortical	adj.	[ˈkɔːtikəl]	皮层的;皮质的;有关脑皮层的

cowardly	adj.	['kauədli]	胆小的;怯懦的
cramped	adj.	[kræmpt]	狭窄的
creativity	n.	[ˌkriːei'tivəti]	创造力
credit	vt.	['kredit]	相信;信任;把……归给
crevasse	n.	[kri'væs]	裂缝;裂隙
criterion	n.	[krai'tiəriən]	(批评判断的)标准;准据;规范
cross-link	n.	['krɔslink]	交叉结合
cue	n.	[kjuː]	暗示;线索
cult	n.	[kʌlt]	异教
custody	n.	['kʌstədi]	保管

cardiovascular disease		心血管病
case study		个案研究
category membership		某类别的成员资格
central nervous system		中枢神经系统
cerebral Cortex		大脑皮层
chronic disease		慢性病
Cincinnati Children's Hospital Medical Center		辛辛那提儿童医疗中心
client-centred therapy		以求诊者为中心的治疗法
clinical psychology		临床心理学
cognitive activity		认知活动
cognitive approach		认知研究方法
cognitive mechanism		认知机构
cognitive schema		认知模式
color constancy		颜色常性
common-sense	n. [ˌkɔmən'sens]	常识(尤指判断力)
compulsive buying		强迫购买
concrete concept		具体概念
conditioned reflexe		条件反射

conscious free will			有意识的自由意志
consumer goods			消费者商品
consumer psychology			消费者心理
contagious disease			接触传染病
the Copenhagen-Medici model			哥本哈根－梅第奇模型
coronary artery disease			冠心病
"criterion contamination" problem			"标准污点"问题
critical attribute			重要属性

D

debilitate	vt.	[di'biliteit]	使衰弱；使虚弱
decay	n.	[di'kei]	腐朽；腐烂；衰减；衰退
decrement	n.	['dekrimənt]	消耗
deficit	n.	['defisit]	赤字；不足额
definable	adj.	[di'fainəbl]	可定义的
dehumanizing	adj.	[diː'hjuːmənaiziŋ]	失去人性的
deliberate	adj.	[di'libəreit]	深思熟虑的；审慎的
deliberately	adv.	[di'libərətli]	故意地；审慎地
demeanor	n.	[di'miːnə]	行为；风度
demystification	n.	[diːˌmistifi'keiʃən]	非神秘化启蒙
deprivation	n.	[ˌdepri'veiʃən]	剥夺
derive	v.	[di'raiv]	得自
desynchronize	vt.	[diː'siŋkrənaiz]	[心]使去同步；使失同步
detect	v.	[di'tekt]	察觉
determinant	n.	[di'təːminənt]	决定性因素
determinism	n.	[di'təːminizəm]	决定论
deviation	n.	[ˌdiːvi'eiʃən]	背离
device	n.	[di'vais]	装置；设计
devout	adj.	[di'vaut]	虔敬的；诚恳的
diabetes	n.	[ˌdaiə'biːtiːz]	糖尿病；多尿症

英文	词性	音标	释义
diagnose	v.	['daiəgnəuz]	诊断
diagnostic	adj.	[,daiəg'nɔstik]	特征的
diagnostician	n.	[,daiəgnɔs'tiʃən]	诊断医生;诊断专家
diameter	n.	[dai'æmitə]	直径
diarrhea	n.	[,daiə'riə]	痢疾;腹泻
dichotomy	n.	[dai'kɔtəmi]	二分法
differential	adj.	[,difə'renʃəl]	差别的;关于或显出差别的
diffuse	v.	[di'fju:z]	散播;传播;扩散;(使)慢慢混合
dignity	n.	['digniti]	尊严;高贵
dilemma	n.	[di'lemə]	进退两难的局面
diligent	adj.	['dilidʒənt]	勤勉的;勤奋的
dimension	n.	[di'menʃən]	因素
discomfort	n.	[dis'kʌmfət]	不便之处;不适
discordant	adj.	[dis'kɔ:dənt]	不调和的;不和的;[乐]不悦耳的,不和谐的
discount	n.	['diskaunt]	折扣
discrepancy	n.	[dis'krepənsi]	相差;差异;矛盾
discrimination	n.	[dis,krimi'neiʃən]	辨别;歧视
disentangle	v.	['disin'tæŋgl]	解脱,解开纠结;松开;解决(纠纷)
dismantle	v	[dis'mæntl]	拆开;分解
disorder	n.	[dis'ɔ:də]	紊乱;疾病
displacement	n.	[dis'pleismənt]	移置;转移;取代;置换;位移;排水量
disposition	n.	[dispə'ziʃən]	性情;脾气
disproportionate	adj.	[,disprə'pɔ:ʃənit]	不成比例
disruption	n.	[dis'rʌpʃən]	中断;分裂;瓦解;破坏
disruptive	adj.	[dis'rʌptiv]	使破裂的;分裂性的
distal	adj.	['distəl]	末梢的

distinct	adj.	[dis'tiŋkt]	截然不同的;独特的
distinctiveness	n.	[dis'tiŋktivnis]	特殊性;独特性
distortion	n.	[dis'tɔːʃən]	扭曲;变形;曲解;失真
distress	n.	[dis'tres]	悲痛;穷困;不幸;危难;忧伤
distressing	adj.	[dis'tresiŋ]	悲伤的;使痛苦的;使烦恼的
distribute	v.	[dis'tribju(ː)t]	分配
divergence	n.	[dai'vəːdʒəns]	分歧
divinely	adv.	[di'vainli]	凭借上帝的力量
division	n.	[di'viʒən]	分割;区分
dizygotic	adj.	[ˌdaizai'gɔtik]	[生]两合子的;两受精卵的
dizziness	n.	['dizinis]	头昏眼花
dominion	n.	[də'minjən]	主权;领土;统治权;支配;控制
dovetailing	adj.	[dʌv'teiliŋ]	燕尾连接楔形接合
drive	n.	[draiv]	(人的)本能需要;欲望
drowsy	adj.	['drauzi]	昏昏欲睡的;催眠的;(街、市等)沉寂的
dual	adj.	['dju(ː)əl]	双重的
duplicate	v.	['djuːplikeit]	复写;复制
dynamics	n.	[dai'næmiks]	动态

deductive reasoning	演绎推理
deep structure	深层结构
defense mechanism	自卫机能
depressed level	抑郁水平
depth perception	深度知觉
difference threshold	差别阈限
dream analysis	梦的分析
drive-reduction theories	动机减少理论
dream condensation	梦的凝缩

dream content			梦的内容
dream displacement			梦的转移
dwelling house			住宅
Dream Work			梦的运作

E

effector	n.	[i'fektə]	神经效应器
ego	n.	['i:gəʊ]	自我
elaborate	v.	[i'læbərət]	详细阐述
electrode	n	[i'lektrəud]	电极
elevate	vt.	['eliveit]	举起;提拔;振奋;提升……的职位
elicit	v.	[i'lisit]	得出;引出;抽出;引起
elucidate	v.	[i'lju:sideit]	阐明;说明
elusive	adj.	[i'lu:siv]	难懂的;难捉摸的
empathic	adj.	[em'pæθik]	移情作用的
empirical	adj.	[em'pirikəl]	完全根据经验的
empirically	adv.	[em'pirikəli]	以经验为主地
empiricism	n.	[em'pirisizəm]	经验主义
enact	v.	[i'nækt]	扮演
endocrine	adj.	['endəukrain]	内分泌(腺)的
endogenous	adj.	[en'dɔdʒənəs]	内源性的
endopsychic	adj.	[,endəu'saikik]	灵魂中的
endorphin	n.	[in'dɔ:fin]	内啡肽
endorse	v.	[in'dɔ:s]	核准;批准或给予支持
enduring	adj.	[in'djuəriŋ]	持久的;不朽的
enforce	vt.	[in'fɔ:s]	强迫;执行;坚持;加强
engrain	vt.	[in'grein]	染成木纹色;使根深蒂固;[喻]使遍体渗透
enormous	adj.	[i'nɔ:məs]	巨大的;庞大的;<古>极

			恶的；凶暴的
ensemble	n.	[ə:n'sɑ:mbl]	整体；全体
entity	n.	['entiti]	实体
enzyme	n.	['enzaim]	[生化]酶
epinephrine	n.	[,epi'nefrin]	肾上腺素
epiphenomenon	n.	[,epifi'nɔminən]	附带现象；偶发症状
episode	n.	['episəud]	一段情节；[音]插曲,插话
equilateral	adj.	[,i:kwi'lætərəl]	等边的
equilibrium	n.	[,i:kwi'libriəm]	平衡
equivalent	adj.	[i'kwivələnt]	相等的；相当的；同意义的
Eros	n.	['irɔs,'erɔs]	爱神；愿望；性爱
erroneous	adj.	[i'rəunjəs]	错误的；不正确的
escape	v.	[is'keip]	逃过（注意）
essential	adj.	[i'senʃəl]	本质的；实质的；基本的；精华的
establishment	n.	[is'tæbliʃmənt]	体制
estimate	n.	['estimeit]	估计；评估
ethologist	n.	[i'θɔlədʒist]	生态学研究者；习性学者
eudaimonic	adj.	[ju:'daimənik]	幸福说的；快乐说的
evaluation	n.	[i,vælju'eiʃn]	估价；评价；赋值
evoke	v.	[i'vəuk]	唤起；引起
exaltation	n.	[,egzɔ:l'teiʃən]	兴奋
excessive	adj.	[ik'sesiv]	过多的；过分的；额外
excretion	n.	[eks'kri:ʃn]	（动植物的）排泄；排泄物
excruciating	adj.	[ik'skru:ʃieitiŋ]	极痛苦的；折磨人的
expectancy	n.	[ik'spektənsi]	期待；期望
expenditure	n.	[iks'penditʃə]	支出；花费
explicit	adj.	[iks'plisit]	清楚的；直率的
extraneous	adj.	[eks'treinjəs]	无关系的；外来的；[化]外部裂化,[化]新异反射

extraversion	n.	[ˌekstrə'və:ʃən]	外向性；外倾性
extremity	n.	[iks'tremiti]	末端；极端
excited level			兴奋水平
experimental psychology			实验心理学

F

facility	n.	[fə'siliti]	设备
facet	n.	['fæsit]	方面
falsify	v.	['fɔ:lsi,fai]	伪造
fatigue	n.	[fə'ti:g]	疲乏；疲劳；累活；[军]杂役
feeble	adj.	['fi:bl]	弱的；软弱的
fiber	n.	['faibə]	纤维物质
fidget	v.	['fidʒit]	坐立不安；烦躁；慌张；（不安地或心不在焉地）弄；玩弄
filter	v.	['filtə]	过滤
fissure	n.	['fiʃə]	裂缝；裂隙
fixated	adj.	[fik'seitid]	异常依恋
flagship	n.	['flægʃip]	旗舰
flexible	a.	['fleksəbl]	灵活的
flip	adj.	[flip]	无礼的；冒失的；轻率的
fluctuation	n.	[ˌflʌktju'eiʃən]	波动；起伏
forebrain	n.	['fɔ:,brein]	前脑
forelimb	n.	['fɔ:lim]	前肢
formative	adj.	['fɔ:mətiv]	格式化的
formulation	n.	[ˌfɔ:mju'leiʃən]	明确地表达；作简洁陈述
freestanding	adj.	['fri:stændiŋ]	独立的
fuse	v.	[fju:z]	熔合

faculty psychology			官能心理学
fixed action pattern			固定行为模式
free association			自由联想
frontal lobe			前叶
functional psychology			机能主义心理学

G

generalization	n.	[ˌdʒenərəlaiˈzeiʃən]	一般化；普遍化；概括；广义性
generate	v.	[ˈdʒenəˌreit]	产生
generative	adj.	[ˈdʒenərətiv]	生成的
generosity	n.	[ˌdʒenəˈrɔsiti]	慷慨；宽大
genital	adj.	[ˈdʒenitl]	性心理发育早期的
germ	n.	[dʒəːm]	芽
gland	n.	[glænd]	腺
glandular	adj.	[ˈglændjulə]	腺(状)的
glasnost	n.	[ˈglɑːsnɔːst]	公开性；公开化
glucose	n.	[ˈgluːkəus]	葡萄糖
grocery	n.	[ˈgrəusəri]	食品杂货店；食品；杂货
gross	adj.	[grəus]	显著的

gender differences	性别差异
general economy of nature	普通自然经济
generalized anxiety disorder	综合焦虑型混乱
genetic method	遗传研究法
Gestalt principles of perception	格式塔感知原理
gray matter	灰白质

H

hallmark	n.	['hɔːlmɑːk]	特点
harassed	adj.	['hærəst]	疲倦的;厌烦的
hazy	adj.	['heizi]	朦胧的;烟雾弥漫的
hedonic	adj.	[hiː'dɔnik]	享乐主义的
hemisphere	n.	['hemisfiə]	大脑半球
hereditary	adj.	[hi'reditəri]	遗传的
heredity	n.	[hi'rediti]	遗传;形质遗传
heritability	n.	[ˌheritə'biləti]	遗传可能性
herpes	n.	['həːpiːz]	疱疹
heuristics	n.	[hjuə'ristiks]	探索性的方法或过程
hideout	n.	['haidaut]	躲藏处
highlight	v.	['hailait]	使显著
hindbrain	n.	['haindbrein]	后脑
hindlimb	n.	['haindlim]	(动物或昆虫的)后肢;下肢
hippocampus	n.	[ˌhipə'kæmpəs]	海马
hitherto	adv.	[ˌhiðə'tuː]	迄今;至今
homeostasis	n.	[ˌhəumiəu'steisis]	(社会群体的)自我平衡;原状稳定
homicide	n.	['hɔmisaid]	杀人;杀人者
hormonal	adj.	[hɔː'məunəl]	荷尔蒙的
hormone	n.	['hɔːməun]	荷尔蒙;激素
hostility	n.	[hɔs'tiliti]	敌意;恶意;不友善;敌对;对抗;反对
humanistic	adj.	[ˌhjuːmə'nistik]	人文主义的
humanity	n.	[hjuː'mæniti]	人性
humiliate	v.	[hjuː'milieit]	羞辱;使丢脸;耻辱
hyperactivity	n.	[ˌhaipə'ræktiviti]	活动过度;极度活跃
hypnosis	n.	[hip'nəusis]	催眠

hypothalamus	n.	[ˌhaipəuˈθæləməs]	丘脑下部
hypothesis	n.	[haiˈpɔθisis]	假设
hysteria	n.	[hisˈtiəriə]	歇斯底里;癔症

health psychology	健康心理学
hereditary modes of response	遗传的反应模式
Homo sapiens	智人(现代人的学名)
human immunodeficiency virus (HIV)	人体免疫缺损病毒;艾滋病病毒
human nature	人性
humanistic approach	人本主义研究方法
humanistic perspective	人本主义的观点
hydraulic drive	流体动力驱力

I

id	n.	[id]	本我
idiosyncrasy	n.	[ˌidiəˈsiŋkrəsi]	(个人的)气质;习性
imagery	n.	[ˈimidʒəri]	意象;形象化的描述
immunization	n.	[ˈimjuːnaiˈzeiʃən]	免疫性
impair	v.	[imˈpɛə]	削弱
impending	n.	[imˈpendiŋ]	迫近
implementation	n.	[ˌimpləmɛnˈteʃən]	执行
implication	n.	[ˌimpliˈkeiʃən]	暗示
implicit	adj.	[imˈplisit]	暗示的;含蓄的
impressively	n.	[imˈpresivli]	令人难忘地
impulse	n.	[ˈimpʌls]	神经脉冲;刺激;冲动
in utero	n.	[inˈjuːtərəu]	在子宫内;未出生
inborn	adj.	[ˈinˈbɔːn]	天生的;生来的
incentive	n.	[inˈsentiv]	动机
incongruence	n.	[inˈkɔŋgruəns]	不一致

index	n.	['indeks]	索引;[数学]指数;指标;(刻度盘上)指针
indicator	n.	['indikeitə]	指示物
indifference	n.	[in'difrəns]	不关心
induce	vt.	[in'dju:s]	劝诱;促使;导致;引起;感应
infantile	adj.	['infəntail]	婴儿的
inference	n.	[infərəns]	推论
infinite	adj.	['infinit]	无穷大的;无限的
inherit	v.	[in'herit]	经遗传而获得
initial	n.	[i'niʃəl]	(名字的)首字母;最初的
initiation	n.	[i,niʃi'eiʃən]	开始
initiate	v.	[i'niʃieit]	开始;发动;传授
innate	adj.	['ineit]	先天的;天生的
insensitivity	n.	[in,sensi'tiviti]	不敏感
instigate	v.	['instigeit]	鼓动
instinct	n.	['instiŋkt]	本能
institution	n.	[,insti'tju:ʃən]	制度
insulate	v.	['insjuleit]	使绝缘;隔离
intact	adj.	[in'tækt]	完整无缺的;尚未被人碰过的;(家畜)未经阉割的
integrate	v.	['intigreit]	使成一体;使结合;使合并
interact	v.	[intər'ækt]	互相作用;互相影响
interaction	n.	[,intəR'ækʃən]	交互作用
interconnected	adj.	[,intə(:)kə'nektid]	互相连接的
intermediary	n.	[,intə'mi:diəri]	中间物;媒介物
internalize	v.	[in'tə:nə,laiz]	使内在化
interplay	n.	['intə(:)plei]	相互影响
interpolation	n.	[in,tə:pəu'leiʃən]	篡改;插补
intersection	n.	[,intə(:)'sekʃən]	交叉
intervene	v.	[,intə'vi:n]	(指时间)介于其间

intervention	n.	[ˌintə(:)'venʃən]	干涉
intricate	adj.	['intrikit]	错综复杂的
intrigue	vt.	[in'tri:g]	激起……的兴趣；用诡计取得
intrinsic	adj.	[in'trinsik]	固有的；内在的；本质的
intuition	n.	[ˌintju(:)'iʃən]	直觉
intuitive	adj.	[in'tju(:)itiv]	直觉的
inverse	n.	['in'və:s]	反面
invoke	v.	[in'vəuk]	求助于；使用或应用
involuntary	adj.	[in'vɔləntəri]	不受意志控制的；不由自主的
issue	v.	['iʃu:]	发布

ideal personality	理想人格
idiographic case study method	特殊规律个案研究法
illness ideology	疾病意识
immune system	免疫系统
employee motivation	员工激励
impulse buying	冲动购买
individual case	个案
inductive reasoning	归纳推理
inflamed appendix	阑尾炎
information processor	信息处理器
inhibitory interneuron	抑制中间神经元
inner dispositions	内在性情
internal secretion	内分泌物
instinct theories	本能理论
intelligence test	智力测验
internal experience	内在经验
internal mental process	内在心理加工

intuitive perception 直觉感知

J

jitters	n.	['dʒitəz]	神经过敏
joint	n.	[dʒɔint]	关节
justifiable	adj.	['dʒʌstifaiəbl]	有理由的

job performance 工作表现

K

kinesthetic receptors 运动觉感受器

L

latency	n.	['leitənsi]	潜伏期
latent	adj.	['leitənt]	潜在的;潜伏的;隐藏的
lax	adj.	[læks]	松的;松懈的;不严格的
legitimate	adj.	[li'dʒitimit]	合法的;合理的
lightly	adv.	['laitli]	轻松地;容易地
limbic	adj.	['limbik]	边的
linear	adj.	['liniə]	线的;直线的;线性的
lobe	n.	[ləub]	(脑、肺等的)叶
locomotion	n.	[ləukə'məuʃ(ə)n]	运动;移动;运动力;移动力
longevity	n.	[lɔn'dʒeviti]	长命;寿命;供职期限;资历
longitudinal	adj.	[lɔndʒi'tju:dinl]	经度的;纵向的
lynching	n.	[lintʃiŋ]	处私刑

level of equilibrium 平衡水平
linear perspective 线条透视
linguistic relativity hypothesis 语言相对性假说
lotus of control 控制点

M

magnitude	n.	[ˈmægnitjuːd]	量；大小
maintenance	n.	[ˈmeintinəns]	维护；保持
maladaptive	adj.	[ˌmæləˈdæptiv]	不适应的；适应不良的；
mammal	n.	[ˈmæməl]	哺乳动物
manic	adj.	[ˈmeinik]	狂躁的
manifest	v.	[ˈmænifest]	表明；证明
manifestation	n.	[ˌmænifesˈteiʃən]	显示；表现
manipulate	v.	[məˈnipjuleit]	（熟练地）操作；巧妙地处理
manipulation	n.	[məˌnipjuˈleiʃən]	处理；操作
martyr	n.	[ˈmɑːtəri]	烈士
masculine	adj.	[ˈmɑːskjulin]	男性的；男子气概的；阳性的
mechanism	n.	[ˈmekənizəm]	机制
mediator	n.	[ˈmiːdieitə]	调停者；仲裁人；[宗]中保（指耶稣）
mediate	v.	[ˈmiːdiet]	仲裁；调停
medulla	n.	[meˈdʌlə]	延髓；骨髓
metabolism	n.	[məˈtæbəlizəm]	新陈代谢；变形
metaphor	n.	[ˈmetəfə]	暗喻
metaphysical	adj.	[ˌmetəˈfizikəl]	形而上学的；纯粹哲学的；超自然的
microelectrode	n.	[ˌmaikrəuiˈlektrəud]	微电极
microorganism	n.	[ˌmaikrəuˈɔːgəniz(ə)m]	微生物
microscopic	adj.	[ˌmaikrəˈskɔpik]	微小的
midbrain	n.	[ˈmidˌbrein]	中脑
mine	v.	[main]	挖掘；开采；布雷；破坏
modality	n.	[məuˈdæliti]	形式；形态
moderator	n.	[ˈmɔdəreitə]	调解者
modification	n.	[ˌmɔdifiˈkeiʃən]	修改；修正

英文	词性	音标	中文
monitor	v.	['mɔnitə]	监控
monocular	adj.	[mɔ'nɔkjulə]	单眼的
monograph	n.	['mɔnəugrɑːf]	专论
mononucleosis	n.	[ˌmɔnəuˌnjuːkliː'əusis]	单核细胞增多症
monozygotic	adj.	[ˌmɔnəzai'gɔtik]	[动]单卵的;单精合子的
morpheme	n.	['mɔːfiːm]	词素
morphine	n.	['mɔːfiːn]	吗啡
morphinelike	adj.	['mɔːfiːnlaik]	类似吗啡的
morphology	n.	[mɔː'fɔlədʒi]	[生物]形态学;形态论;[语法]词法;词态学
motivational	adj.	[ˌməuti'veiʃənəl]	动机的;有关动机的
motive	n.	['məutiv]	动机;目的
motoneuron	n.	[ˌməutə'njuərɔn]	运动神经元
moulding	n.	['məuldiŋ]	塑造
multi-faceted	n.	[ˌmʌlti'fæsitid]	多面的
multiplicity	n.	[ˌmʌlti'plisiti]	多样性
musculature	n.	['mʌskjuətʃə]	肌肉组织
musculoskeletal	adj.	[ˌmʌskjuləu'skelitəl]	肌与骨骼的
myelin	n.	['maiəli(ː)n]	髓磷脂;髓鞘
myelinated	adj.	['maiəlineitid]	有髓鞘的
myelinization	n.	[ˌmaiəlinai'zeiʃən]	髓鞘化;髓鞘形成
myopic	adj.	[mai'ɔpik]	近视的
mystic	n.	['mistik]	神秘主义者

material goods	物质商品
mental health professional	心理健康专家
mental image	心理想象
mental model	智力模型
mental representation	精神方面的代表
Minneapolis Gas Company	明尼阿波利斯天然气公司

Minnesota Multiphasic Personality Inventory			明尼苏达多项个性检查表
monocular cue			单眼线索
motor cortex			运动皮层
motor neurons			运动神经元
multiple assessments of personality variability			人格可变性的多重评估

N

nag	v.	[næg]	困扰;使烦恼
nativist	n.	['neitivist]	先天论者;本土主义者
nausea	n.	['nɔ:sjə]	反胃;晕船;恶心;作呕
neocortex	n.	[ˌniəu'kɔ:teks]	新(大脑)皮层
Netherlands	n.	['neðələndz]	荷兰;地区名
neural	adj.	['njuərəl]	神经系统的;神经中枢的
neurobiologist	n.	[ˌnjuərəubai'ɔlədʒist]	神经生物学家
neurology	n.	[njuə'rɔlədʒi]	神经学;神经病学
neuron	n.	['njuərɔn]	神经细胞;神经元
neuropsychology	n.	[ˌnjuərəusai'kɔlədʒi]	神经心理学
neurosurgeon	n.	[ˌnjuərəu'sə:dʒen]	神经外科医生
neurosurgery	n.	[njuərəu'sə:dʒəri]	神经外科
New Guinea	n.	[nju:'gini]	新几内亚岛(位于太平洋)
nociceptor	n.	[ˌnəusi'septə]	伤害感受器
nocturnal	adj.	[nɔk'tə:nl]	夜的;夜曲的
nomothetic	adj.	[ˌnɔmə'θetik]	基于普遍性科学规律的
nonsensical	adj.	[nɔn'sensikəl]	无意义的;荒谬的
norepinephrine	n.	['nɔˌrepi'nefrin]	去甲肾上腺素
norm	n.	[nɔ:m]	标准;规范
normative	adj.	['nɔ:mətiv]	标准化的
notion	n.	['nəuʃən]	观念;想法
notorious	adj.	[nəu'tɔ:riəs]	恶名昭彰的;声名狼藉的
novice	n.	['nɔvis]	新手;初学者

numbing	adj.	['nʌmiŋ]	使麻木的;使失去感觉的
nut	n.	[nʌt]	狂热者
nerve fiber			神经元;神经纤维
nervous system			神经系统
neural impulse			神经脉冲
non-verbal concept			非言语概念
norm violation			违背常规
normal level			正常水平
nucleus raphe			脑干缝际核

O

obesity	n.	[əu'bisiti]	肥胖;肥大
obsess	v.	[əb'ses]	迷住;使困扰
obsessive	adj.	[əb'sesiv]	强迫性的;分神的
obstetric	adj.	[ɔbs'tetrik]	产科的
oecology	n.	[iː'kɔlədʒi]	生态学;社会生态学
omnipresent	adj.	[ɔmni'preznt]	无所不在的
onset	n.	['ɔnset]	攻击;进攻;有力的开始;肇端;[医]发作
ontogeny	n.	[ɔn'tɔdʒini]	[生]个体发生;个体发生学
operationalise	v.	[ˌɔpə'reiʃənlaiz]	使用于操作;使开始运转;实施
opiate	n.	['əupiət]	鸦片制剂;麻醉剂
oral	adj.	['ɔːrəl]	口部快感
organism	n.	['ɔːɡənizəm]	生物;有机体
orientation	n.	[ˌɔ(ː)rien'teiʃən]	方向;方位;定位;倾向性;向东方
originate	v.	[ə'ridʒineit]	起源;发生
orthodox	adj.	['ɔːθədɔks]	正统的;传统的;保守的;

			东正教的
outgrow	v.	[aut'grəu]	过大而不适于;出生;长出;年久丧失(某种习惯,兴趣等)
outlook	n.	['autluk]	景色;风光;观点;见解;展望;前景
outmoded	adj.	[aut'məudid]	过时的
outset	n.	['autset]	开端;开始
overlap	v.	['əuvə'læp]	重叠
overwhelm	vt.	['əuvə'welm]	淹没;覆没;受打击;制服;压倒

obsessive-compulsive disorder　　强制强迫型混乱
occipital lobe　　枕叶

P

pack	v.	[pæk]	挤(塞,装)满
palpitation	n.	[pælpi'teiʃ(ə)n]	心悸
panic	n.	['pænik]	惊慌;恐慌;没有理由的
paradoxical	adj.	[,pærə'dɔksikəl]	荒谬的
parallel	v.	['pærəlel]	相应;平行
parameter	n.	[pə'ræmitə]	参数;参量;<口>起限定作用的因素
parsimonious	adj.	[,pɑ:si'məunjəs]	吝啬的;节俭的
pathological	adj.	[,pæθə'lɔdʒikəl]	病理的;病态的
perceive	v.	[pə'si:v]	感知;感到;认识到
percept	n.	['pə:sept]	知觉的对象
perceptible	adj.	[pə'septəbl]	可察觉的;显而易见的
perception	n.	[pə'sepʃn]	感知;感觉
perceptual	adj.	[pə'septjuəl]	知觉的

perch	v.	[pə:tʃ]	栖息
perimeter	n.	[pə'rimitə]	周界
peripheral	adj.	[pə'rifərəl]	周围的;外面的
periphery	n.	[pə'rifəri]	外围
persistence	n.	[pə'sistəns]	坚持;持续
personality	n.	[ˌpə:sə'næliti]	个性;人格
perspective	n.	[pə'spektiv]	透视画法;透视图;远景;前途;观点
pervasive	adj.	[pə:'veisiv]	普遍深入的
petty	adj.	['peti]	小的;琐碎的
phallic	adj.	['fælik]	生殖器的
phenomenological	adj.	[fiˌnɔminə'lɔdʒikəl]	现象的
phenylalanine	n.	[ˌfenəl'æləni:n]	苯基丙氨酸
phenylketonuria	n.	[ˌfenəlˌki:tə'njuəriə]	[医]苯丙酮尿;苯丙酮酸尿症(一种先天性代谢异常)
phobia	n.	['fəubjə]	恐惧症
phoneme	n.	['fəuni:m]	音位;音素
photosynthesis	n.	[ˌfəutəu'sinθəsis]	光合作用
phylogeny	n.	[fai'lɔdʒini]	语系发生;发展史
physiological	adj.	[ˌfiziə'lɔdʒikəl]	生理学的
physiology	n.	[ˌfizi'ɔlədʒi]	生理学
physostigmine	n.	[ˌfaisəu'stigmi:n]	[药]毒扁豆碱(一种眼科缩瞳药)
pictographic	adj.	[ˌpiktə'græfik]	象形文字的
pictorial	adj.	[pik'tɔ:riəl]	图示的
pin	n.	[pin]	大头针;别针
pituitary	adj.	[pi'tju(:)itəri]	脑垂体的
placebo	n.	[plə'si:bəu]	安慰剂
plausible	adj.	['plɔ:zəbl]	似是而非的

polarize	v.	['pəuləraiz]	(使)偏振;(使)极化;(使)两极分化
pons	n.	[pɔnz]	脑桥
posit	v.	[pɔzit]	安置
posttraumatic	adj.	[ˌpəusttrɔː'mætik]	[医]外伤后的
postulate	n.	['pɔstjuleit]	假定;基本条件;基本原理
potentially	adv.	[pə'tenʃ(ə)li]	潜在地
practitioner	n.	[præk'tiʃənə]	从业者
precipitate	vt.	[pri'sipiteit]	猛抛;使陷入;促成;使沉淀
predisposition	n.	[priːdispə'ziʃən]	性向;倾向;易患病体质
prejudice	n.	['predʒudis]	偏见;成见;损害;侵害
premature	adj.	[ˌpremə'tjuə]	太早的;未成熟的
premise	n.	['premis]	前提
preoccupation	n.	[pri(ː)ˌɔkju'peiʃən]	当务之急
prerequisite	n.	['priː'rekwizit]	先决条件
pressing	adj.	['presiŋ]	紧迫的
pressor	n.	['presə]	增压物质
presumption	n.	[pri'zʌmpʃən]	推测;假定
prevail	v.	[pri'veil]	普遍
primate	n.	['praimit]	首领;大主教;灵长类的动物
prioritise	v.	[prai'ɔritaiz]	把……区分优先次序
probe	vt.	[prəub]	(以探针等)探查;查明
procedure	n.	[prə'siːdʒə]	方式;完成某事的途径
profusion	n.	[prə'fjuːʒən]	丰富
prognosis	n.	[prɔg'nəusis]	预后
proliferation	n.	[prəuˌlifə'reiʃən]	增殖;分芽繁殖
prolong	v.	[prə'lɔŋ]	延长;拖延
prolonged	adj.	[prə'lɔŋd]	延长的
prominently	adv.	[prɔminəntli]	显著地
prone	adj.	[prəun]	倾向于

英文	词性	音标	中文
propel	vt.	[prə'pel]	推进;驱使
proportion	n.	[prə'pɔ:ʃn]	比例;均衡;面积;部分
propose	v.	[prə'pəuz]	计划;建议;向……提议;求(婚)
proposition	n.	[ˌprɔpə'ziʃən]	命题
protocol	n.	['prəutəkɔl]	草案;协议
prototype	n.	['prəutətaip]	原型;典型事例
provision	n.	[prə'viʒən]	供应;(一批)供应品;预备;防备
provisional	adj.	[prə'viʒənl]	临时的
proximity	n.	[prɔk'simiti]	接近;邻近
psyche	n.	['saiki(:)]	灵魂;精神
psychiatry	n.	[sai'kaiətri]	精神病学;精神病治疗法
psychic	adj.	['saikik]	精神的
psychical	adj.	['saikikəl]	灵魂的;精神的
psychoanalytic	adj.	['saikəuˌænə'litik]	心理分析的
psychopathology	n.	[ˌsaikəupə'θɔlədʒi]	精神病理学
psychophysics	n.	['saikəu'fiziks]	精神物理学
psychosexual	adj.	['saikəu'sekʃuəl]	性心理的
pursuit	n.	[pə'sju:t]	事务
pygmy	n.	['pigmi]	俾格米人

panic disorder	恐慌型混乱
parietal lobe	顶叶
perceptual bias	知觉偏见
perceptual constancy	知觉常性
periaqueductal gray	近沟区灰质
peripheral nervous system	外围神经系统
personality characteristics	个性特点
personality traits	个性特征

phylogenetic psychology	进化心理学
physiological arousal	生理激励
physiological drives	生理动机
physiological mechanism	生理机制
physiological needs	生理需求
physiological psychology	生理心理学
physiological state	生理状态
pictographic script	象形文字的原稿
positive health	积极的健康
positive psychology	积极心理学
posttraumatic stress disorder	伤后压力型混乱
prescriptive rules	法定规则
primary effect	最初印象
projection neuron	投射神经元
Psychiatric disorder	精神病型的混乱症
psychic determinism	精神决定论
psychical process	心理过程
psychoanalytic approach	心理分析的研究方法
psychoanalytic perspective	心理分析的观点
psychodynamic conflict	心理动力冲突
psychological adjustment	心理调节
psychological anatomy	心理解剖学
psychological disorders	心理混乱
psychological function	心理机能
psychological maladjustment	心理失调
psychology of structure	构造心理学
psychosexual stage	性心理阶段

Q

Q-sort technique	Q 分类技术

R

racing	adj.	['reisiŋ]	比赛的
radiate	v.	['reidieit]	放射;辐射;传播;广播
rarity	n.	['rɛəriti]	稀有
rating	n.	['reitiŋ]	评价;地位
rational	adj.	['ræʃənl]	理性的;合理的;推理的
reactor	n.	[ri(:)'æktə]	反应堆
rear	v.	[riə]	养育
rebus	n.	['ri:bəs]	(猜字的)画谜
receptor	n.	[ri'septə]	感觉器官;感受体
recipe	n.	['resipi]	处方
reciprocal	adj.	[ri'siprəkəl]	相互的
recollect	v.	[,rekə'lekt]	回忆;记忆
recrudescence	n.	[,ri:kru:'desns]	复发;再发作
rectangular	adj.	[rek'tæŋgjulə]	矩形的
refine	v.	[ri'fain]	精练
refinement	n.	[ri'fainmənt]	精致;(言谈,举止等的)文雅;精巧
reflex	n.	['ri:fleks]	反射(作用);本能的反应
regress	n.	['ri:gres]	退路
regression	n.	[ri'greʃən]	衰退
regulate	v.	['regjuleit]	控制;调节
reinforcement	n.	[,ri:in'fɔ:smənt]	加强
relapse	n.	[ri'læps]	回复原状
relay	v.	['ri:lei]	转达;转播
reliability	n.	[ri,laiə'biliti]	信度
relive	vt.	['ri:'liv]	重新过活;再体验
rendering	n.	['rendəriŋ]	透视图
replica	n.	['replikə]	复制品;复写;酷似

repression	n.	[ri'preʃən]	压抑作用
reproach	n.	[ri'prəutʃ]	责备
repugnant	adj.	[ri'pʌgnənt]	不一致的
respiration	n.	[ˌrespi'reiʃən]	呼吸
respondent	n.	[ris'pɔndənt]	回答者
retard	v.	[ri'tɑ:d]	延迟;使减速;阻止;妨碍;阻碍
retardation	n.	[ˌri:tɑ:'deiʃən]	延迟
retardate	n.	[ri'tɑ:deit]	白痴;低能者
retarded	adj.	[ri'tɑ:did]	智力迟钝的;发展迟缓的
reticent	adj.	['retisənt]	沉默寡言的
reticular	adj.	[ri'tikjulə]	网状的
retina	n.	['retinə]	视网膜
reverse	v.	[ri'və:s]	交换……的位置;使变位
reverse	n.	[ri'və:s]	相反
revert	v.	[ri'və:t]	回复
rift	n.	[rift]	裂缝;裂口;断裂;裂谷;不和
rigor	n.	['rigə]	精确
rigorous	adj.	['rigərəs]	严密的
rigorously	adv.	['rigərəsli]	严格地
rote	n.	[rəut]	死记硬背;机械的做法;生搬硬套
route	v.	[ru:t]	按规定路线发送
rudimentary	adj.	[ru:di'mentəri]	根本的;未发展的

reciprocal determinism	相互决定论
reticular activating system (RAS)	网状激活系统
reticular formation	网状结构
retinal disparity	网膜像差

role-based personality variability　　基于角色的人格可变性
Rorschach inkblots test　　罗夏墨迹测验

S

saint	n.	[seint]	道德崇高的人
salient	adj.	['selijənt]	易见的；显著的；突出的；跳跃的
schematic	adj.	[ski'mætik]	示意性的
schizophrenia	n.	[ˌskitsəu'fri:niə]	[心]精神分裂症
schizophrenic	adj.	[ˌskitsəu'frenik]	精神分裂症的
screen	v.	[skri:n]	审查
scrutiny	n.	['skru:tini]	详细审查
secretion	n.	[si'kri:ʃən]	分泌；分泌物（液）
segmented	adj.	['segməntid]	分割的；分段的
semantics	n.	[si'mæntiks]	语义学
sensation	n.	[sen'seiʃən]	感觉
sensitivity	n.	['sensi'tiviti]	敏感；灵敏（度）
sensory	adj.	['sensəri]	知觉的；感觉的；感觉中枢的
serial	adj.	['siəriəl]	连续的
serially	adv.	['siəriəli]	连续地
shadowing	n.	['ʃædəuiŋ]	阴影
shortcut	n.	['ʃɔ:tkʌt]	捷径
Siamese	n.	[saiə'mi:z]	暹罗人[语]；暹罗猫
sibling	n.	['sibliŋ]	兄弟；姐妹；同胞；同属
signify	v.	['signifai]	表示；意味
similarity	n.	[ˌsimi'læriti]	相似性
simultaneously	adv.	[siməl'teiniəsli]	同时地
sinner	n.	['sinə]	罪人
sinus	n.	['sainəs]	窦；穴；湾；凹处
skeletal	adj.	['skelitl]	骨骼的

skull	n.	[skʌl]	头盖骨;头骨
slaughter	v.	['slɔːtə]	屠杀
smother	v.	['smʌðə]	窒息
sociobiological	adj.	[ˌsəuʃiəuˌbaiə'lɔdʒikəl]	社会生物学的
sociological	adj.	[ˌsəuʃiə'lɔdʒikəl]	社会学的;社会学上的
solely	adv.	['səu(l)li]	仅仅
somatic	adj.	[səu'mætik]	细胞体的;肉体的
sore	n.	[sɔ, sɔə]	痛处
specialty	n.	['speʃəlti]	专业
species	n.	['spiːʃiz]	种类;(原)核素
specify	v.	['spesifai]	详细说明
spectrum	n.	['spektrəm]	范围
spill	vt.	[spil]	使溢出;使散落;洒;使流出;使摔下;倒出
spinning	n.	['spiniŋ]	纺纱
spontaneously	adv.	[spɔn'teinjəsli]	自然地;本能地
stability	n.	[stə'biliti]	稳定性
stable	adj.	['steibl]	稳定的
stalk	n.	[stɔːk]	柄;柄状物
stance	n.	[stæns]	姿态
status	n.	['steitəs]	身份;地位;情形;状况
stepwise	adj.	['stepˌwaiz]	逐步的
stereopticon	n.	[ˌstiəri'ɔptikən]	立体感幻灯机
stereotype	n.	['stiəriəutaip]	定型;典型;[印]铅版;陈腔滥调;老套
stereotyped	adj.	['steriəutaipt]	套用陈规的
stigmatize	vt.	['stigmətaiz]	打烙印;诬蔑
stimulus	n.	['stimjuləs]	刺激物;促进因素;刺激
stochastic	adj.	[stəu'kæstik]	随机的
stressor	n.	['stresə]	[心]紧张性刺激

subject	n.	['sʌbdʒikt]	受实验者
submissiveness	n.	[səb'misivnis]	柔顺；服从
subsist	v.	[səb'sist]	维持生活
substantial	adj.	[səb'stænʃəl]	重要的；有价值的；坚固的
substitution	n.	[ˌsʌbsti'tju:ʃən]	代替；置换
successive	adj.	[sək'sesiv]	连续的
successively	adv.	[sək'sesivli]	接连着；继续地
superego	n.	[ˌsu:pər'egəu]	超我
superficial	adj.	[sju:pə'fiʃəl]	表面的
superposition	n.	[ˌsju:pəpə'ziʃən]	重叠；重合
susceptibility	n.	[səˌseptə'biliti]	易感性；感受性
susceptible	adj.	[sə'septəbl]	易受影响的；易感动的；容许……的
syllogism	n.	['silədʒizəm]	三段论
symbolic	adj.	[sim'bɔlik]	象征的
synaptically	adv.	[si'næptikəli]	突触地
syntactic	adj.	[sin'tæktik]	依据造句法的
syntax	n.	['sintæks]	句法
synthesis	n.	['sinθisis]	综合；合成
sales promotion			商品促销
sample size			试样量，样本大小
self-consciousness			自我意识
self-identity			自我身份
self-image			自我形象
self-motivation			自我激励
sense organs			感觉器官
sensory adaptation			感觉适应
sensory input			感觉输入

sensory neurons	感觉神经元
sensory receptor cells	感觉接收细胞
sensory system	感觉系统
shape constancy	形状常性
situational factor	外在因素
size constancy	大小常性
skin diving	轻装潜水
social anxiety disorder	社会焦虑混乱症
social behavior	社会行为
social category	社会范畴
social norms	社会规范
social phobia	社会恐惧症
social phobia self-test	社会恐惧症自我测试
social psychology	社会心理学
social status	社会地位
social-cognitive perspective	社会认知观点
somatic nervous system	细胞体神经系统
somatosensory cortex	身体感觉皮层
species life	物种的生命
spinal cord	脊髓
stages of development	发展阶段
stereotyped form	刻板形式
surface structure	表层结构
symbolic consumption	象征性消费
systematic zoology	系统动物学

T

taxonomy	*n.*	[tækˈsɔnəmi]	分类法;分类学
tease	*adj.*	[tiːz]	取笑;奚落;欺负;

			嘲弄
temple	n.	['templ]	太阳穴
temporal	n.	['tempərəl]	当时的;暂时的
terminology	n.	[ˌtə:mi'nɔlədʒi]	术语学
testable	adj.	['testəbl]	可测试的
thalamus	n.	['θæləməs]	视神经床;丘脑
Thanatos	n.	['θænətɔs]	死的愿望
thermal	adj.	['θə:məl]	热的;热量的
thermostat	n.	['θə:məstæt]	自动调温器;温度调节装置
threshold	n.	['θreʃhəuld]	阈
thymus	n.	['θaiməs]	胸腺
tissue	n.	['tisju:]	组织
topicality	n.	[ˌtɔpi'kæliti]	时事性
tornado	n.	[tɔ:'neidəu]	旋风;龙卷风
torture	n.	['tɔ:ʃtə]	折磨;痛苦
trait	n.	[treit]	特性
transcutaneous	adj.	[ˌtrænskju(:)'teinjəs]	经过皮肤的
transduce	v.	[trænz'dju:s]	转换
transduction	n.	[træns'dʌkʃən]	换能;转换
transference	n.	['trænsfərəns]	移动;转送;转让
transistor	n.	[træn'zistə]	[电子]晶体管
transmit	v.	[trænz'mit]	传输;转送
trigger	v.	['trigə]	引发;引起;触发
tumor	n.	['tju:mə]	肿瘤
typhus	n.	['taifəs]	斑疹伤寒
tyrosine	n.	['tirəsi:n]	[生化]酪氨酸

taxonomic psychology		分类心理学
temporal lobe		颞叶

texture gradient			结构级差
theories of learning			学习理论
to lead . . . astray			引入歧途
trait perspective			特性的观点
transistor radio			晶体管收音机

U

underlie	v.	[ˌʌndəˈlai]	成为……根据；作为……的基础
underlying	adj.	[ˈʌndəˈlaiiŋ]	潜在的
undertake	v.	[ˌʌndəˈteik]	着手做；从事
uneventfully	adv.	[ʌniˈventfuli]	太平无事地
ungainly	adj.	[ʌnˈgeinli]	笨拙的
unmyelinated	adj.	[ˌʌnˈmaiəlineitid]	无髓鞘的
utilise	v.	[ˈjuːtilaiz]	利用
utterance	n.	[ˈʌtərəns]	言辞；言论

unconscious mental causes	无意识心理原因
unconscious process	无意识过程
verbal concept	言语概念

V

vague	adj.	[veig]	不明确的；含糊的
validity	n.	[vəˈliditi]	效度
variability	n.	[əˌvɛəriəˈbiliti]	可变性
variable	n.	[ˈvɛəriəbl]	[数]变数；可变物；变量
vent	v.	[vent]	放出；排出；发泄
verbally	adv.	[ˈvəːbəli]	用言辞地
verify	v.	[ˈverifai]	证明；证实

vicinity	n.	[vi'siniti]	邻近;附近;接近
vigilant	adj.	['vidʒilənt]	警惕着的;警醒的
violation	n.	[ˌvaiə'leiʃən]	违反;违背;妨碍;侵害
vis-à-vis	prep.	[viːzɑːˈviː]	同……相比;关于
visceral	adj.	['visərəl]	内脏的
visual	adj.	['viʒuəl]	视觉的
visualization	n.	[ˌviʒuəlai'zeiʃən]	形象化;可视化
volition	n.	[vəu'liʃən]	意志
volitional	adj.	[vəu'liʃənəl]	意志的
vulnerable	adj.	['vʌlnərəb(ə)l]	易受攻击的;易受……的攻击
voluntary	adj.	['vɔləntəri]	故意的

vertical position　　　　竖直[Y轴]位置
visual cortex　　　　　　视觉皮层
visual perception　　　　视觉,视知觉

W

wavelength	n.	['weivleŋθ]	波长
wend	v.	[wend]	走;离开
will	v.	[wil]	用意志力使;主观促成
wiring	n.	['waiəriŋ]	线路

white matter　　　　　　　　白质
whole unit　　　　　　　　　单位整体
Whorfian hypothesis　　　　　沃夫假说
within-individual variability　 个体内部可变性
work of displacement　　　　梦的转移作用
working conditions　　　　　　工作环境

X

xenophobic　　*adj.*　　[ˌzenəʊˈfəʊbik]　　恐惧(或憎恨)外国人的；恐外的

Y

yearning　　*n.*　　[ˈjəːniŋ]　　向往

REFERENCES

[1] BOOTZIN R, BOWER G, CROKER J. Psychology today: An introduction[M]. New York: Von Hoffmann Press, 1991.

[2] CONNER M. Initiation and maintenance of health behaviors[J]. Applied Psychology: An International Review, 2008, 57(1):42-50.

[3] DAVIDOFF L. Introduction to psychology[M]. New York: McGraw-Hill Education, 1987.

[4] DRENTH P. Psychology: is it applied enough? [J]. Applied Psychology: An International Review, 2008, 57(3):524-540.

[5] FELDMAN R. Essentials of understanding psychology[M]. New York: McGraw-Hill Education, 1997.

[6] FREUD S. The interpretation of dreams [M]. Hertfordshire: Wordsworth, 1997.

[7] GROBSTEIN P. Variability in brain function and behavior[J]. The Encyclopedia of Human Behavior, 1994(4): 447-458.

[8] HILL G. Advanced psychology through diagram [M]. Oxford: Oxford University Press, 1998.

[9] HOLMES D. Abnormal psychology[M]. New York: Harper Collins College Publishers, 1994.

[10] LAHEY B. An introduction to psychology [M]. New York: McGraw-Hill Education, 2001.

[11] LIPPA R. Introduction to social psychology [M]. Belmont: Wadsworth Publishing Company, 1990.

[12] LIPPKE S, ZIEGELMANN J P. Theory-based health behavior

change: developing, testing, and applying theories for evidence-based interventions [J]. Applied Psychology: An International Review, 2008, 57(4):698-716.

[13] MADDUX J E. Positive psychology and the illness ideology: Toward a positive clinical psychology[J]. Applied Psychology: An International Review, 2008, 57(1):54-70.

[14] MAYERS D. Psychology[M]. 2nd Edition. New York: Worth Publishers Inc. ,1989.

[15] PETRI H. Motivation: Theory, research, and applications[M]. Belmont: Washington Publishing Company, 1990.

[16] SELIGMAN M. Positive health[J]. Applied Psychology: An International Review, 2008, 57(1):3-18.

[17] TITCHENER E B. The postulates of a structural psychology[J]. Philosophical Review,1948,7(5):449-465.

[18] WADE C, TAVRIS C. Psychology [M]. New York: Harper Collins College Publishers,1993.

[19] WORTMAN C, LOFTUS E. Psychology[M]. 3rd Edition. New York: Alfred A. Knopf. Inc. , 1988.

[20] 丛伟,李建明. 大学心理学英语教程[M]. 北京:北京科学技术出版社,2004.

[21] 沈德灿,沈政选. 心理学专业英语教程[M]. 北京:北京大学出版社,2001.